A Secret Gift

*How One Man's Kindness—
and a Trove of Letters—
Revealed the Hidden History of the
Great Depression*

TED GUP

CENTER POINT PUBLISHING
THORNDIKE, MAINE

This Center Point Large Print edition
is published in the year 2010 by arrangement with
The Penguin Press,
a member of Penguin Group (USA) Inc.

The text of this Large Print edition is unabridged.
In other aspects, this book may vary
from the original edition.
Printed in the United States of America
on permanent paper.
Set in 16-point Times New Roman type.

ISBN: 978-1-60285-925-8

Library of Congress Cataloging-in-Publication Data

Gup, Ted, 1950–
  A secret gift / Ted Gup. — Large print ed.
    p. cm.
  Originally published: New York : Penguin Press, c2010.
  ISBN 978-1-60285-925-8 (library binding : alk. paper)
  1. Canton (Ohio)—Biography. 2. Canton (Ohio)—Economic conditions—20th century.
  3. Canton (Ohio)—History—20th century. 4. Stone, Samuel, 1887–1981.
  5. Benefactors—Ohio—Canton—Biography.
  6. Benevolence—Ohio—Canton—History—20th century. I. Title.
  F499.C2G87 2010b
  977.1′62—dc22
                                                    2010026679

For my mother, Virginia,

Her sister, Dorothy,

And in Memory of Minna and Sam

And the Good People of Canton,

to whom so much is owed

Other states indicate themselves in their deputies—but the genius of the United States is not best or most in its executives or legislatures, nor in its ambassadors or authors, or colleges or churches or parlors, nor even in its newspapers or inventors—but always most in the common people, south, north, west, east, in all its states, through all its mighty amplitude.

—WALT WHITMAN, 1855

It was the ordinary pities and fears consumed us.
We gathered on porches; the moon rose;
we were poor.
What audience would ever know our story?
Beyond our windows shown the actual world.

We gathered on porches; the moon rose;
we were poor.
And time went by, drawn by slow horses.
Somewhere beyond our windows
shown the actual world.
The Great Depression had
entered our souls like fog.

—FROM "PANTOUM OF THE
GREAT DEPRESSION,"
DONALD JUSTICE

Contents

A
Secret Gift

I.

A Christmas Carol

The Offer

[Christmas is] the only time I know of, in the long calendar of the year, when men and women seem by one consent to open their shut-up hearts freely, and to think of people below them as if they really were fellow passengers to the grave, and not another race of creatures bound on other journeys.

—CHARLES DICKENS,
A CHRISTMAS CAROL
(DECEMBER 1843)

It was Sunday, December 17, 1933, a cold and drizzly day, when B. Virdot's plan began to take shape. That evening, outside the First Presbyterian Church, beneath its soaring twin battlements, hundreds of families gathered. Parents took their children's hands and climbed the wide sandstone steps to enter the gothic sanctuary. Here, at the center of this beleaguered city, the faithful had come for generations. President William McKinley himself had been married here. But on this night, they assembled to hear a reading of Charles Dickens's *A Christmas Carol*. It was a tradition of long standing, but during this bleak holiday season, it took on special meaning. Pressed shoulder-to-shoulder in the stiff-backed pews, they were drawn from every corner of the city: church elders, men and women of privilege, jobless millworkers, tradesmen forced to sell their tools, bankrupted shop owners, widows trying to hold on to their children.

At the front of the sanctuary was a crèche with the baby Jesus, and around it, stunted pine trees festooned with tinsel and glistening ornaments. Festive greenery hung from the choir loft above. For many of these children it was all the Christmas they would see. They listened as Dr. Delbert G. Lean, professor of oratory from nearby Wooster College, read of the miserly Ebenezer Scrooge, of the ghosts that tormented him, and of a gift that transformed one poor family's Christmas. Only one who had lived such a life—who had lost his home, seen his father tossed in debtor's prison, and been pressed into factory labor as a child, as Dickens had—could understand what such a tale might mean to these congregants.

Malnourished parishioners must have salivated to hear the words "There never was such a goose . . ." and fought back tears as Tiny Tim proclaimed, "God Bless us, everyone." They too hungered for someone to bless them with a Christmas dinner, to lift them, if only for a moment, out of their misery. Then, one by one, they shuffled past the Reverend James Wilson Bean, steeling themselves against a frigid night and, for many, an empty cupboard.

The pastor too returned to his home, which, like many, had grown accustomed to the soft knock of the hoboes and the homeless, hoping that a walk needed shoveling or a step, mending—in exchange for a sandwich and a cup of coffee. Some members of the church's board would have been glad to be rid of Bean. His outspoken sympathies for the poor were fine, but at that moment the church could ill afford to think of anything but its own survival. Bean's pay had been cut. The "benevolences," as the fund for the needy was called, had been slashed. Church accounts had been frozen with the failure of the Dime Savings Bank in October 1931, forcing it to make do with the few dollars left in petty cash. Attendance was plummeting. Even among the stalwarts, some were losing faith—in themselves, in one another, and in God.

Christmas was a week away, but for many, it meant just another day to get through. For four years, Canton's 105,000 citizens had been battered by the Great Depression. Around town, parents were using strips of tires to extend the life of worn-out shoes, the union mission was bursting with the homeless, and scrawny children in patched coats were scavenging for coal along the B&O Railroad tracks. Many of those lucky enough to still have homes had sold the furniture, beds and all, and huddled together on bare floors or sat on old orange crates. So it was around the country. And B. Virdot saw it all.

Newspapers, selling for three cents a copy, were shared, family to family, and read by kerosene lamp. For many, electricity was a luxury as remote as a ride on the bus or a visit to the doctor. Children went to school on empty stomachs. Many would not learn the meaning of the word *breakfast* until years later. In back alleys, dogs and cats were left to fend for themselves and could be seen pawing through refuse for scraps. Thousands of Canton's depositors were shocked to discover their banks padlocked, their savings gone. Mothers and fathers did what they could to hide their despair from the children—and from each other. All the while, the asylum, the county poorhouse, the city orphanage, and the reformatory swelled with the casualties of the Hard Times. It was a landscape Dickens would have recognized.

Far off in Washington, a new president had proclaimed earlier in the year that "the only thing we have to fear is fear itself." In Canton, and across the country, it didn't feel that way. By Christmas 1933, two million Americans were homeless. Tens of thousands rode the rails in search of a job. One in four Americans was out of work. In Ohio, it was worse. There the jobless numbered more than one in three. And in industrial centers like Canton some put the number at 50 percent. There was no purpose in counting. No relief was to be had.

Until then, Canton had always been a proud city

where skilled and unskilled hands alike had found opportunity. Its immigrant-rich labor pool, the centrality of its location, the convergence of railroads, and the richness of its mineral deposits had given rise to major industries, like Hoover, Timken, Diebold, and Republic Steel. The sweepers, roller bearings, safes, and steel they produced could be found worldwide. Now some forges were idle and cold. Many assembly lines were reduced to skeleton crews that went through the motions of maintenance, turning out the lights, and going home.

Like towns and cities across the land, Canton was sinking fast, mired in a systemic failure so pervasive that it bred more resignation than revolution. No institution existed—neither government, church, nor charity—to stem the misery. Bankruptcies mounted. Families were evicted over and over and over again. To some in this city notorious for graft and vice—by one count it had 108 brothels, outnumbering even its churches—it seemed that crime alone flourished. Dubbed "Little Chicago," its corruption-fighting city editor had been gunned down by the mob seven years before. His posthumous Pulitzer couldn't save the dying newspaper.

That Christmas of 1933 was a time when consumption meant TB, not a shopping spree, and the stigma of the dole was as hard to face as hunger itself. Prohibition had ended two weeks earlier, but who could afford a drink? Nothing was thrown out, and a new product called Scotch tape helped mend the torn and tattered. *The Lone Ranger* premiered on radio, bringing a masked outsider to the rescue of communities unable to save themselves. Even the weather had turned against them. That Friday, two days before the Dickens reading, a freakish storm had pummeled Canton. Its torrential rains set a record, and its lightning and thunder filled the December skies with an anger rarely seen so late in the year.

"Do you think we will get out of this Depression just because we got out of all the others?" asked humorist Will Rogers. "Lots of folks drown that's been in the water before."

NO ONE UNDERSTOOD the Hard Times better than Mr. B. Virdot. And so, that same Sunday, December 17, 1933, he arranged to have an ad placed in the Monday morning edition of the *Canton Repository*. It was no bigger than a playing card and appeared on page 3. And there, it might have gotten lost above an ad for Blue Arrow gasoline and next to a story in which scientists touted the prowess of the "tiny gene." But the ad was not lost. A mere 158 words, it would catch the eye of the entire town, be passed from household to household, then spread by word of mouth well beyond, making news as far away as New York. It read in full:

In Consideration Of
The White Collar Man!

Suppose if I were confronted with an economic situation where the bread of tomorrow is the problem of today—there is a question in my mind if I would accept charity directly offered by welfare organizations. I know there are hundreds of men that are confronted with economic problems and think, feel and act the same way.

To men or families in such position the maker of this offer, who will remain unknown until the very end, will be glad if he is given an opportunity to help from 50 to 75 such families so they will be able to spend a merry and joyful Christmas.

To such men or families that will request such financial aid, the writer pledges that their identity will never be revealed. Please write:

B. VIRDOT,
GENERAL DELIVERY,
CANTON, OHIO

In writing, please familiarize me with your true circumstances and financial aid will be promptly sent.

Even before the ad appeared, it created such a stir in the newsroom that the editors decided to write a front-page story about the offer, assuring it citywide attention. The headline read: MAN WHO FELT DEPRESSION'S STING TO HELP 75 UNFORTUNATE FAMILIES: ANONYMOUS GIVER, KNOWN ONLY AS "B. VIRDOT," POSTS $750 TO SPREAD CHRISTMAS CHEER. The story noted that five years earlier—before the crash and the Depression—the benefactor had enjoyed all the comforts of life and "money poured in." Then the Hard Times caught up with him. Two years earlier—1931—he was broke and "headed into bankruptcy.

"But there were friends who believed in him," the story went on, "and creditors who had confidence that he would come back. He hung on, and fought." The story was a Depression-era parable of the Good Samaritan and a plea to others not to give up. There was also an ominous reference to the donor's "remembrance of much darker days." Just how the writer knew this much of the donor is unclear. Perhaps he was privy to the secret, or perhaps some intermediary shared this information with him.

The gift, the paper explained, was meant for those who might otherwise "hesitate to knock at charity's door for aid." Such hesitation went beyond the stigma attached to accepting charity. Canton's streets, like those of other Depression-era

24

towns, teemed with grifters and con artists. An offer like B. Virdot's was sure to draw as much suspicion as hope. Was this stranger who hid behind a false name really on the up-and-up? To the skeptics, the paper offered words of reassurance: "This is a genuine Christmas gift, involving no strings and no embarrassment to the recipients."

"The name, 'B. Virdot,' is of course, fictitious," the paper observed. "Perhaps the name 'Kris Kringle' is fictitious too, but the genuineness of the spirit of giving he represents has never been questioned."

Not surprisingly, within two days, the post office was deluged with letters addressed to "Mr. B. Virdot, General Delivery, Canton, Ohio." And though the offer was specifically addressed to the "White Collar Man," it ignited a wave of appeals from men and women alike, from the elderly and from children. There was Harry Stanley, a blacksmith out of work for two years, who hoped his five small children might have something for Christmas; there were James Burson, a cook whose last job was in July 1931, and Dan Jordan, a Timken Company policeman whose pay and hours had been slashed and who fretted about his four children, two of whom were deaf; there was Joe Rogers, an unemployed janitor, and Charles Minor, a jobless steeplejack living on bread and coffee; there was Ervin Neiss, a pipe fitter swamped by hospital bills and locked out from his own life savings by the American Exchange Bank, and Ethel Dickerhoff, a mother of nine whose husband was a plumber with no work in sight.

The letters came from every walk of life—from a roofer, a car dealer, a locksmith, a millworker, a carpenter, a stonecutter, a musician, a grocer, a farmer, an ex-con, a butcher, a bell captain, a roofer, a railroad man, a cobbler, a bricklayer, a bookie, a pastor's assistant, and an array of fallen executives that read like a Who's Who of city notables. In a postscript, former bookkeeper Richard E. Anderson wrote, "I am an office man." But by then he'd been reduced to years of odd jobs. And there were children who secretly took up their pens and pencils and asked on behalf of parents too proud to seek help themselves, children like twelve-year-old Mary Uebing, whose widowed mother was trying to feed six.

How many letters came in—whether it was hundreds or thousands—no one knows. And true to his word, within days, the shadowy B. Virdot sent out the promised checks, all of them arriving before Christmas. Initially he had intended to send ten dollars to some seventy-five families, but he found himself unable to turn away so many worthy appeals, so he doubled the recipients and halved the amount to five dollars. Today, five dollars doesn't sound like much, but back then, it would have been worth closer to one hundred dollars. For many, it was more than they had seen in a long time. In 1933, you could get a loaf of bread for seven cents, a pound of ground beef for eleven cents, a dozen eggs for twenty-nine cents. Eighteen cents bought a gallon of gas. The newly passed minimum wage was thirty-three cents, but many counted themselves lucky to make a dollar a day.

B. Virdot never imagined his modest checks would reverse the course of the Great Depression, but they did allow for many a child to go to bed with a full stomach, for presents to miraculously appear, for enough coal to heat the house that week and into the next, and some token payment for the family doctor who'd looked after a son's polio, a daughter's jaundice, or a father's tuberculosis. Given that many families had six, seven, or eight children, the 150 checks cumulatively reached a wide swath of Canton's neediest.

But B. Virdot's gift was more than just a long shot at a lottery. It raised the spirits of thousands with the knowledge that someone—one of their own—cared. He had invited them to share with him their years of pent-up grief, disillusionment, and feelings of worthlessness, burdens that could not be shared with loved ones without the risk of breaking their spirits. That Christmas, even those B. Virdot did not choose received more than a glancing blessing from his gift.

But who was this B. Virdot? There must have

been rampant speculation. Perhaps the donor was one of Canton's millionaires, a Hoover, a Timken, or some other highborn son of privilege able to ride out the Depression in style. But they had not known any such "darker days," as hinted at in the *Repository*. Perhaps, then, he was a man of the people, someone more like themselves who had also suffered. Had he perhaps been sitting there amid the congregants of the First Presbyterian Church, himself moved by Dickens's tale of redemption? Perhaps he belonged to St. John's, the nearby Catholic church. The deed itself shed little light on the man. But it was so Christian an act, this gift, with its wish that its recipients have a "merry and joyful Christmas." Whoever he was, he must surely be a person of faith to shore up the faith of so many. And what had he endured—again, that reference to "darker days"—that he could understand so well what so many in government and charities did not—that those without were not without pride?

For seventy-five years, B. Virdot's identity remained a secret. The letters seemingly vanished and B. Virdot went quietly to his grave, joined in time by all who had written to him. But the mystery surrounding his gift lingered: Who among so many needy had been chosen for such a gift? Did it make any difference in their lives? Who was B. Virdot and why all the secrecy? Finally, what in his own life had so moved him to make such a gift?

In the decades that followed, Canton once again enjoyed the blessings of prosperity. The factories boomed once more, the forges glowed, and the vacant storefronts came back to life. For many, Christmas became a time of overindulgence, when presents were piled high and food and drink were in abundance. Memories of the Hard Times grew mercifully dim, but so too did its lessons. Three generations later, it was as if none of it had happened—the Great Depression and B. Virdot's gift both seemed beyond remote, mere figments of that collective imagination called "history."

And there, this tale might well have ended, but it did not.

Mr. B. Virdot's Story:
The Suitcase

June 24, 2008. That day, my son Matt and I drove three hours from our log cabin in Bucksport, Maine, south to Kennebunk, to surprise my mother, Virginia. It was her eightieth birthday. After dinner, she took us to her storage room under the attic eaves. There was something she said she wanted me to have. I stood in the center of the room, surrounded by the artifacts of her downsized life—a century-old brass cash register, a bronze stand for umbrellas and walking canes, an ivory mah-jongg set, a crated chandelier. She made straightaway for an old black suitcase that lay on a shelf, wedged between Grandfather's adding machine and some Pyrex dishes. On top of it was a box of memorabilia and a wooden case of serving cutlery.

Mother freed the suitcase from its niche and set it on the floor. Inside, she said, were some "old papers"; exactly what, she did not know. But she knew about my interest in family history and my passion for research and, eager to clear out storage space in the cramped attic, she'd decided to make a present of the suitcase. Twice widowed, she had begun to pare away her belongings, not wishing to leave my sister Audrey and me with the sort of monumental cleanup she'd faced when her mother, Minna, passed three years earlier.

Like me, Minna was a pack rat. Both of us were teased for our inability to throw anything away. We were the family archivists. For us, every old scrap of paper—be it a canceled check, the stub of a movie ticket, a book of unused World War II ration stamps—held a narrative that could fill an afternoon. Clearing out the detritus of Minna's ninety-seven years fell to her two surviving daughters, who had neither the time nor the patience to sift through the thousands of pages she'd accumulated. Much of it went out with the trash. That the suitcase and its contents escaped this fate was something of a miracle.

The next morning I loaded the suitcase, unopened, into the car, along with our backpacks and gear, and returned to the cabin. I slid the suitcase under my bed, where it remained for days. Then, one evening, I remembered it, and placed it on my bed. I studied it for a moment. But for a few bruises, it looked to be in decent shape. The corners were frayed and there were places where the faux leather had been scraped clean down to the gray boarding underneath, but the hinges were strong and the latches retained their snap. The suitcase measured eleven by eighteen inches and was six inches deep, with a black leather handle, pebbled to the touch. It was too big to be a briefcase, too small to be of much use as luggage.

Taped to the top of the suitcase was a four-by-six-inch piece of paper, with notes written in faded blue ink in my grandmother's hand: "Memoirs: Minna's Baby Book, etc., Mother and Father, Sam's Clippings and Pictures, Sampler, Baby Dress, Wedding Book, Family Misc." Beside one latch was a blue tag, evidence that it had once been shipped by Allied. It was one of a dozen moves the suitcase had endured on its journey from Canton to Miami to Kennebunk.

I popped open the latches. It released a musty smell, a mix of old papers, decayed suitcase lining, and air long trapped within. The top inside of the case had five yellowed pockets of varying sizes, each with a snap. I imagined what each might have held in its day—perhaps a brush, a comb, a mirror, a nail file, tweezers. The suitcase was crammed with old papers, stacked tightly, one upon the other.

On top was a large and tattered ten-by-thirteen-inch yellow envelope written in my grandfather Sam's hand: "PERTANING XMAS GIFT DISTRIBTION." He never was much for spelling.

Inside the packet was a tight sheaf of letters. I withdrew a handful. All of them were dated December 18, 1933—the week before Christmas. Among the letters I found a tiny black passbook from Canton's George D. Harter Bank. It recorded a single deposit of $750. There were also some 150 canceled checks, each neatly signed "B. Virdot." I had no idea what to make of any of it. The name "B. Virdot" sounded vaguely familiar, but why, I did not know. Even by my grandmother's standards of hoarding, this collection of papers—canceled checks, all of them for five dollars, the passbook with an account opened and emptied within a week, the mass of letters—seemed unworthy of saving. Perhaps, I speculated, they were remnants of some exotic Christmas promotion my grandfather had staged at his clothing store.

I skimmed the first lines of a few of the letters but the handwriting was poor and put me off. I soon lost interest in them, distracted by more recognizable treasures—my grandmother's baby book, letters from Sam and Minna's courtship, dozens of faded black-and-white photos from the 1920s and 1930s, files from my grandfather's business. The hours passed. It grew late and I was tired. I gathered up the contents of the suitcase, which now lay scattered across my bed, and set them back in the suitcase in the order in which I had found them, placing the packet of letters to this stranger, Mr. B. Virdot, back in its original position on top of all else. I then closed the suitcase, fastened the latches, and slid it back under my bed. I promptly forgot about it.

Then, some days later, I found myself again sorting through the suitcase, but this time I was drawn to the envelope marked "PERTANING XMAS GIFT DISTRIBTION." This time I withdrew all the letters. There appeared to be a couple hundred. They were in no particular order, but someone—presumably my grandmother—had gone to some trouble to keep them all carefully together and safe. I began to read through them, beginning with those that looked most legible. They spoke of hunger and cold, of endless searches for work, of dead ends and growing doubts. I was startled by their candor and disturbed by the grim terrain they described. The street names and landmarks were all familiar to me. The writers poured their hearts out to this B. Virdot, describing their anguish in such detail that it made me uncomfortable, as if I were peering through a keyhole into the misery of strangers, or eaves-dropping on others' prayers. How, I wondered, had these letters and their appeals found their way into my grandparents' hands?

It was then that I found, folded into quarters, a front-page section of the *Canton Repository* dated December 18, 1933. The paper was yellowed and torn at the edges. I gently unfolded it and set it on the bed, searching the page for some reference to my grandparents. There was none to be found. There was a story about a fatal car crash and another about two freighters caught in a Pacific gale. There was an account of a steel strike and a brief note about a burglary that netted the robbers twenty-five dollars. But there was nothing to link any of this to my grandparents.

Then I noticed, at the bottom of the page, with a tear running up the center of the story and dissecting the headline, an account of a mysterious donor named "Mr. B. Virdot." As I read it, I felt a cold shiver pass up my spine. The contents of the envelope, the letters, the canceled checks, all began to fall into place. I searched for B. Virdot's offer referred to in the story but could not find it. I searched again and again. Nothing. Finally, my eyes fell upon it on page 3, a tiny ad so easily missed it seemed a wonder anyone found it. I read it over twice and then again. Here, before me, the seventy-five-year-old secret had been revealed.

B. Virdot was my grandfather. His name was Sam Stone.

THAT EVENING I called my mother to share my discovery, but it was something she had known her entire adult life. Her mother had let her in on the secret when she was considered old enough to honor Sam's wish and to keep it in the family. The moniker "B. Virdot," she said, was constructed from the names of Sam and Minna's three daughters: Barbara, Virginia, and Dorothy, known as "Dotsy." My mother was the "Vir" in "B. Virdot."

She also explained why the name sounded familiar. In the late 1930s and early 1940s, when the three girls were not yet teenagers, Sam would take them jetting across Turkey Foot Lake in his sleek twenty-seven-foot Chris-Craft Custom Runabout, with its varnished mahogany and 350-horsepower engine. Just above the waterline was stenciled the boat's name—*The B. Virdot*. It was a county away from Canton and no one made the connection between the name and the mystery donor of years earlier. He liked such inside jokes, parading before the world clues to his identity that only he could decipher. That was where I had heard the name B. Virdot, from stories about the speedboat and my mother's halcyon summer days on the lake.

But in 1933, when my mother was just five, she had known nothing of her father's gift. Preserving the secret had been critical to its success. Many of those who wrote to B. Virdot were known to Sam Stone, as he was known to them. He passed them on the streets, frequented the same restaurants and shops, and sent his daughters to school with their children. In his store he measured their sleeves, cuffed their pants, squared their shoulders, and sold them their overalls. And they, in their countless trades and callings, attended to his needs. It was only the promise of anonymity on both sides of the divide that had persuaded his fellow townsmen to speak freely and to come forward. They were proud men and women, acutely sensitive to the situation they found themselves in, and would never have felt comfortable writing such letters to anyone whose face they might recognize or see again. Their appeal to B. Virdot was less an application for relief than it was a prayer for deliverance. It just so happened to carry a local address.

But in solving one mystery, I had given birth to another. Why had my grandfather done such a thing? And why, over the course of four decades and countless conversations with him, had he never mentioned it? In my mind I retraced my memories of him, searching for some clue he might have dropped along the way. There was nothing that tied the man I knew to the benefactor others knew only as B. Virdot.

As a child I called him "Sambo." He stood a stout five feet five, and was bald and barrel-chested, with Popeye-like forearms. His eyes were soft and brown and looked out on the world through thick lenses. Somewhere I have a photo of him in his eighties wearing my father's red flannel pajamas. The legs were long by nearly half a foot. I watched him climb the steps, his Chaplinesque figure trying not to trip over them. He looked like a melted candle and laughed at his own comic figure.

There was an impishness to him and a mimelike quality, as if there were more to be learned from his movements than his words. Mother recalls nights watching him teach himself to ice skate, taking a dining room chair out on frozen Turkey Foot Lake and dancing with it as if it were his partner. That image—in his pas de deux under the stars—and countless other exuberant moments invited none of the modern psychobabble suggesting early trauma or scarring. There was always about him a sense that what you saw was exactly what you got. It was a tactic that served him well.

At every party, he was the toastmaster. His remarks tended to be wooden and grandiloquent, sounding vaguely like a Marx Brothers caricature of high society. It was how the formally educated sounded to him. I have a tiny joke book of his in which he jotted down his favorite punch lines. It's divided into three sections, "Safe," "Caution," and "Danger." The first two are all but blank. "Danger" is packed with off-color entries. To me he was a grandfather so mischievous and impulsive that even as a child I felt I should keep a close eye on him.

He was also a magician. He could withdraw a quarter from behind my ear or from my navel and make it vanish with a sweep of his hand. He knew the eyes saw what they wanted to see, and no more. He played this to great advantage in his magic and in his life. The more public his persona, the less, it seemed, he had to hide. He courted the limelight in part perhaps because it gave him control over others' attention and kept it from straying into private realms.

The Sam I knew was well-to-do. The Sam my

mother knew was downright rich. My mother grew up with a live-in butler and maid, Steve and Hermene, a Hungarian couple, in a summer cottage on a lake and a Tudor home with a library and a well-tended garden. Mother and her two sisters wanted for nothing. As a senior in high school, my mother was treated to a luxurious full-length beaver coat. But such wealth was to come only after 1933, and some portion of it was gone before I really knew my grandfather. He had lived with great poverty and wealth, and made his peace with both.

The Hard Times he'd known had not waited for the Depression. I knew nothing of the years before 1918, when he turned thirty. No one was privy to those years, and any attempt to pry into them was instantly deflected with humor or a story. He told me only that he was born in Pittsburgh and graduated from the "School of Hard Knocks." He spoke of working in a coal mine, a job he despised. He said he scoured dirty soda bottles until the acid ate his fingertips. As he told the story decades later, his thumb gently caressed the tips of his digits as if they still needed soothing. He said he learned to swim after being pushed off a barge in Pittsburgh's Monongahela River. But no narrative reached back as far as childhood, adolescence, or early manhood. All his many stories seemed to abruptly run out of track before arriving there.

He looked upon his life as an alchemist might

have viewed base metals, transforming sorrow and treachery into gilded tales of mirth and high jinks. I remember him telling me about the first suit he bought. It had taken him months to save for it. He related how proud he was carrying it home in the box the salesman had handed him. But once home, he discovered that instead of a suit, the box held nothing but a brick. He returned to the store and demanded his money back. The salesmen ignored him. Sam laughed when he recounted the story. It was the laugh of a man whose idea of vengeance was grounded in living large and well. Twenty years after being cheated, he owned a chain of clothing stores that stretched across four states and held a thousand suits.

He told me that he was once lured to board a train in the middle of the night, bound for where, he did not know. All he knew was that there was a job for him at the other end. When the train arrived—I think it was Chicago—he and hundreds like him were ordered to follow closely behind those who had brought them, to race through the darkness and stop for nothing and no one. This he did, until, in the melee that followed, he was bloodied and struck by the fists of strikers and the clubs of company guards. He had been duped into being a strike breaker. Again, he laughed. A onetime socialist-turned-capitalist, he'd seen the faults in both and was a true believer in neither.

My grandfather often quoted lines of verse and

aphorisms that expressed both his optimism and his determination to let go of the past. In 1959, when my grandmother was ill, he wrote her: "More than ever, I tried to bring to life my old slogan that you are familiar with—'Each night I bury the record of today, for every morning a soul is born anew, and I do not permit the disappointments of today or yesterday to reflect on the possibilities of tomorrow.'"

When my grandparents passed they left to my mother odds and ends of furniture, some miniature silver pieces, a bottle of forbidden absinthe, and a bronze sculpture of an athlete in midjump clearing a hurdle. The latter, titled *The Jumper*, was one of Sam's prized possessions, one that he had as long as anyone could remember. Standing about eighteen inches high, it is a handsome piece, the figure muscular and balletic. It was prominently displayed in Sam's office in Canton. It followed him through a succession of offices, homes, and apartments, through up times and down, first in Canton, and later in Florida. We knew nothing of its origins or its sculptor. But wherever Sam went, it was there on display. I admired it even as a child.

I came to believe that for Sam, who was not a collector of art, the sculpture represented his personal triumphs over so many hurdles. I had not yet discovered that the sculpture had a deeper, more personal link to Sam, that it was yet another of those clues to an encrypted life. In my mind I revisited all his stories and toasts, reexamined the few possessions he'd left behind, reread his letters and postcards, and still I had the sense that the jovial and mischievous Sambo I knew was a man of secrets. Indeed, as it would turn out, finding the identity of B. Virdot was the easy part. Discovering the true identity of Sam Stone would put my sleuthing skills to the ultimate test.

IN THE WEEKS and months after I had been given the suitcase, I found myself repeatedly returning to its contents. I would withdraw the B. Virdot letters by the handful and lose myself in their words. These were the voices of my hometown speaking from the depths of the Great Depression. All but one were handwritten, some in pen, others in pencil. Some letters, like that from the painter Bill Gray, were six pages long; others, like that from fourteen-year-old Helen Palm, were just a few lines on a single page, a simple plea for food and clothing. Anna DeWalt sought money to pay for her husband's funeral. (In Canton, there were both a commercial building and a street named for a DeWalt family.) August Liermann hoped Christmas dinner for his eight children might be more than what little he had—"two string ends of ham." Fourteen-year-old Betty Taylor had gone without a winter coat. Hazel Baum hoped to buy milk and fresh eggs to soothe her husband, Edward's, ulcers. Frances Lindsay secretly sought help for the family of Willis Evans, which, though down on its luck, had taken others in. And forty-three-year-old Lloyd Stover, once a skilled ironworker who built bridges and now a part-time janitor, would put the money toward feeding his family of four.

Most were from the city, but some were from the farms and rural reaches just outside town; many wrote in secret, lest their families discover their desperation; some notes were barely literate and written on irregular scraps of paper or envelopes steamed open to create a page; Clara Brenner, a mother of seven and wife of an out-of-work railroad brakeman, wrote hers on a postcard; others were written on the formal stationery of long-defunct businesses. The latter came from onetime executives with polished prose and perfect penmanship. Their names and titles were embossed at the top of the pages, but their words described paupers' lives. George D. Coldren, once a prominent real estate agent, wrote his letter on the back of an "Application to Purchase" that carried the name of his company, whose offices had been in the First National Bank Building. Black and white, foreign-born and native alike, the scions of privilege and privation—all of them leveled by the same Hard Times.

My grandfather kept only those 150 letters to whom he had sent checks. (The others would doubtless have weighed upon him.) How many letters he may have received is unknowable. I searched for some hint of how he had triaged the mass of appeals, how he decided who would get relief and who would not. There was nothing. Among the letters was a smattering of thank-you notes as well as pages from a typed ledger, a detailed account of each dispersal. If words of encouragement had accompanied the outgoing checks, as was suggested in some of the incoming thank-you notes, there was no record of them in the suitcase.

I wondered why, given all the secrecy surrounding this gift, he and my grandmother had taken the trouble to save the letters. Again, they left no clues. Did they see in them some historical value, wishing to preserve the voices of a struggling town? Was it a matter of routine record keeping? Did they foresee the day when a curious grandchild might stumble upon them? All unanswered questions. But it was my good fortune that the suitcase found its way into my hands. I was the author in the family. A former investigative reporter with the *Washington Post*, I had always been drawn to the extraordinary lives of "ordinary people." I was fascinated with history, and felt an attachment to my hometown undiminished by thirty-five years' absence. And the discovery could not have been more timely.

As I read the letters, America was descending into the worst economic times since the Great

Depression. Canton was once again suffering double-digit unemployment, its soup kitchens and shelters overwhelmed. Unable to provide for all the needy, shelters were giving the homeless bus tickets out of town in the hopes that someone down the line could help. It was no accident that candidate Barack Obama would choose Canton as the location to deliver his campaign's closing argument on October 27, 2008, telling the stricken community what it already knew too well: "We are in the midst of the worst economic crisis since the Great Depression."

In reading the letters, I couldn't help but wonder whether I was peering into the past or glimpsing the future. As the specter of new Hard Times gripped Canton and the nation, as the ranks of the needy swelled, the benevolent spirit of Mr. B. Virdot reappeared with the discovery of this weathered old suitcase. It was as if some genie in a bottle had simply been waiting for his time to come round again, waiting for a grandson and another generation, hard-pressed, to summon him.

As a student of history, I thought I understood the Great Depression. I had seen the black-and-white photos of Dorothea Lange and Walker Evans, read Steinbeck and other writers of the period, and knew the outlines of the New Deal. For me the Depression was a series of disjointed images—breadlines; soup kitchens; the Dust Bowl; FDR in an open car, teeth clutching a cigarette holder. The Depression I knew was a chapter in a history book, fertile ground for scholarship and film. But it had been sapped of its immediacy.

That was before I read these letters. It would be some months before I recognized what a rare, perhaps unique, historical trove had literally been placed in my hands. There are many extant letters from the period, and oral histories aplenty that record the trauma of those years, but here before me was a contemporaneous account of an entire community, written with an intimacy and candor that only the perpetual assurance of secrecy could have produced. Because these letters were never intended for the public eye, they are among the most unvarnished and compelling accounts of those years. Collectively they preserve the struggle not merely of an individual or a family but of an entire town at the very time that it was being ravaged by the harshest poverty America had ever known. In the minute details of their lives can be seen the stirrings of vast societal and political changes that would reshape the nation, and the emergence of a generation so respected that three-quarters of a century later its descendants would hail it as "the Greatest."

But early on, I saw in the letters only the suffering of my hometown. Some of the signatures—Haverstock, DeHoff, Dick, Vogt—were names that were known to me. The return addresses framed the universe of my childhood. And yet the landscape was barely recognizable. Such desolation as the letters described seemed light-years from the tree-lined streets and manicured lawns of my upbringing. Born in 1950, I had grown up in an America where there was always a net beneath my feet, where recessions were hailed as "buying opportunities," and where euphemisms pillowed every fall from fortune. I had come to view the Depression as a historical blip, as when a plane in an otherwise cloudless sky hits a small pocket of bad air.

But true "Hard Times," the ones severe enough to be capitalized, meant more than declining wealth or momentary setbacks. The B. Virdot letters were a portal into a Dantean landscape. Here, there was no bottom, no cushion to the fall, just an abyss threatening to swallow loved ones whole. These letters were the entrance to that netherworld. This chorus of plaintive voices, long stifled, were again vying for the attention of a stranger—this time, the grandson of B. Virdot.

I read them and reassured myself that I did so from a safe distance. Social Security, Medicare, the Federal Deposit Insurance Corporation (FDIC), and unemployment were there to catch us if we fell. As a child of prosperous times, I believed that there could be no second Depression. Like polio, it was a thing of the past. Mine, I believed, was an age in which regulation moderated risk—only the rash and the reckless had anything to fear, and I was neither.

But in absorbing the news, it was impossible not to hear at least a faint echo of Hard Times in my own—the layoffs, the foreclosures, the bank failures, the bankruptcies, the swooning stock market, the Ponzi schemes and speculators. Iconic industries collapsed. A new vocabulary took hold, one that included *TARP* and *toxic assets*. By June 2009, two million more Americans were out of work than in the depths of 1933. Granted, the percentage was smaller—10 percent versus 24 percent—but that was little comfort to the sixteen million jobless. By year's end, 140 banks had failed, another 500 were on the precipice, and the FDIC was running on fumes. "Too big to fail" had become an ironic epitaph.

How long the aftereffects of the Great Recession would last, no one knew, and even many of those who had seemingly outrun the storm were faced with preparing for its longer-term consequences. Reading the letters put things in perspective. They reminded me of the difference between discomfort and misery, between the complaints of consumers forced to rein in their spending and the keening of parents whose children went hungry night after night.

That evening of June 24, 2008, when my mother handed me the suitcase, she had no idea its contents would touch so many lives—hers, mine, and the descendants of those who had written the letters. To us, it seemed, at the very least, fortuitous that the letters should surface after a seventy-five-year repose, and that the gift that illuminated a community in need so long ago might do so once again. But though I am an author, it did not yet occur to me that this was a story for a wider audience. It was about my grandfather, my neighbors, my hometown. I saw it all in personal terms.

The letters helped me understand what our neighbors had endured and how the legacy of their suffering shaped the character of my community and my family—why it was that grace was said before meals, why the chance to work overtime was seen as a blessing, why sacrifice was the only thing to be taken for granted. I read the letters as the backstory to my own life and that of my hometown, not yet seeing in them the backstory of a nation.

And even if the B. Virdot letters were worthy of being shared with those beyond Canton, I felt chastened by the secrecy that sealed them and my grandfather's role. Promises had been made. How could I, even after so many decades, dishonor him and them by making it all public? The right of privacy may have ended with the writers' deaths, but should not their pride and dignity outlive them?

Late in the summer of 2008 I put the suitcase

away and forgot about it. In the ensuing months, America's economy cratered. My family too was touched. My sister lost her job. My mother's travel business collapsed. The house across the street was foreclosed and vacant. And once again, neighbors began to reference the Great Depression. By late 2008, Americans began to provision themselves financially and emotionally against something they had only heard about—"the Hard Times."

Then, one night at three in the morning in mid-November 2008, I sat up in bed and recognized the letters for what they were—not a dusty archive but a time capsule addressed to the present, one that had taken on a sense of urgency. And so I got out of bed and wrote about B. Virdot's gift. The next morning I hesitantly e-mailed the story to the *New York Times*, fearing they would dismiss it as too parochial or personal. The response from the editor was immediate: "Remarkable. How do we know it's true?" I offered proof—photocopies of the letters. The piece ran on the op-ed page three days before Christmas, on December 22, 2008—seventy-five years to the day when the B. Virdot checks arrived in Canton's neediest homes. Within twenty-four hours it was the second-most e-mailed story in the *New York Times* and drew e-mails from as far away as England, China, Italy, Japan, Israel, Saudi Arabia, and Brazil. Only then did I begin to grasp the power of B. Virdot's gift.

In America, President George W. Bush and then

Barack Obama would pour hundreds of billions of dollars into the wilting economy, prop up megacorporations, and invoke lofty Rooseveltian rhetoric. But it was the smallness of B. Virdot's gift—a mere five dollars—that was its magic, not an act of governmental grandiosity but a gesture of human compassion. In a country reeling from the likes of Bernie Madoff, the avarice of hedge fund managers, and the potentates of failed financial institutions, the story of B. Virdot's gift came as welcome relief.

It stood as a rebuke to those whose creed had been "More is better." Against the billions being doled out, the B. Virdot dollars were dwarfed, and would have been lost in the first rounding off of even the most modest relief effort. It was precisely that, its puniness and its purity, which gave it its transformative power, then and now. It was too small to put even a dent in the Great Depression but just enough to fend off the sense that no one cared and nothing could be done. For one moment, in one forgotten town, one man managed to shrink the vastness of the Depression to a human scale.

Reading the letters to B. Virdot also reminded me that community is more than collective self-interest. The Depression was a calamity that brought incalculable suffering to the greedy and the innocent alike. There is no romanticizing the wreckage it wrought. But it also rid us of our sense of entitlement and made us take inventory of our intangible wealth. The Depression was like a great anvil upon which our national character was beaten into shape. It forged an indomitable spirit we later recognized as "the Greatest Generation."

Still, I was unsure if writing for the *Times* had been the right thing to do. I worried that my grandmother would not have approved. The day the *Times* story ran I returned home and found phone messages from readers. But first I had to wade through old messages that had to be saved or erased. One of these was from my grandmother. She had passed away three years earlier, but I had not been able to bring myself to erase her voice. Now, on this day, she spoke to me again—this time, from the grave:

"Dearest Wonderful Ted . . . I am so proud of you. . . . Thank you for your wonderful love of me and your devotion. God Bless you. . . . I love you, darling . . . Minna." Once more I saved the message. I could not help but feel she had given me her blessing to continue. And so I did.

Over the ensuing year I combed through thousands of pages of documents in an effort to track down the descendants of those who had written to B. Virdot. I wanted to know what had become of them. Did they survive? Did they go on to prosper? Did they become part of some permanent underclass? Did they know about the B. Virdot gift, and if so, did it make a difference in their lives?

I began my research by reading all the letters, then focused on about fifty that seemed representative of the rest. Over time, I developed a methodology that served me well in locating the descendants of those who wrote to B. Virdot. I began with the Canton city directory from 1933 that alphabetically listed the residents, their trade, employer, spouse, and sometimes their children. From there I searched by name in the U.S. Censuses for 1910, 1920, and 1930. This provided me such vital information as age, family members, place of birth, national origin, date of naturalization, native language, and level of literacy. It also gave me a snapshot of the immediate community, listing the same information about their neighbors. I combed through World War I draft registration forms and land records. In Canton's probate court, I searched wills, death records, and marriage licenses. The latter allowed me to trace the lives of daughters who later took their husbands' last names.

Death records provided me not only the cause of death and place of burial but the names of the attending physician and the parents of the letter writers. Parents' names allowed me to track family histories going back in time. Taking the date of death from the death certificate, I could find the person's obituary in the newspaper, and that gave me a condensed life story of the deceased, and, even more important, the names of surviving family members, which allowed me to come forward in time to the present. I also pored over ships' passenger lists and naturalization records and microfilmed copies of the *Canton Repository*. I was given access to the county's orphanage records and the state's prison records.

There my work ended—with regard to documents—and began with regard to people. Using various online search sites and telephone directories I tracked down the survivors. Over the course of the next sixteen months, I interviewed about five hundred descendants, many of them multiple times. To my surprise, seventy-five years after B. Virdot made his offer, nearly all the descendants still called Canton "home." Many lived within five miles of where their parents or grandparents had written their letters during the Great Depression.

I read them the letters. Many wept. They provided me with personal stories and family albums, and helped me trace lives across the generations. They shared with me what wisdom, if any, had been handed down from that awful time. I walked the streets and alleyways of my hometown seeing them with new eyes, guided by the voices of the letters. My years as an investigative reporter prepared me well for such a quest.

But I was not prepared for what I was to learn about my grandfather, the man they knew as "B.

Virdot." The same suitcase that contained the letters held tantalizing leads to the identity of Sam Stone, a man whose background was as mysterious to his own family as it was to the recipients of his largesse. For his children and grandchildren, the revelations related to B. Virdot were just the beginning. The same repositories of public records that helped me track down the descendants of those who wrote to Mr. B. Virdot also yielded clues about my grandfather's past. It took months to clear away decades of fabrication and deception—even today, given my feelings for the man, it is hard for me to utter the word *lies*—before I could begin to understand what drove him to make such a gift.

For a year I imagined myself on two parallel pursuits—the one to track down the identities of those who wrote to B. Virdot, the other to discover the true identity and motivation of my grandfather. But over time I came to see the two quests converge. The more I discovered of Sam's secret past, the better I understood the struggles of those he helped. Conversely, the more I learned of those whom he had chosen to aid, the more insight I gained into Sam himself. Only when I could step back far enough was I able to see that the tiny pixels of these myriad individual lives all came together in the face of my grandfather, and that pieces of Sam's own fragmented and secretive life were reflected in each of their stories.

II.

In Consideration of the White Collar Man

It's a recession when your neighbor loses his job;
it's a depression when you lose yours.
—HARRY S. TRUMAN

A Man of Means

Sam, the inveterate prankster, had a favorite trick, one that amused him well into his eighties. He would tape a thread to a dollar bill and leave it in the middle of the hallway outside his apartment, the other end of the thread extending under his door and resting in his hands. His eye would be fixed to the peephole until someone came upon the bill and stooped to pick it up. Then he would give the thread a swift jerk and snatch the bill away before the passerby could lay a finger on it. He could scarcely control his laughter.

In an envelope, I have one of those dollar bills, the long thread still taped to its underside. Like many of his tricks, this one was rooted in Sam's own life. Time and again the prospects of good fortune and better times had been cruelly snatched away from him. But by 1927, he had finally established himself as a respected merchant. He was then thirty-nine. His Canton store, Stone's Clothes, provided him and his new bride with a solid living. He had investments in real estate, and a lifestyle he could never before have imagined. Then came the crash of '29 and it nearly wiped him out. He had allowed himself to become overextended in real estate, the clothing store that he had nurtured was failing, and, like so many businessmen of that period, he stood on the brink of bankruptcy. It was a severe setback, but he'd endured worse. Through it all he did what he could to insulate his wife from financial worries, holding to his routine and concealing whatever doubts he had. A few years later he would recognize that same trait in many of those who wrote to his alias, B. Virdot.

After the reversals of 1929, it took Sam three years to get back on his feet. He worked frightful hours, saved what he could, and turned customers' sensitivities to price to his advantage with promotions such as "Buy a suit and get an extra pair of pants free." His own rough edges, his lack of pretension, and his empathy for their struggles helped him win over the workingman and those just eking by. In him, they recognized one of their own. Like them, he was scrappy, determined to keep what was his, and to win back that which had been lost—even if it meant giving chase to a shoplifter and tackling him blocks away, as he was known to do.

By the fall of 1933 Sam had reestablished himself and his business. Like many businesses that survived those years, his store had become not merely a place to shop but a refuge where men fatigued by years of disappointment and rejection could engage in friendly banter and be valued for more than what was in their pockets. He had a gift for drawing laughter from the dourest of circumstances. It proved to be no small asset in those years.

By late 1933, he was in the enviable position of being able to take advantage of business opportunities others could not. Stores were closing all around him, and retail chains, desperate to raise cash, sought to unload their marginal operations at a fraction of their worth. On September 1, 1933, Sam purchased the Kibler Company and its nine menswear stores in Ohio, Illinois, and West Virginia. But even in the depths of debt, he had sworn that he would repay his creditors, and even those willing to have accepted fifty cents on the dollar were paid in full, though it took years.

As the decades passed, Sam continued to enjoy a life of comfort and luxury, pocked with intermittent setbacks. At home he had a private stash of Beluga caviar, but nothing, in his view, beat the hot dogs served at Woolworth's lunch counter. In later years, when he belonged to the Jockey Club, he drove such a clunker that he was mistaken for the help. It was always as if he were straddling two worlds, prepared to exit one or the other at a moment's notice. To the end, he imagined himself a peasant, unable to swallow his own good fortune. And the way he said the word *peasant* commanded respect. Even in the best of times he saw himself as the man who came upon the dollar bill with the unseen thread attached.

Sam knew the value of hard work but also the caprice of fortune. It was reason enough for his alter ego, B. Virdot, to focus on other "white collar men" whose fate so mirrored his own. He understood them as well as he understood himself. These were men who had invested much of their lives in their work and whose businesses, like his own, carried their names, elevating their personal success in the good times, but exposing their failure to public scrutiny.

Looking out across Canton that Christmas of 1933, what Sam saw resembled nothing so much as a dark version of Monopoly, the board game invented by an out-of-work heating engineer named Charles Darrow and first distributed in 1933 in Philadelphia. But instead of expansion, the sole object was survival. Where one landed in life seemed to have less to do with strategy than with dumb luck and a roll of the dice. Men of means—financial and social pillars of Canton—were brought low, their possessions sold off one by one, their grand homes vacated, their office suites traded in for a broom, a paint brush, or a snow shovel. One minute they were at the pinnacle of success, the next, holding their hand out to a stranger named "B. Virdot." Sam Stone knew firsthand about such vulnerability and what such a fall truly meant—a loss measured not only in dollars and cents but also in self-esteem.

• • •

OF ALL THE letters, none would have resonated more with Sam than the one from George Monnot, who, like Sam, was self-made, a family man, and someone who cared deeply about his community. Their paths doubtless crisscrossed countless times, making it all the more imperative to the success of the B. Virdot offer that Sam's true identity be veiled.

Monnot's name appears in a multivolume history of Stark County that contains sketches of Canton's most prominent and privileged citizens. Published in 1928—a year before the stock market crash and the cascading events that became the Depression—it offers a freeze-frame of Canton at its financial apogee, a time when fortunes and positions seemed secure. The names that appear both in this celebratory volume and on the list of Mr. B. Virdot's checks provide an index of who fell the furthest. When B. Virdot addressed his offer to the "white collar man," it was the likes of George Monnot that he had in mind.

The trajectory of Monnot's career and life closely tracked that of industrial America. In 1905, just two years after Henry Ford incorporated the company that would bear his name, a prescient George W. Monnot looked beyond his modest Canton bicycle shop and opened the city's first Ford dealership. From there his fortunes would rapidly ascend along with Ford's. By 1920, half of all cars in the United States were made by Ford.

The first transcontinental highway—the Lincoln Highway—built in 1928, passed right through Canton, running one short block from Monnot's Ford showroom, and bringing with it a constant flow of traffic. But Monnot's success had not just been a matter of luck. Like Sam, he had proven himself to be a shrewd businessman, surviving when so many lesser rivals did not. In 1916, Canton boasted some twenty car dealerships. Eight were gone before World War I ended. Only three outlasted the depression of 1921.

By 1928, Monnot was accorded three full pages in the *History of Stark County Ohio* and a full-page formal portrait. Dressed in suit and tie, a perfect part in his hair, he looked like the exemplar of corporate America. By that year, his Ford dealership, bearing the name Monnot & Sacher, occupied an entire city block and had a cavernous showroom. The company even had its own eleven-person band that dressed in tuxes and performed under the name of The Monnot & Sacher Serenaders.

In Canton, the Monnot name was well known, the family pedigree widely respected. George Monnot was born in Canton on September 29, 1878, of French stock. His family had helped settle the county a generation earlier. His father, a councilman active in the city's political and religious life, had two sons—George and Richard, and two daughters—Barbara and Joan.

George's wife, Alice, was a socialite and belonged to the Canton Women's Club. Monnot was a prominent member of the Better Business Bureau, the Canton Chamber of Commerce, the Canton Club, and the Brookside Country Club. (As a Jew, Sam Stone was barred from belonging to the last two.) The county history said of Monnot that "he is keenly and helpfully interested in everything that pertains to the welfare and progress of the city and his cooperation can at all times be counted upon to further any plan or measure for the general good. He finds his diversion in golf and hunting and is a lover of all outdoor sports, but he never allows these to interfere with the conduct of his commercial interests."

The fawning portrait noted that "he has developed an enterprise of mammoth proportions. He deserves much credit for what he has accomplished, for he started out in the business world without financial aid soon after entering his teens and has steadily worked his way upward through determination and ability until he is now numbered among the foremost business men of his native city."

To an outsider, he seemed to have it all. Each day Monnot would lunch at Bender's, a fashionable downtown tavern and restaurant where Sam Stone also lunched daily, then stop for a fine cigar at Simpson's and play the tip sheets.

Monnot also had a summer home and a thirty-five-foot yacht at nearby Turkey Foot Lake—not far from where my grandfather had a cottage. It was likely that the two businessmen knew each other, as they traveled in the same orbit. Only one block separated Monnot's dealership from Sam Stone's clothing store.

But just one year after that county history celebrated Monnot's achievements, the stock market crashed. It was 1929. Henry Ford furloughed between twenty-five thousand and thirty thousand workers. The Great Depression was making itself felt everywhere, and Canton was no exception. His grandchildren were told that Monnot's reluctance to lay off some of his employees, notwithstanding his own dire straits, hastened his financial failure. In 1931 Monnot lost his business and his splendid brick home in the upscale Ridgewood neighborhood—the same neighborhood where Sam Stone had lived before business reversals had forced him out of his home. Monnot moved himself, his wife, and his four children into cramped quarters on Woodward Place, more alley than street. His neighbors—the few who could find jobs—were steelworkers and tradesmen.

One of the city's most admired businessmen, he was now struggling to feed his family. He had nothing but his pride and now he was even prepared to put that at risk by reaching out in response to an offer he read in the newspaper from a man named B. Virdot. That day he picked up a pen and wrote these words:

CANTON O. DEC 18-1933
B. VIRDOT GEN. DEL.

Dear Sir:

Your interesting and benevolent article appearing in the Repository prompted me to write and advise how the depression left the writer.

For 26 years was in the Automobile business prosperous at one time and have done more than my share in giving at Christmas and at all times. Have a family of six and struggle is the word for me now for a living.

Xmas will not mean much to our family this year as my business, bank, real estate, Insurance policies are all swept away.

Our resources are nil at present perhaps my situation is no different than hundreds of others. However a man who knows what it is to be up and down can fully appreciate the spirit of one who has gone through the same ordeal.   •

You are to be congratulated for your benevolence and kind offer to those who have experienced this trouble and such as the writer is going through.

No doubt you will have a Happy Christmas as there is more real happiness in giving and making someone else happy than receiving. May I extend to you a very Happy Christmas.

GEORGE W. MONNOT
1329 WOODWARD AVE. NW
CANTON O.

Three days later, on December 21, 1933, check number 22 for five dollars, signed by "B. Virdot," was sent to George W. Monnot. A thank-you note soon followed:

CANTON, OHIO DEC. 27-1933

My Dear Mr. B. Virdot,

Permit me to offer my sincere thanks for your kind remembrance for a Happy Christmas.

Indeed this came in very handy and was much appreciated by myself & family.

It was put to good use paying for 2 pairs of shoes for my girls and other little necessities. I hope some day I have the pleasure of knowing to whom we are indebted for this very generous gift.

At present I am not of employment and it is very hard going. However I hope to make some connection soon.

I again thank you on behalf of the family and an earnest wish is that you have a most Happy New Year.

SINCERELY YOURS
GEORGE W. MONNOT
1329 WOODWARD AVE NW
CANTON OHIO

Beyond that letter, George Monnot could never bring himself to speak of the losses he had suffered. Nor did he ever recover. He refused to declare bankruptcy and, like Sam, insisted that he would repay his debts no matter how long it took. It would, by family accounts, take a decade— well into the 1940s. Even after his business failed, George Monnot remained an inveterate inventor and dabbler. From the Ford dealership, he had salvaged his massive workbench and great wooden tool chest. In the basement of his home he spent endless hours working on projects and schemes, hoping that one or another might restore him and his family to a measure of financial security and position. He was always just one invention away from making it again. The army, in World War I, had been poised to buy the "Hydrocar," an amphibious vehicle he had designed, but the military lost interest with the signing of the armistice.

In short order, Monnot went from owning a thousand cars to owning none. He and his wife had to travel by city bus. He worked until age and health forced him to stop. At seventy-five he was diagnosed with pancreatic cancer and died two months later, on February 27, 1949. On a chill Tuesday morning, March 1, 1949, a Requiem High Mass was sung in his honor at Canton's St. John's Catholic Church and the following morning he was buried in the church cemetery.

But the real epitaph to this once shining career was written on his death certificate. Under "Occupation," he is listed as "Stock Clerk, Hercules Motor." He had indeed become a casualty of the Great Depression, a grand entrepreneur now working as a clerk. As for the giant Hercules Motor plant on the edge of Canton, it was once the world's largest maker of combustion engines and supplied the power to Willys jeeps, landing craft, armored cars, picket boats, and trucks that helped win World War II. The 600,000-plus-square-foot plant sat on twenty-six acres and during the war years operated twenty-four hours a day, seven days a week, employing fifty-eight hundred men and woman. The company produced eighteen thousand engines a month. Monnot, in his own small way, was a part of that effort.

Monnot's precipitous fall from fortune was particularly hard on Alice, his widow. For her, the Depression never ended. For decades after, she was forced to face not only the loss of wealth and position but that of identity and friends as well. She was no longer a part of that elite social circle in which she had long been the center. Instead of vacations in Cuba, a summer home by the lake, and exquisite furniture, she had social security checks. Instead of the grand home, she had a dismal basement apartment. Few visitors ventured down the stairs past the exposed pipes into the spartan one-bedroom apartment where she lived out her life.

But it was perhaps Monnot's eldest son, George E. Monnot, who paid the steepest price during the Depression. A superior student, he yearned to go to college to become an engineer. Instead, to help support the family through those years, he wielded a broom at Weber Dental Manufacturing Company and watched as some of his well-heeled peers went off to college and pursued professions. But over time Monnot rose through the ranks and became a company executive. Later, he wintered in Florida, but the memories of pre-Depression wealth persisted. In his 1994 obituary, it is said of his son George E. Monnot that "He spent much of his youth enjoying the Turkey Foot Lake area and sail boat racing at the South Shore Yacht Club."

The younger son, Richard J., would also reflect back on the earlier days of comfort. When peeved with his wife, Jeannette, he would say, "When we had a maid . . ." But she would cut him off midsentence. Richard Monnot spent thirty-three years working the furnaces at, of all places, Canton's Ford plant, which as late as 1986 employed some nine hundred workers. In 1988 the plant was shut down.

The B. Virdot check that Christmas of 1933 had gone to buy shoes for Monnot's two daughters, Barbara and Joan. That too must have touched Sam. He then had daughters of his own, the youngest named Barbara. But Monnot's daughter Barbara never fully escaped the Depression mentality. She rarely spoke of it directly, but she also, like many who survived it, never complained and was exceedingly frugal. After she died in 1998, her son Tom Haas discovered drawers of old underwear and linens and a host of other things that his mother could not bring herself to throw away. She had become something of a packrat, unable to part with something she might conceivably need later. She lived on social security and never tapped into the investments that accrued from her husband's pension—investments that totaled $400,000 when she died. From what the Monnot descendants call "the good times"—the days before the Great Depression—

the Monnots were able to hold on to only a few baubles, passing from George and Alice to daughter Barbara and finally to grandson Tom. Among these were some fragile glass Christmas bulbs to decorate the tree.

On a rainy day in early March 2009, I sat with Tom Haas in the dining room of the McKinley Grand Hotel. Through the window we looked out on where Monnot's bike shop stood a hundred years before. Now it is an empty space dubbed "Bicentennial Park," one of many parks and playgrounds that attempt to fill the void left by exiting merchants and residents. We mused at our being brought together by the B. Virdot gift. Monnot and my grandfather had to know each other, says Haas. They traveled in the same circles, had businesses virtually across the street from each other, dined at the same restaurant, and boated on the same small Portage County lake. And yet Monnot never knew the identity or proximity of his benefactor.

Now here we were, the grandsons, poring over an old scrapbook—a photo of the South Shore Yacht Club, of three children in a canoe, of a sailboat—the only evidence of a lifestyle otherwise erased by the Depression. Over a cup of coffee, Tom Haas reads his grandfather's letter for the first time and simply shakes his head. There is an unspoken bond between us, our grandfathers joined by Hard Times and common interests, our own link forged by a letter that surfaced a lifetime later.

But the grandchildren too would find their way in the world. A granddaughter, Martha, got a master's degree in education and married Herbert J. Lanese, who would become president of McDonnell Douglas Aerospace.

The huge wooden chest of tools that George Monnot used, first to repair bicycles and later to assemble Ford Model Ts, is now with another grandson, Jeffrey Earl Haas. This grandson too had a modest childhood, having grown up in a third-floor apartment above a drugstore. But the real inheritance, Jeffrey says, was not the tool chest but the lessons his mother, Barbara, handed down to him from the Depression, lessons in how to manage one's affairs. Barbara Monnot was something of a miser and her sons too were raised to believe in the value of saving, the dangers of excessive debt, and the importance of hard work. Today, at sixty-five, George Monnot's grandson Jeffrey enjoys many of the material comforts that his grandfather had also once known. He divides his time between a home in America and one in England that is on the famous Wentworth golf course and near both Windsor Castle and Ascot Racecourse. A collector of ancient Greek coins and an avid scuba diver, the retired Procter & Gamble vice president owns a Mercedes and a Porsche. No Fords.

Seventy-five years after George Monnot wrote his appeal to Mr. B. Virdot, he would still be able to recognize much of Canton, though not even his favorite restaurant, Bender's (originally, Bender's Hofbrau Haus), was immune to the Depression. In 1932 it closed its doors, but it reopened six months later under new ownership. In some ways, the Depression literally gave Bender's a new lease on life. When the American Exchange Bank failed, its executives, John Raymond Jacob and his son, Wilbur Henry Jacob, decided to try the restaurant business and leased Bender's from the founder's widow. John Raymond Jacob was a formidable figure weighing some three hundred pounds. He'd made much of his money in the travel business helping to bring German immigrants to Canton. (My grandmother Minna Adolph's first meal in Canton, getting off the train in 1912 as a five-year-old, was at Bender's.) Its German murals, of which Jacob was so proud, were covered over in World War I when the United States was at war with that nation, but were restored after the armistice.

Today, a dark round oak table indistinguishable from that at which Monnot and my grandfather, Sam Stone, lunched with other business leaders in the good days before the Depression is there still. But now it is the grandsons' and granddaughters' turn to gather around it beneath the old tin ceiling and talk of Canton's future. The women are no longer required to use the "Ladies' Entrance," though what was their dining room is still referred to as the "LDR," or "Ladies' Dining Room," a carryover from the days when the main dining room was largely off-limits to them, as was the bar that featured a row of brass spittoons.

In 2002, Bender's observed its one hundredth anniversary, still serving its famed turtle soup, Camp Cagle pickerel, and Bender's fries. That the tavern still stands is a miracle. On January 1, 1988, it was engulfed in flames and nearly consumed, but the arsonist (never brought to justice) failed to bring the venerable restaurant down. Its sandstone façade is lit by antique gaslights and blackened by the fire and years of exposure to wind and soot. It has catered to the likes of Guy Lombardo, Eddie Cantor, Roy Rogers, Tiger Woods, the Grateful Dead's Bob Weir, evangelist Billy Graham, baseball's Early Wynn and Cy Young, überathlete Jim Thorpe, and, it is whispered, the mobster Baby Face Nelson. But it is generations of Canton's own families—the Monnots, the Stones, and thousands of others—who, coming out of the cold, have placed their feet upon its sandstone lintel until it has been worn down into a bowl, like some ancient grindstone.

The Depression left its mark on Bender's as it did on everything else. Decades afterward, there was still an effort to conserve even the last trace of butter. The paper that wrapped the butter was subjected to heat, because the butter would surrender to the flame before it would to the wax. And when diners' plates were gathered after their meals, the butter was scraped into a common cask and heated until it purified. When patrons dipped their lobster into drawn butter, they were unknowingly dipping not only into the leavings of an earlier diner but into the legacy of the Great Depression as well.

Like much of Canton's industrial prowess, the once formidable Hercules plant where Monnot and thousands of other citizens worked is now relegated to the past. Today, the plant, which between 1915 and 1999 produced more than two and a half million engines, is empty, the company gone. Abandoned but not forgotten, the site is on the National Register of Historic Places. Grand plans for developing the site ran headlong into the Great Recession.

As for the vast building that once housed Monnot's Ford dealership, it suffered a fire that destroyed its top floor in 1947, and underwent a host of transformations, first as home to Caxton Press, then Thurin's furniture store, and then a Robert Hall department store. But since 1978, the huge showroom has been something that would surely have pleased George Monnot. It is a museum for classic cars. In the midst of it all is parked a gleaming Model T, and at night, with the lights low, one can imagine the ghost of Mr. Monnot proudly showing off this, his latest model.

But as Christmas 2008 approached, George Monnot might also find the economic landscape of Canton eerily familiar. The American auto industry was in shambles. In 2008, the stock of his beloved Ford Motor Company plummeted to historic lows—one dollar a share. And in the deepening recession, hundreds of Ford dealerships across the country closed their doors. At Canton's Downtown Ford Lincoln Mercury dealership, owner Brad Black says what George Monnot himself said: "I haven't laid anybody off yet. I probably should have." But what has kept Black's head above water, he says, are the Depression-era lessons his parents passed on to him—not to spend everything he made, but to save, and not to take on excessive debt. Others, says Black, were less disciplined. "They were living on the edge when times were good. One hiccup, and it took them down." A black-and-white photo of the enormous Ford dealership that Monnot once owned now hangs in his waiting room.

Just months later, Chrysler declared bankruptcy. Then, on June 1, 2009, General Motors filed for bankruptcy, saying it would cut some 21,000 more jobs, close 14 plants, and cut loose 2,000 of its 6,000 U.S. dealerships. Even George Monnot had not witnessed such calamity in his beloved auto industry.

Blizzard

There were many like my grandfather, Sam Stone, who had made their own way into that select circle of Canton's leading businessmen. But some few were to the manor born, princes and heads of long-established family businesses, part of the city's upper crust, which, generation after generation, enjoyed positions of privilege. They too were not safe from the Depression. Within a matter of years—for some, just months—they found themselves destitute, scratching for pennies and feeling as if they had let down their families, their employees, and their community. As Sam Stone himself learned more than once, the bright line that separated the favored class from those below them could dissolve almost overnight, exposing the fragile divide between the haves and have-nots.

Among those who experienced such a precipitous fall was Frank J. Dick, a man seemingly marked for success from birth. He was the son of the founder of Joseph Dick Manufacturing Company, established in 1874. Dick was of pioneer stock. His family came from Alsace-Lorraine and settled in Stark County in 1837. The company his family founded was renamed Blizzard Manufacturing for its agricultural device that blew feed into silos. It served a global market and was the largest maker of agricultural machines in the state. Its plant took up an entire city block. Frank Dick's father, Joseph, had been a major part of the Canton community and beyond, hobnobbing with the city's power brokers and social elite. He received dozens of patents for his agricultural inventions, and his contributions to the community were well known. He was a member of the school board, a director of the Board of Trade, and vice president of the Canton Home Savings and Loan Company.

"Progressive, enterprising and liberal, [Joseph Dick] has been largely instrumental in promoting the general welfare and industrial thrift of the city of Canton and is in every way worthy of the high place he holds in public esteem," noted an 1892 profile. The family even gifted a fabulous altar to St. John's Catholic Church.

The mansion where Frank Dick lived until he was twenty-seven was an imposing Victorian edifice on Tuscarawas Street. It was built in 1890 of wood and stone, some of it imported from Europe. Boasting twenty-two huge rooms, it claimed eight fireplaces, five chimneys, an elevator finished in fine walnut, and, in the basement, a bin designed to hold as much coal as an entire railroad car. The dining table featured fine crystal, the chairs were carved ornately. City luminaries had been frequent guests in the home, recalls a great-grandson.

It was in that home that Joseph and his wife, Rosanna, raised six children in an aura of privilege and refinement. Each child was taught to play at least one instrument, and they formed an orchestra and toured on vacations. Among the boys, Frank J. Dick was the quietest. Soft-spoken, gentle, and, above all, proper, he would become the company's vice president and assistant manager, displaying a talent for both management and invention. Like George Monnot, he was a tinkerer. With his wire-rimmed glasses and somewhat starched personality, he was a formal man. He was never seen without a white shirt and tie. Like his father, he took pleasure in helping others—what he called "the good work." A gifted photographer, he had more of an artist's temperament than a businessman's. His portraiture and landscape pictures all proudly displayed his initials, FJD.

Raised in comfort, he and his wife, Harriet, and children became accustomed to the same. His daughter Florence, born in 1908, attended finishing school, was a young socialite who mingled with Canton's elite, played tennis, and was said to have flown with the famed pioneer aviator Jimmy Doolittle.

Frank Dick, like his father, was a man of influence and of civic involvement. He possessed sound business judgment—which mattered not a jot when the end came for the company. In an effort to resuscitate the firm, Frank Dick pledged everything he had—stock, his home, and all other assets—but to no avail. After more than half a century his business and all he had was gone. He was fifty-seven. In his December 18, 1933, appeal to Mr. B. Virdot, the pain of his circumstances can be heard to fuse with the formality of his upbringing.

"Mr. B. Virdot," he wrote. "The writer is forced by serious business reverses to accept temporary assistance if it is available. I do not of course know to whom I am directing my appeal, but shall immediately give you my identity. I am Frank Dick. Residence 1018 12th St. N.W.

"Possibly you are familiar with the serious business reverses I have suffered but for your information I shall state briefly my position. For thirty-five years I have been a member of The Joseph Dick Mfg. Co. one of Canton's oldest Manufacturing Companies. While with above company . . ." The top of the letter is too tattered to make out, but it picks up with these lines:

> . . . I also owned stock in our company to the approximate value of Sixty-five thousand dollars. . . . Little did we know that the reverse conditions in agricultural would extend over so long a period. Nevertheless our company required additional finances to carry on the good work. Once at this point I personally

endorsed the company's paper and in so doing placed my home valued at approximately thirty-seven thousand dollars, in support of my endorsement.

Agricultural conditions continued to grow worse and our company after weathering the storm for over fifty years ceased to be and I experienced the loss of all of my stock holdings, my home and everything of value I possessed together with thirty-five years of hard work and efforts, leaving me without a dollar to support my family. My dear friend, am sure you are in position to realize what this means. I am sure I would never wish it to befall anyone . . . Would very much appreciate an opportunity of meeting with you personally. I am sure I can give you sufficient evidence and references as to my character and ability, if given the opportunity.

In the meantime I assure you that any assistance whatever will be gratefully received and I am sure that you will never have cause to regret any confidence placed in me.

VERY SINCERELY,
FRANK J. DICK
1018–12TH ST. N.W.

The letter was desperate, the signature elegant. Three days later he received a check for five dollars from Mr. B. Virdot and on December 22, 1933, penned this thank-you note:

My dear friend,

I wish to thank you kindly for the assistance you have given me and I assure you it is very greatly appreciated and I hope that I shall have the pleasure of meeting you personally, offering me the opportunity of expressing my gratitude for this act of friendship.

Before I unfortunately met with business reverses, my greatest pleasure was found in assisting everyone about me in every possible way and I hope that I shall again be in position to carry on the good work.

Wishing you a most enjoyable Christmas and continued success. I am

VERY GRATEFULLY YOURS,
FRANK. J. DICK

What Frank Dick did not say in his letter to Mr. B. Virdot—what others in the Dick family also chose to keep to themselves—was their belief that the company had been the victim of embezzlement, and, worse yet, that the crime might have been perpetrated by a member of the family, though not Frank Dick himself, who was above suspicion. That theft, they said, pushed the firm over the edge. But the family apparently concluded that nothing could bring the company back, that the negative publicity of a criminal trial involving family would only further wound its reputation and its dwindling standing in the community. Even today, descendants speak guardedly of the incident. The idea that one family member would steal from another was something I later learned resonated all too painfully with my grandfather, who, like the Dicks, would decide that pursuing the matter in the courts would bring only more pain.

Compounding the shock of Frank Dick's own losses was the knowledge that the company's failure would profoundly affect the lives of its 150 employees, many of whom had been with the company for decades. Blue blood and blue collar, young and old alike, together found themselves walking Canton's cold December streets looking for work and unable to find it. Among these was James A. Brownlee, who lived one block away from the First Presbyterian Church, where the Dickens tale had been read. He had worked for years as the Blizzard Company's paint foreman. The same day his former boss reached out to B. Virdot, James Brownlee wrote his own appeal for help.

"Mr. B. Virdot," he wrote, "I am doing something I have never did befor, that's ask for that I have not earned or rather inform you I am one who could use the gift you so kindly offer to share . . ."

> I am 73 years old, however I'm feeling not a day over 40. I want to say how I would rather have work to pay for my own way than any other thing. I have never wasted what I earned in fast living and feel proud to be able to say that I have registered for Road Work or bridge painting but so far have not been called. Why I am writing this to you is a mystery to me. Without there's [sic] in your printed (beautiful) offer, the Real Spirit as sung by the Angelic Host at the First Christmas in Bethleham of Judea.

After receiving the five dollars from Mr. B. Virdot, James Brownlee wrote a note of thanks dated December 22, 1933: "Your fine and much appreciated Gift received this AM. And I hasten to thank you and say I am in hearty cooperation with your idea of lessoning the amount and reaching more needy ones. Accept my sincere thanks with my wishes for Many Blessings not only at the coming Christmas Season but throughout the year. Merry Christmas to you and yours. I am

Thankfully Yours, J. A. Brownlee." To this he added a stanza of verse from the popular poet Edgar A. Guest:

He has not lived who gathers gold,
Nor has he lived whose life is told
In selfish Battles he has won,
Or deed of skill he may have done,
But he has lived who now and then
Has helped along his fellowman.

Such a note would have touched Sam Stone. It was the kind of poetry he admired, and Guest was among his favorites. There was nothing coy about it. Its meaning was clear and Sam embraced its sentiments. He had his own ready stock of verses whose homespun wisdom was just waiting for the right occasion. In reading Brownlee's note my grandfather would surely have felt a special kinship.

I suspect he would have found less in common with Frank Dick. When the Blizzard Company went under, Dick lost everything. For him, as with so many other leaders in Canton's business community who now found themselves stripped of wealth, position, and influence, the drop was stunning. For a time Frank Dick hoped that he might convert his longtime hobby of toy making into a new career. Shortly after the failure of the family business Frank Dick incorporated a new company called "Dixtoy," set up works in an empty plant, and spoke optimistically of building a factory of his own. For a time, his mechanical clowns and scooters and wagons were featured in the windows of the five-and-dime, W. T. Grant and Company, in downtown Canton. But launched in the depths of the Depression, when parents were far more concerned with feeding their children than giving them toys, the venture went nowhere.

His grandson, James Vignos, son of Florence Dick—the socialite—said his grandfather never recovered. "He was poor the rest of his life." Frank Dick, the man who had helped oversee a major company, was reduced to eking out a living in woodworking, making and selling children's jigsaw puzzles, pictures burned into wood, and games. It was his only income. In later years, his wife lost her vision and he ended up a boarder in one of Canton's seedier neighborhoods. He never complained. He never talked about what he had lost. But those who knew him could see the toll it had taken.

He increasingly retreated into his woodworking and found escape in creating worlds unto themselves. One of these was an enormous electrified city in miniature, another an animated Christmas scene depicting a girl and her dreams of what Santa might bring. Finally, there was a four-by-three-foot farm scene of wood and metal, composed of 1,032 pieces, including many that moved and made sounds: the cow mooed, the chicken cackled, the train whistled; the people sawed logs, worked at a churn, drove the horses, and washed clothes. The windmill turned and the salesman knocked at the door. It was a universe protected under a glass dome and it was the only part of his world that Frank Dick had any control over.

At ninety, a widower, he was to be found in a gloomy nursing home, sharing a room with three other poor, aging souls. His grandson Robert and his wife, Sally, would visit him weekly. What Sally remembers of those visits is that even in that crowded room with the three other men, Frank Dick invariably wore a shirt and tie—whether he was expecting visitors or not. In my grandfather's words, he was the consummate "white-collar man." But by then his clothes were as tired and old as he was. The knees of the pants had a sheen to them where the material had worn thin, and the collars and cuffs of his shirts were frayed.

Both men lost it all when the company failed—the onetime executive Frank J. Dick and the painter James A. Brownlee. Both lived to be ninety-one. And neither ever recovered. James Brownlee died on August 17, 1951. On his death certificate he is listed as a retired paint foreman for the Blizzard Manufacturing Company, a position he had not held in decades.

Frank Dick died on September 27, 1967. Even his obituary reflected a certain sense of disappointment, referencing only his family pedigree and the factory that had vanished so many years before. The service for him was held at St. John's Church, beneath an ornate altar that his father had given to the church years earlier. Little was passed down from him. The ornate farm he had created, in dire need of repair, was sold to a stranger. Crystal champagne glasses that had been in the Dick family are now with Sally Dick, but are chipped from hitting the spout as a nearly sightless Harriet Dick washed them.

The Dick mansion fared no better than Frank Dick himself. It passed into the hands of Rush D. Hiller, an undertaker, and later was converted into a furniture store. By 1940, appearing "doomed to slow death by deterioration," as the *Canton Repository* put it, the house was turned into efficiency apartments. Later still, it was unceremoniously dismantled. Today, near where the opulent mansion once stood now stands the Canton Inn, which has its own inglorious history. In the late 1990s, police were called to the scene nearly four hundred times because of violence, drug dealing, and prostitution. In 2001, the city, threatening to shut it down, reached an agreement with the owner, who pledged to clean it up. The vast plant where the Dick family designed and produced agricultural equipment for the nation was also torn down. By the late fifties it was the site of a used-car lot.

Like a blizzard, the alleged embezzlement together with the Depression had taken down a venerable company and a respected family. Nor was there a return to the cushy life for the descendants of Joseph Dick. Frank Dick's son, Edward, would spend his days in a Timken steel mill helping to support his aging parents. One of Edward's sons, Robert, would work for Goodyear, and the other, Thomas, for the public library. And in the Dick family tradition, Thomas would play an active role in the community, and later, in Canton's chamber of commerce and the annual parade for the Football Hall of Fame.

For Frank Dick's once-pampered daughter, Florence, the loss of position and wealth was hard to accept. She married Henry Vignos on February 18, 1930, in the depths of the Depression. Though the Dick family had already suffered its grievous financial loss, they did what they could to provide her a stylish wedding, which was featured prominently in that day's "Social Affairs" column of the *Repository*. The paper noted that the marriage "united two of Canton's pioneer families."

"The bride," the paper wrote, "was beautiful in a princess frock of pie crust crepe and she wore a baku straw hat in cocoa shade. Her bouquet was of bronze roses." But the decline in status and wealth took its toll on Florence Dick. Her son, James Vignos, could see the difference between the photos taken of her during what she longingly referred to as "the good times" and those taken in the difficult years after. There was a loss of confidence, observed her son. "For her, the good times were wonderful, then all hell broke out. Friends of hers said she had been full of pep and vigor. I didn't know her that way at all, so I think it probably did a job on her. It crushed her a little."

As a college student, Frank Dick's grandson James corresponded with his grandfather, but he escaped the cycle of poverty. In some ways James Vignos's career more closely resembles that of his great-grandfather, Joseph Dick. James went on to get a Ph.D. in physics from Yale University, and would teach at Dartmouth, later go into industry, and today enjoys retirement in a Boston suburb. Like his great-grandfather, he holds a number of patents.

Hello Bill

When George Monnot needed his showroom painted, when Frank Dick considered painting an office or factory, when my grandfather Sam Stone needed someone to paint his store, it's likely they would have turned to Bill Gray. Most of Canton's leading businessmen relied on Bill Gray. He was one of them, a success story in his own right. Only a few years before 1933, he had had the most prosperous painting business in Stark County. At the pinnacle of his career, "Gray the Painter," as he was known, counted sixty employees. He painted virtually every major business. To ensure that his customers did not have to disrupt their businesses or close shop, he sent his teams of painters in to work all night. He also painted many of the town's homes and even had a man whose specialty was doing the detail work in Canton's churches. Likely he did the First Presbyterian Church, where the Dickens reading was held. In those prosperous days, Bill Gray would take two hundred dollars off the painting bill for stores that sold women's clothes, and in exchange his wife and daughters would be allowed to go in and get the season's newest outfits.

Bill Gray was a prominent figure in the community, active in its social life and its many clubs and societies. He was a bon vivant who counted his membership in such clubs among his most prized possessions, and his fellow members felt the same way about him. He drove an Essex hardtop, rented a lakeside cottage, and moved to Willowdale Lake, a private club where he won prizes for ballroom dancing. A 1927 article in the *Canton Daily News* featured his daughter Marjorie, then fifteen, who each day would swim a half mile from the cottage dock across Willowdale Lake to a bakery, and then a half mile back, returning with a perfectly dry loaf of bread to be toasted for breakfast. Bill Gray was a regular at Bender's, and surely dined in easy sight of George Monnot and Sam Stone. He was tall and thin and jolly, and, busy though he was, his surviving daughter remembers him making time to tell his children stories.

Business was so good that he let the paint companies he represented persuade him to expand into a second major store. That was on the eve of the crash of 1929. Five years later, he had next to nothing.

His December 18, 1933, letter to Mr. B. Virdot chronicles his decline in excruciating detail—but also his resolve to climb back out of the economic crevasse into which he had fallen. That was exactly the sort of grit that would have instantly won over my grandfather. Gray was a workingman who had elevated himself to the ranks of the city's business class, as Sam Stone had done. His six-page letter was written in ink on the very stationery—"Gray the Painter"—that had once been synonymous with entrepreneurialism, and was now reduced to carrying his appeal for help. Sam Stone's offer forged an instant bond with such men, who saw in the words of Mr. B. Virdot a kinship and shared experience. In the wasteland of the Depression, when men rarely felt free to truly open up to one another and share their doubts, Sam Stone had created a rare comfort zone. Those who had long guarded their feelings could finally release them without fear of disappointing others or humiliating themselves. Such trust showed itself in the very first words of Bill Gray's letter.

"Dear Friend," it began:

Your word picture in tonights newspaper hit me squarely in the face, what a blessing it is for me just to tell someone of my painful experiences since July 25, 1931. Someone that will realize, when others cannot or will not.

I'll lay my cards on the table.

Gray the Painter—2 stores The Save The Surface 212-3rd St N.W. and 1438 Tusc. St. W. Wholesale & Retail—Contracting Painting and Decorating. Gray the Painter no longer in the telephone book, not listed in Brad St & Dun. Bankruptcy July 25—1931. Store, fixtures, merchandise, ladders, equipment, business and all gone, after 18 profitable years in the Game. Saved the truck and Household Furniture, which was mortgaged by Loan Co. and is yet. So this is what I have. That which is mortgaged.

I am now living in Summer Cottage at Willow Dale Lake, ½ mile north of McDonaldsville, O. address W. H. Gray. North Canton, O. R.D. #7.

Four in family dependent (2 children going to Jackson Township School.) Thank God all in good health.

Yes I drift back into Canton once or twice a week to look for work & view the once fertile field of endeavor. Once recognized as largest Painting Contractor in Stark Co. with pay rolls running from $1,600 to $2,200 per week for my men and office help & truck drivers. Now begging for painting to do at 40 cents per hour. Yes I am still a Mechanic. Friday of last week was turned down on a paint job because 40 cents per hr was too high, for the customer. I agreed to furnish drop cloth, ladder, brushes & labor for 40 cents per hr then agreed to take part out in tobacco & gasoline. This was at a Roadhouse–Gas Filling Station where in my good times I spent plenty. Well I am trudging home on foot overalls and brushes under my arm.

Yes I have warm clothing. And am not uncomfortable for I have one suit of clothes left from the good old days & just one pair of shoes. No I don't want to complain, because I'll come back again and you'll see it. After I lost my store business & all I rented a barn, rear 715 Cleveland Ave. N.W. No lights, no heat, no water, no toilets, I put in a telephone & got busy, done a little advertising but could not make it go. I was forced to vacate, I could not pay the rent $12.50 per mo. Yes I sacrificed my Club Lodge & all Social & Sport activities to stage a comeback. I've dropped $25,000 Life Insurance Policies, which I had been carrying & had paid for from 8 to 10 years.

But I'll get back and a going some day, and snap off some of those nice big jobs that I once used to call Mine. Today I stood in line at C.W.A. [Civil Work Administration] but that brought me nothing. Two hours later I got a break. A chance to work out my back dues in the Elks Lodge #68 Canton. Painting work to be done about the kitchen, refrigerator, &

stock rooms, which will put me in good standing once again. Bros. Clayton Carver one of the officers of the Elks made me this proposition & you bet I took him up for I am an Elk & want to always be an Elk. Now if Lily Lodge #362 K of P and the (U.C.T.) United Commercial Travelers #41 of Canton would make a like proposition I would be in good standing again in the 3 Secret 7 Fraternal orders I once belonged & in some held office. Friend I am not complaining to you. You wanted to know my true condition. Here it is, all these facts above mentioned are true & real & you can check me up on same.

You may read between the lines a few more things. My wife, family & myself had to forego aside from what I told you. No I don't want charity, I want work, I want to get agoing again. My earnest desire is that I can retain my health & get jobs that I may fulfill my obligations to my children as a parent. Before I close I want to tell you something-You whoever you are, you are doing a most wonderful piece of good work & sympathy & charity to just that class that are most forgotten & the public refuses to consider. Whether the writer shares in your kind offer or not, you have made me feel good, and if more of the unfortunate *Has Beens* would write you & empty out their painful burdens to one that has taken such a unique plan of encouragement, the road would be easier to travel & this world a better place to live in. May God bless you & may the best men win. Your open letter is a tonic to a guy that can take [it] on the chin. Yours for a Happy Christmas and always a Brighter New Year Coming.

Thanks for this priveledge

AGAIN JUST BILL GRAY

B. Virdot's check for five dollars arrived four days later, on December 22, and on that day, Bill Gray wrote:

Kind Friend

Mr. B. Virdot

Merry Christmas to you. I rec'd your check for $5.00 today. Thanks for same. You can be assured that it will be spent for something useful & I know that this fine gift of yours is much needed at this time & I'll always remember you for it and again I want to thank you for it & I know each one you have helped will appreciate your kind offering. A Merry Christmas &

Always a Happy New Year

I AM BILL GRAY
NORTH CANTON, OH. R.D. #7

Bill Gray, like so many who wrote to Mr. B. Virdot, wanted not a handout but a job. It was the hope of many that in reading their letters the mysterious B. Virdot would reach out to them with an offer of employment, a part-time position, or someone to contact who might know Someone. During the Depression, that "Someone" was capitalized because he or she might have an inside track on a possible job. In those leanest of days a job went unfilled only as long as the time it took for someone to get wind of it.

Many of those who wrote to B. Virdot invited him to their homes. "Here it is," wrote Bill Gray, "all these facts above mentioned are true & real & you can check me up on same." In an era of scams, Gray and scores of others wanted the donor to see for himself that things were as described—or worse. In the Canton the 1920s and the Depression, a fellow couldn't be too careful, and the well meaning and trusting were prime targets for the unscrupulous. Those who wrote the letters were constantly exposed to flimflammers and schemers. Sam Stone was not a child himself, and it may well be that among the many considerations that led him to operate behind the mask of B. Virdot was this: its anonymity shielded him from the connivers who would have been eager to make his acquaintance. But those who wrote to Mr. B. Virdot inviting him to inspect their homes and their lives had a purer aspiration—they hoped that if he visited and attached a face to their hard-luck stories he might find work for them. His gift was most welcomed, to be sure, but the relief it brought was transient and their misery was not.

Bill Gray was the son of Urias, a cigar maker, and Catherine Gray. He was the oldest of four children. He had a brother Charles, who worked as a foreman on the large painting jobs; a brother Roy; and a sister, Carrie, a nurse. Gray and his wife, Viola, had four children, Marjorie, Robert, Betty Jane, and Grace Ruth. In 1933, at the time he wrote to B. Virdot, he was forty-seven.

But even today, three-quarters of a century later, there are more than dusty memories from those Hard Times. Bill Gray's eldest child, Marjorie Markey, turned ninety-seven on October 10, 2009. She lives in the County Home in Ohio's rural Wyandot County, 108 miles due west of Canton. She remembers the Depression only too well. She was forced to drop out of high school after the crash of '29 to help support the family. In 1933, she was twenty-one and had long been working as

"Gray the Painter's" bookkeeper, so she saw firsthand the economic maelstrom and what it meant for her father.

She remembers how he did all he could to protect the family from the worries that consumed him, but she also remembers the sound of his steps late at night pacing across the bedroom floor above. She remembers the terrible headaches that afflicted him, how underneath his straw hat he concealed a white kerchief he had soaked in cold water and tied around his head to relieve the throbbing ache. And she remembers how a lifetime of business acumen counted for nothing, how the steady flow of income was reduced to a trickle, and then, nothing. On top of the losses he suffered, there was the embarrassment, the sudden unseemly slide from prominence to subsistence, and all of it so terribly public.

But Bill Gray was determined to provide for his family, and if it meant finding another path, so be it. He picked up any odd job he could find. From the Amish, he bought Old Trail sausage and rounds of cheese that he cut into smaller sections. A first-class salesman even in the worst of times, he found just enough buyers for these foods to keep his own family fed. He would dig for potatoes at a farm, for himself and his aging parents and neighbors. That too would have touched Sam Stone, who shared whatever good fortune he had with those of his siblings in need. Another of Bill Gray's daughters,

Gloria Hawkins, now eighty-eight, still remembers the big iron skillet and the dinners of fried potatoes and eggs. Another Depression-era supper at the Gray home was mush—a porridge or pudding made from cornmeal that was allowed to set, then sliced and served with a bit of syrup over top. "We ate a lot of mush," recalls Marjorie, suggesting that the sweetness of the syrup more than made up for the repetitiveness of the meal.

But it was not enough for Bill Gray that he could feed his own family. He also went door-to-door soliciting canned foods for others—"the poor." It was a tradition in his family. His mother, Katy, had always put together baskets of provisions for the needy, and Bill Gray carried on the tradition even when he had little himself. (His daughter Gloria later volunteered for Meals On Wheels, and today her daughter, Connie, devotes her Thursdays to delivering Meals On Wheels.)

Groceries were sold a mere five doors away at Youngen's, at the corner of Rowland Avenue and Ninth Street. The Grays rarely had the money to pay for them, but a routine evolved whereby on Saturday evenings, Bill Gray and his father, Urias, would stop in and pay off what they owed or at least what they could afford, hoping to start a fresh tab come Monday. John Youngen lived above the grocery and was liked by the Gray children, who would often poke their heads in the door and ask, "Would you give us a weenie?" Mr. Youngen obliged. The hot dog was eaten on the spot and added to the tab. Dr. Kelly, who made house calls to the Gray family and had delivered the children, knew he would have to be patient if he was to receive some semblance of payment, but some was better than none.

It seemed that winter mornings in Depression Ohio were particularly cold. Precious coal had to be conserved. The Gray children dressed in front of the oven, which was fired up just before school. In 1933 Marjorie Gray got married. Also that year her mother-in-law, Jennie Markey, inherited a sizable sum of money that was placed in a Fort Wayne bank for safekeeping. The bank failed and the entire inheritance was lost.

Bill Gray did eventually get back on his feet, though never to the degree he enjoyed before the Depression. He found work with American Oil and Paint, a Cleveland roofing company headed by millionaire C. D. Rogers. Gray covered much of the state selling tar and other roofing materials. And he did well enough that fifteen years after his letter to Mr. B. Virdot, he could afford to retire to a modest home in Ohio's rural Wyandot County. There he pursued his hobbies: hunting rabbits and pheasants, fishing, and baseball. He volunteered to announce the evening games of the adult softball league and sometimes even sold snacks to those who had come out to watch.

To his grandson, William Markey, he was a

hardworking man who never spoke of the Hard Times. Bill Gray enjoyed a long and peaceful retirement. One day in 1959, while driving down Route 23, a country lane south of the county, he pulled off onto the side of the road, shut off the engine, put his head back, and died right there. He was seventy-six. Bill Gray's beloved business—"Gray the Painter"—is long since forgotten, but there remains one curious testimonial to him and to his painting skills. It is there in the tiny town of Upper Sandusky, Ohio, and is painted in his own hand, in huge black letters against the white outside wall of the Elks Club on Route 30. It says, simply, HELLO BILL. It was once a customary greeting among Elk Club members nationwide, a practice that goes back to the turn of the last century, but which has long since fallen into disuse. Bill Gray painted the sign in the late 1940s. Today it's a kind of local landmark in Upper Sandusky, visible to passersby from far off. But to the descendants of Bill Gray, it is also the final salutation to "Gray the Painter."

Gassed

To many, like my grandfather, who entered the Depression as adults, it was neither the first trial they faced nor even the most severe. Their lives had already been tested by tragedies and terrors that now seem remote: influenza that wiped out millions, the Great War (ghastly even by modern standards), Old World pogroms, deadly workplaces, all created the expectation that life would be short and trying. Many of those who wrote to B. Virdot, even those who had enjoyed a measure of success, had come of age in a time so pocked with hardship that it did not even merit a mention in their letters. To dwell on such specifics would have been beneath them. Their creed was self-discipline, not self-indulgence.

This too my grandfather would have understood. Aside from a few carefully selected stories, Sam Stone never said a word of the true conditions of his youth. Men and women of that era were eager to distance themselves from the duress of their early lives. It was part of the allure of America that the past could be left behind, that men and women could reinvent themselves. Besides, it was a given that others had suffered similarly. There was little therapeutic value to be gained from opening up old wounds, and it was impolite to pry. Nothing in my grandfather's day was as out of fashion as self-pity. Only to later generations, coddled by prosperity, analgesics, and concerns over leisure and longevity, would such flinty self-reliance seem extraordinary or explorations of one's sorrows become so common as to be featured on daytime TV. Those who grow up in today's society, determined to snuff out risk and surrounded by smoke detectors and seat belts, may find it hard to imagine the perilous lives their grandparents faced.

Coming of age in America, even before the Depression, meant running a gauntlet of hardships that for many included outrunning persecution, poverty, infant mortality, diseases (tuberculosis, polio, influenza, malaria, typhus, dysentery, and cholera), industrial accidents, and a world war. In 1900, when much of the Depression-era generation was still young, only one in twenty-five could look forward to reaching sixty-five. One in five newborns died before the age of five and the average life span of a male infant born that year was forty-eight years. It was a nation without antibiotics, Social Security, or Medicare. Against such a backdrop, one's familiarity with tragedy and expectations of life were dramatically different from those of today. People were not unconscious of their burdens but, having known little else, could barely imagine being free of them. So fraught with risk and hardship was their world that the idea of voicing one's particular plight would have struck many as curious, even presumptuous. After all, what did they expect?

Georgianna Pryor, in her letter to B. Virdot, wrote: "We do not come within the class of those who have had and lost. It seems we've never had anything to lose. My husband has tried hard, but we are still just a poverty-stricken family, not unlike countless others." At the time she wrote the letter her six children were all quarantined with whooping cough.

Charles Stewart's early exposure to hardship scarred him literally but did not even warrant a mention in his letter to B. Virdot. He wrote:

Dear Sir-

I read the article or item in the Canton Repository, yet I hesitate in even writing or asking aid from a person or organization of any kind.

Practically my entire working career has been a white-collared job, until April, 1930. Since that date I have been unable to obtain any kind of steady employment. I did manage to obtain a day now and then during the summer, which kept the wolf from the door, or at least wouldn't allow him entrance. I applied to the Service Director for work, to be paid in groceries, but he stated he couldn't assist me in any way.

My last position I held was with the Klein-Heffelman-Zollars Co. as collector, which was in April, 1930.

For myself, I can get along on nothing, but I have a wife and daughter to think of beside myself — and they certainly need shoes and clothing. We have been trying to get along on cast off clothes from other persons, but it's rather a hard chore.

I am unable to obtain factory employment, on account of not being able to pass their physical examinations due to Tuberculosis which has partly destroyed one lung.

Should I be fortunate enough to be one of the 50 or 75 family men granted aid, I request that you supply your real name, so that this may be repaid with interest when the writer obtains remunerative employment.

I trust I have made myself clear in all details.

I AM RESPECTFULLY,
C. LEROY STEWART
335 CLEVELAND AVE. S.W.
CANTON, OHIO

Stewart's eloquence was matched by his penmanship. Each letter was formed with a spare upright discipline, the writing of a proud man. But what he doesn't say reveals most about himself and his times.

For that, one must speak with the only child of Charles and Gertrude Stewart, Ruth Brown. She was eleven at the time her father wrote to Mr. B. Virdot, but knew nothing of the letter or the five dollars that her father received days later. But she does know her father's story. One of six children, he was born in 1896 and raised on a farm in tiny White Fox, Ohio. Sometime in 1917 or 1918 he married Gertrude Wilson, who was thirteen years his senior.

On April 29, 1918, at twenty-two, Charles Stewart volunteered for service in the army and was assigned to Company F, 112th U.S. Engineers. On July 10, 1918, he joined the American Expeditionary Force. He soon found himself in the midst of World War I's deadly trench warfare. One evening, he and a dozen others were ordered to go over the top, crossing no-man's-land in the face of heavy gunfire. They seized two German machine-gun nests and returned to the trench. Stewart's hand was bloodied from shrapnel. He refused to be taken to the hospital.

But the date he would never forget was September 26, 1918. That was the day the Allies advanced against the Germans in the Argonne

Forest; for Americans, one of the bloodiest of all battles. Within six weeks, more than 26,000 members of the Allied Expeditionary Force were dead. Another 96,000 were wounded. In the early bombardment some 800 mustard gas and phosgene shells rained down on the Germans.

During the battle, Stewart himself was exposed to mustard gas. The powerful agent seared his lungs and incapacitated him. On October 18, he found himself in an army base hospital in Toul, France. When the armistice was signed on November 11, 1918, Stewart was still unable to get out of bed. Thanksgiving came and went. His unit went home, but he could not. In January, he was moved to yet another hospital, where he remained until January 21, 1919. It was not until four months after he was first hospitalized that he was fit enough to come home. On February 10, 1919, Stewart was honorably discharged. He had survived the war, but he would never escape it.

Even when he returned to America, he carried with him the damage to his lungs. Immediately following the war, he moved to Canton and worked as a clerk in a factory and later as a bookkeeper. He lived a quiet life, lost himself in Zane Grey novels, tended his garden, and provided for his family, his wife, Gertrude, and daughter, Ruth. But he lost his job during the Depression and thereafter took whatever work he could find—which in his increasingly fragile condition was not much. In 1930, he worked as an enumerator for the U.S. Census. The Stewart family had an apartment they enjoyed rent-free in exchange for the couple cleaning and maintaining the building. But even with Gertrude working as a maid in other people's homes, they came up short.

Their daughter, Ruth, was hardly aware that they were poor. Still, she could not afford a movie at the Palace Theater or an evening at Bender's fashionable tavern. But eighty-seven-year-old Ruth Stewart Brown insists she never suffered or wanted for anything. She hopscotched and roller-skated her way through the worst days of the Depression, and in the evenings enjoyed games of euchre with Mom and Dad in the apartment. "You survived and that was it," she says. Like so many during the Depression, Ruth did not have far to look to see others in worse shape, and the few who enjoyed a measure of luxury or ease were too distant to see and, if they were sensitive at all, too discreet to put their good fortune on display.

Over time, and long after the Depression lifted, the Stewarts managed to get their feet on the ground somewhat. Charles kept the books for a printing company and later clerked for the Canton Police Department. Ten years after writing to Mr. B. Virdot, the Stewarts purchased their own home at 814 High Avenue Southwest. But through it all, Charles Stewart had to cope with his exposure to mustard gas. He had a constant sinus condition and was forever blowing his nose. His wife, fearing germs, would boil his handkerchiefs. But the source of his distress was rooted in events that occurred decades earlier. Throughout the 1930s, 1940s, and until his final labored breath on July 20, 1955, at age fifty-nine, not a year passed when he was not in and out of veterans' hospitals as doctors tried to attend to his lungs.

Decades later, a descendant of Charles Stewart, his great-grandson Evan Jet Brown, is a sheet-metal worker who has had his own taste of both economic hard times and war. These days, like many in Canton—and across the country—he is caught up in a constant scramble to find work to support his young family. In the early summer of 2008 he was helping to rebuild a local high school but facing an imminent layoff—and not his first. Not long after speaking with me, he was out of work for months—but at least there was unemployment. A father of two, he now commutes two hours to a job in Wooster, Ohio. When we last spoke he was standing on a twelve-foot ladder, keyhole saw in hand, cutting a hole in drywall to make way for a heating duct at Wooster Hospital, and knowing that a month from then he would be out of work yet again.

Half a dozen years earlier he was serving on the front in the war on terrorism. The former marine sergeant, in five years of service, was deployed to Afghanistan, Iraq, Yemen, the United Arab

Emirates, Kosovo, and the Horn of Africa, and was even on the USS *Nassau* when, in December 2002, it boarded a North Korean ship carrying SCUD missiles to Yemen. Like his great-grandfather, he is reluctant to speak of his time in the service. "We don't really talk about it," he says. "We just did it, that's all. I don't tell anybody." Charles Stewart would have saluted such silence.

FOR SOME THE decline from positions of stature to empty pockets and worn-out shoes was almost more than they could bear. It was not merely the loss of possessions, nor even the years of work and sacrifice with nothing to show for it. For some, it was also the humiliation that came with failure, made all the worse for those whose lofty expectations of themselves had been realized and then dashed by the Depression and circumstances over which they had no control. Those who had enjoyed prominence now had to cope with the loss of self-esteem, the severing of bonds with established social circles, and the lack of prospects that stretched before them. There are no figures in Canton for how many took their own lives during the Depression, but it is certain that some did commit suicide and others at least contemplated it. The B. Virdot gift did not restore fortunes or friendships, but it may have convinced some not to give in to despair. For some, it appears the offer by B. Virdot may have been enough to restore confidence and counter the daily barrage of bills and bad news.

J. L. White lived on Tuscarawas Avenue, just four doors away from what had been the Dick family mansion. He had owned two stores and lost them both in 1929, the same year Sam Stone nearly lost his. He had diligently saved his money only to discover, like so many others, that his savings were lost when his bank failed. "If I [had] only known at that time," he lamented. Now he was unsure how he was going to feed his seven children. In his letter to Mr. B. Virdot, he wrote: "Your encouraging letter and generous offer in Repository of 18 December has again given me the courage to try again. Yesterday evening just before I read your letter was thinking of things that no person should. Four years ago I was a successful business man. . . . I am down flat. But since reading your letter will say that I am not out yet."

Such dark thoughts were not his alone. But the outpouring of letters that greeted the B. Virdot offer—J. L. White's among them—signaled that its power and appeal had less to do with the prospect of receiving a check than with the affirmation it offered that others cared and were concerned for them. Despite widespread unemployment and block after block of poverty, those suffering often felt profoundly isolated and abandoned by government and society at large. Washington had not yet demonstrated its commitment to address the suffering. The New Deal had not yet made itself felt upon the land, and the poor were desperate for some evidence that their plight mattered to anyone other than themselves. B. Virdot's gift was modest, but the gesture behind it was not. To those like J. L. White, who momentarily lost their way, overcome by the gloom all around them, B. Virdot's offer was seen as a small beacon, but enough to help them find their way back from the precipice.

Mr. B. Virdot's Story:
The Promise

There is nothing to prove that any of these men—George Monnot, Frank Dick, Bill Gray, Charles Stewart, or J. L. White—were personal friends of the real B. Virdot, Sam Stone, though in a town of Canton's size, it would be hard to imagine that their lives would not have intersected. Sam's store, Stone's Clothes, was located in the heart of the downtown on the busy corner of Tuscarawas Street and Market Avenue, a minute's walk from the courthouse, the banks, Bender's, the First Presbyterian Church, and the *Repository*'s newsroom. All those who benefited from this gift would have walked by his shop countless times and at least known of him. But whether he knew them on a personal level or not, it was not mere affection or commercial connections that moved him to do what he did. The Sam Stone I knew always identified with the struggles of workingmen and -women.

And Sam's own financial troubles neither began with the Depression nor ended in 1933. Today many Americans think the Depression extended a few miserable years, starting with the crash in 1929 and ending in the midthirties. But as the men and women of Canton could attest—as Sam himself knew well—the Hard Times arced across the entire decade and, but for a brief respite in the middle, never loosened their grip. There was just enough time in the midthirties for the exhausted to drop their guard and catch their breath before the second blow landed.

In Sam's life and so many others, prosperity was that dollar bill lying on the floor that a hidden hand might snatch away. Just when Canton seemed to emerge from the Depression, as factories began to rehire and the pile of bills began to shrink, the town and the nation were hit by a devastating second wave of Hard Times that again drove unemployment skyward. In 1937, Canton's misery was exacerbated by a series of bitter and sometimes violent strikes that disabled some of its most prominent employers—Republic Steel, Timken, and Hercules Motor Corporation—tossing additional thousands out of work. The headlines of riots, National Guardsmen, rock throwers, dynamite, and injured strikers were not Canton's alone.

Caught in this economic downdraft were many of the town's leading merchants, Sam Stone among them. He was forced to move the family from their stately Ridgewood Tudor into a cramped bungalow in one of the town's modest working-class neighborhoods. My mother, then in her last years of elementary school, remembers her life being upended—twice changing schools, saying good-bye to friends, parting with some of the comforts she'd grown accustomed to, and sensing the tensions that come with such reversals. Like George and Alice Monnot before them, the Stones discovered how quickly some society friends could turn their backs on them. Short of cash, they lived for a time on traveler's checks left over from an earlier cruise to Central America and the Panama Canal.

By September 1938, Sam Stone found himself in bankruptcy court with suppliers clamoring for the $205,000 owed them. Under a court agreement he pledged to pay his creditors thirty-five cents on the dollar. But in the years thereafter, despite the agreement, he insisted on paying off each debt in full and did, as noted in a later Dun & Bradstreet report. (That same report suggested that Sam was getting younger and younger, as it pushed his date of birth forward five years, to 1893.)

Periodic reversals were as much a part of Sam's life and outlook as the good times, and continually chastened him to remember that the line between the down-and-out and himself was not drawn in indelible ink. I heard him say as much many times, especially in those moments when he was about to enjoy his own good fortune. A cracker with caviar would trigger a memory of a tougher time, to which he would refer, but only obliquely.

That Christmas of 1933, he knew how lucky he was and that he could just as easily have been one of the many supplicants to B. Virdot, a role he invented, I believe, in part to pay homage to the fickle nature of fortune. He always saw himself in the sunken eyes and hard-luck faces of those around him, particularly those who had fallen so far and so fast. Even decades later, he would speak of them as one might speak of a lost sibling. But unlike others in a position to help who merely said, "There but for the Grace of God, go I," or dashed off checks to local charities, Sam Stone was driven to do something more. I am convinced that he felt the need to actually connect with them, to reach out in a human way that would provide not only momentary financial relief but some measure of spiritual comfort as well. His was an elaborate scheme whose true benefits were intended to be a multiple many times over the actual dollars that went out across the city. In 1933, when so many suffered in silence and isolation, such a release was as close to therapy as most would experience.

From the beginning, I sensed that the gift was uniquely rooted in Sam's life, a life about which I knew next to nothing. The key was the anonymity of his gift. Promising the needy that their names would never be known was an insightful and compassionate way to persuade the souls of a beaten-down community that their candor would pose no threat to them, that they could safely express their financial and emotional needs free of the threat of exposure or humiliation. As for the donor's anonymity, at first blush, it seemed to be a reassurance to the needy that even if they should know the giver or encounter him thereafter, they need feel no embarrassment. And it offered the donor a buffer against the potential barrage of desperate appeals and knocks at his front door.

But I suspected that behind the veil of anonymity that cloaked the donor was something more than pragmatism, more perhaps even than humility and selflessness. For my grandfather, it was also a way of concealing himself from further public inquiry, as if such scrutiny might produce more information than he wanted to disclose. For a man who loved to be the center of attention at a party but who deftly dodged any questions asked of his early years, the gift was not only an act of charity but something of a risk. No matter how slight, it raised the possibility that his true identity might be discovered, that such attention could undo the life he had so carefully stitched together, a life I would discover was rife with falsehoods and documentary fabrications. If that was his concern, it was ultimately borne out—but seventy-five years later, when the gift and the suitcase that held it found their way into the hands of his grandson.

I was determined to shine a light on those early chapters of his life that had long been denied me and all those who loved him, and to discover the link between what I came to think of as "the missing years" and the gift. This was not my first foray into Sam's past. That had come in 1982, twenty-six years before I ever heard of B. Virdot. I had begun to research my family history for an article for the *Washington Post Sunday Magazine*. I was getting married and thinking more about my forebears—who they were and how their lives might have shaped my own. I applied my investigative skills to fleshing out the lives of my ancestors, relying on birth records, death certificates, city directories, census reports, wills, passenger lists, deeds, and other documentary evidence.

It was easy work piecing together the lives of my grandparents—all except for the branch that ended with my grandfather Sam Stone. Of his early life I knew little and could find even less. The records that had effortlessly revealed themselves to me for the other three grandparents were a cul de sac when it came to Sam. Even Pittsburgh proved to be a dead end. I tried every possible permutation of his name—Sam, Samuel, S.J., Samuel John. I enlisted the help of locals and city clerks, searched old newspapers and genealogical archives. I grilled relatives. Nothing.

I had more than a passing interest in Sam. He had always been a favorite, a bad boy whose wanderlust, roving eye, and sleight of hand hinted at a life led outside the margins. From Kenya, he had returned with a zebra-skin drum for me. From Lagos, Nigeria, he came back with the name of a pen pal. I had a drawer filled with postcards and letters he'd sent from Zanzibar, Madagascar, Uganda, and other far-off lands. Both of my grandfathers were named Samuel, but I always preferred to believe that my middle name— Theodore Samuel Gup—was for him, not my father's father, a scholarly but starched rabbi. As an investigative reporter who had spent years under the *Washington Post*'s Bob Woodward, I knew how to work the records, and yet I could find nothing of my own grandfather's past.

Like Superman, Sam seemed to have suddenly popped up on the planet in the late 1920s, leaving a full thirty years unaccounted for. Once or twice I had asked my mother, but she too had no answers. Somehow she and everyone else had grown comfortable with the idea that Sam had no past— or that if he did, he must have had good reason to bury it.

So I turned to Minna, Sam's widow. Earlier inquiries had gotten me nowhere, which was strange given that she and I were so close. She was my confidante, and I, hers. I told her of my frustration trying to retrace Sam's life. She had generously walked me through her own family's lineage, but, after fifty-four years of marriage, she seemed to know nothing of Sam's. I pressed the case.

That's when she dropped all pretense of ignorance and made me promise—actually swear an oath—that as long as she was alive I would not ask anything more of Sam's past. The reporter in me tried to get at the reason for her resistance. I got nowhere. Finally, I surrendered and gave her my word. I would not delve into Sam's life as long as she was alive. That was that. But it did not stop me from wondering what could possibly be so sensitive. Sam was dead. As a devoted grandson, I dropped the matter completely. But as an investigative reporter I could not resist running the universe of possible scenarios that might explain her demands of me. Was Sam a bigamist? Did he have another family that might come forward and claim his estate? Had he been a wanted man? Was Sam Stone even his real name? And finally, did Minna have the answers, or merely fear them?

Long before, there had been signs that something was amiss; I just didn't see them. I had some vague knowledge growing up in Canton that several of his relatives—my relatives—lived around us, but I didn't know their names or of what relation they were to me. In fact, I was never allowed to mention them. Doing so brought a sharp rebuke from my mother. It hadn't occurred to me that she could be protecting me from something.

We lived on Twenty-second Street Northeast. Just up the street was a small house that I passed each weekday on my walks to and from Belle Stone Elementary School. I was forbidden from stopping there or talking to the people who lived there. I had come to look upon the house as a kind of Hansel and Gretel cottage where I might be taken captive or transformed. Many years later, as an adult, I learned that it was the home of one of Sam's brothers. In my mind, it had some vague association with murder and mayhem. When I was seven I had overheard something, snippets of conversation about "murders," the details of which would not make themselves known to me for years to come.

There were other hints that not all was as it appeared in Sam's life. In 2005, when my grandmother Minna's health was failing, I discovered an ancient strip of film, from which I had prints made. They were taken the day of Minna and Sam's wedding in 1927. In the black-and-white photo, Sam and Minna are embracing in the backyard of my great-grandmother's home. I noticed that no one else was in the photos. I had two of the pictures framed and sent to Minna. Later, when I visited her at the nursing home, I saw them by her bedside. I asked what had become of the wedding party. There wasn't one, she said.

On January 13, 2005, my grandmother Minna left us. Her ashes were buried beside Sam's remains in Canton's Westlawn Cemetery. It didn't occur to me then, indeed not until three years later, when my mother gave me the suitcase, that I was now free to follow the path of Sam's life wherever it might lead.

III.
The Bread of Tomorrow

You are doing a very good thing and I wish there were a lot more people like you. The people who are lucky enough to have no worry where the next meal is coming from don't realize how it is to be like we are and a lot of others.

—LETTER FROM RUTH AMAN TO MR. B. VIRDOT

Beginning Again

When Sam Stone first appeared in Canton in 1918, he was thirty and living in a single rented room. He held at least two jobs, one in a clothing shop, the other as a freelance ad man. A 1920 magazine, *The Metro Annual*, features an oval photo of a young Sam Stone in cravat and coat, and says of him, "Samuel: This young man eats advertising, sleeps with it and works with it. Short of Stature with a winning smile that covers his entire face, he is a new member and will undoubtedly . . ." But the page is torn and the rest of the sentence is lost. The magazine was right. Sam got little sleep. His feverish schedule left him exhausted. To stay awake driving between jobs he would suck on lemon drops.

Sam was a young man in a rush, anxious to shed his past, impatient to prove himself. He'd come to the right place. Canton in the 1920s was full of just such people. The town welcomed newcomers and immigrants, no questions asked—the kind of place where one might even reinvent oneself. Those with rough edges and a penchant for cutting corners would have felt right at home. Bootleggers, bookies, prostitutes, officials on the take, and schemers of every description mingled freely with miners and millworkers and shopkeepers.

"Little Chicago," as Canton was then known,

was on the Lincoln Highway, at the crossroads of corruption between New York and "Big Chicago." The *New York Times*, in July of 1926, offered its readers a sampling of the lexicon of Canton's underworld: a plainclothes policeman "is a 'sport,' a uniformed officer is a 'harness bull.' Dope peddlers are known variously as 'shovels,' 'reindeers' or 'angels.' Likewise a pistol is a 'silencer' or a 'six best friends' if it happens to hold six cartridges.'" The portion of town where crime was most concentrated was "The Jungle." There were plenty of honest, hardworking men and women living in Canton, but even they had grown blasé about the rackets and the vice, as long as they knew their place. "Public indifference" was the phrase cited by the *Times*. Unlike some cities, business in Canton's many brothels was all but dead on the weekends. That was the customers' family time. And if a john died in flagrante delicto, the police could be counted on to arrange for the body to be found in a more proper setting—they could do no less for the family. For all its flaws, the town was tolerant, forgiving, and oblivious to pedigrees.

In such a place, it took Sam little time to establish himself, acquiring a men's clothing shop on Tuscarawas, one of the city's main commercial streets. It proudly bore his name, Stone's Clothes. Beside him was Petropoulos & Xynos, the shoeshine business of two Greek immigrants; a confectionary run by Italian immigrants, the Marsinos; and a barbershop belonging to native-born Lester Link. From Sam's store could be seen the imposing Stark County Court House with its four gilded angels blowing trumpets from a soaring bell tower. By the 1920s he was one of Canton's up-and-coming merchants.

Evidence of Sam's success is to be found in the suitcase that holds the B. Virdot letters. There is a menu dated July 10, 1922, from aboard the RMS *Majestic*, at the time the world's largest ocean liner. Once Germany's prized SS *Bismarck*, it had passed to the Brits under the Treaty of Versailles and was now the flagship of the White Star Line. That evening, Sam had a choice of "Sea Bass, Petits Paysanne, Roisettes of Mutton, St. Germain, or Philadelphia Chicken, Chipolata." It appears that Sam also had a traveling companion, doubtless a lady friend. The personalized menu notes that it is for "Mr. Stone and Party."

From another such card in the suitcase it seems that he had become a man not only of means but of some leisure as well. He did not return from abroad for at least five weeks. On a card dated August 17, 1922, he waxed poetic: "Grotesque and massive . . . wind tossed and rugged; limitless distances, blue waters bulwarked against the most wonderful ship in the world—and wine . . . and more wine—and life full of the gladness of living. That's the night before the last night on board the

131

steamer 'Paris.' " During the voyage he was served his first artichoke. He attacked it with knife and fork until someone suggested it be taken apart delicately, leaf by leaf. That was not how Sam approached life.

On his passport application dated May 2, 1921, he wrote "I solemnly swear that I was born at Pittsburgh, on or about the 1st day of March, 1889, that my father Jacob Stone was born in Russia, and is now deceased. That he emigrated to the United States from the port of [unknown], on or about [unknown], 1875 . . ." He said his father had been naturalized as a citizen of the United States on May 15, 1883, as shown by the accompanying Certificate of Naturalization.

But in a thorough search of the records, I could find no evidence of his naturalization. I scoured the U.S. Census but could turn up no reference to the family living in Pittsburgh in that period. In my sweep of all documents, I found nothing to support any of the claims made on his passport application. That's because, as I would discover over the ensuing months, it was all pure fantasy. There was no such naturalization in 1883. And contrary to Sam's sworn statement, his father, Jacob, was not born in Russia and was still very much alive at the time he applied for the passport. Almost everything Sam Stone wrote and swore to was fictitious. It pains me to admit it, even now, but in so doing, he had knowingly committed a federal crime. If found out, it would likely have led authorities to a host of other misrepresentations and ultimately put him and his hard-earned reputation in serious jeopardy.

Sam had written that the purpose of his trip to Switzerland, Romania, France, Italy, and Jugo-Slavia was to explore the export and import business. But the State Department and Canton's local postmaster general had their doubts. Their suspicions were piqued by a confidential interview with W. G. Saxton, a cashier with Canton's First National Bank, who informed investigators that he suspected Sam's true purpose was to visit relatives. It mattered because at the time the country was traumatized by the influx of poor immigrants and demanded of passport applicants that they swear their purpose was not to aid in bringing more foreigners into the country.

As the investigators eyed Sam's passport application, his May 18 departure drew closer. Given the wealth of supporting documentation, including a birth certificate, they were unable to challenge it. Despite their suspicions, he was granted a passport, which arrived by special delivery just days before his scheduled departure. But the contradictions and inconsistencies in his story would surface again and again, and the lies would grow ever more convoluted until even when he wanted to tell the truth he could not. In a town like Canton in the 1920s, where the underworld flourished and the authorities took little note, taking such liberties with the truth might have seemed petty enough, but the potential consequences would weigh upon him for decades to come, and the more he gained in wealth and stature, the more he had to fear from the truth.

Grief

I did not need to know the story of his life to know that Sam had suffered. His childish jokes were often the only glimpse we would get of his childhood. "I am on a seafood diet," he used to say, then pause. "I eat all the food I see." As he delivered the punch line, he would rub his ample belly. Sam was amused by the very notion of a diet and the idea that one might be in so privileged a position as to be able to choose what one eats. We, his family, understood without his ever having to say so that behind the joke was a memory of hunger. When, in his ad, he wrote the words "the bread of tomorrow," he was not speaking metaphorically. In the world from which he came and the one to which his appeal was addressed, bread was the answer to many a prayer. In December 1933 there was real urgency in the words "Give us this day our daily bread . . ."

Many of the letters to B. Virdot refer to bread. For them, it was the focus of their days, upon which they and their loved ones depended. Sixteen-year-old Dorothy Clark, in her letter to B. Virdot, penned, "where you wrote in your column 'The bread of today is the question of tomorrow' was surely true of us this last couple weeks. Sometimes we just eat oats to save bread for the next day for our school lunches." She was one of four children, her thirty-five-year-old father, Clyde, an out-of-work crane operator in a steel mill, so sick he could barely walk.

This was not a classical famine brought on by locusts or crop failure (though the Dust Bowl hardly helped) but an economic drought. The famine it produced was no less harsh—the slow and relentless drain on energy and will that comes from being underfed day in and day out, the stunted growth of the young, the sunken look of the old. It was a cruel form of starvation that lacked finality, withering the spirit as much as the body. In some, it bred resignation and paralysis. In others, it created resentment and even a willingness to break the law.

Those who endured the Depression and saw their children go to bed hungry night after night understood how desperate times could sometimes give rise to desperate actions. Prolonged hunger and want fed into Canton's seamy underbelly of crime, pitting the haves against the have-nots, and fueling a growing perception that the laws were there to protect property not people. That December of 1933, the simple phrase "the bread of tomorrow" was enough to telegraph to one and all the depths to which so many had sunk.

Forty-year-old Paul Kendzora, a onetime coal miner and son of German immigrants, wrote, "There is seven in the family and one working part time so you can realize what our Christmas will be.

I guess we will have to hunt rabbit for dinner . . . I worry until I have the headache all the time."

Bread was also on the minds of Chester and Nancy Young when, on the evening of December 18, 1933, Nancy wrote to B. Virdot. Three years earlier, Chester Young had lost his job. He was also partially blind. They shared their cramped home with their son Robert, twenty-one; his sixteen-year-old wife, Dorothy; a son Chester Jr., age fourteen; a son Alvah, age six; and a daughter, Betty Jane, age four. Their circumstances continued to spiral downward. Nancy Ellen Young took up a pencil and wrote to B. Virdot:

Dear Sir:

I was just sitting in my room this evening looking upon my family and knowing I did not have a cent to my name to even buy them bread, all though they were asking about Santa Claus. My husband is a Parscal Blind and has had no work for about three yers. A $1.00 now and then. There is a family of five. 3 children. And I have ask for help and Mr. Young has try to get work from the Government but can't get it so far. But God only knows the best. We have allways try to be Honest in every way. And I was reading in the paper where you like to help a Poor and needed family out for Xmas. Well I can't get much poor off than I am. Last week we did not have bread for two days. May god bless the giver to help my poor little children out. Now in the God do not think I am lying as you are welcome to come and see me Mr Chester A.Young 1111 3rd St SW Canton Ohio I sure will thank you very much for Help and to make my children a Merry Christmas. God bles you and family. And Merry Xmas & Happy new Year. Answer please thank.

Nancy Young had good reason to fret about her family. She knew the true depths of personal loss, though she made no mention of it in her letter. It was yet another example of the trauma of life in those years and the culture that kept its sorrows to itself. To have fully unburdened herself to Mr. B. Virdot, or to anyone, for that matter, would have been deemed unseemly. No one wanted another's pity, and even in the poorest and hardest hit of families, notions of dignity and privacy were not compromised. As secretive as Sam was about his own past—especially viewed from the vantage point of today—he reflected a broader norm in which that generation seldom shared its woes with the next, perhaps hoping to escape their own grief or provide their offspring with a clean slate, unencumbered by such grimness. Today, in an age of celebrity, where anguish and loss are routinely the stuff of autobiography, we are mystified by that generation's reticence to share its stories. They would have been no less taken aback by our lack of inhibition and disregard for privacy. And what I take to be Sam's secrecy, he and his generation might have seen as their gift to us, fulfilling the dream that we, their descendants, might be liberated from such hardships as they endured.

But there was no such escape for Nancy Ellen Young. What she omitted from her letter was boundless grief. The twenties had brought one funeral after another. The death certificates record a succession of tragedies. On May 1, 1921, they lost their seventeen-day-old infant, Orville. He was born premature and died at home. A year later, on September 27, 1922, their two-month-old daughter, Margaret, died of what was called "inanition"—the fatal exhaustion that comes from lack of nourishment. On August 13, 1925, they lost their six-year-old son, Donald. The cause: acute gastroenteritis. On May 18, 1928, their eight-day-old son, Arnold, also premature, died at home. Four times in eight years, they made the trek to Westlawn Cemetery to bury their children.

Against such losses, the opening sentence of Nancy Young's letter to B. Virdot takes on a more ominous tone: "I was just sitting in my room this evening looking upon my family and knowing I did not have a cent to my name to even buy them bread . . ." In the Young home, food was always an issue, except perhaps for those few days before Christmas when the check from B. Virdot arrived. Whatever transient relief it provided did not end the sorrows in the Young household. Seven years after writing to Mr. B. Virdot, Nancy Ellen Young was dead. She was fifty-one. The cause: pneumonia. In Westlawn Cemetery, she joined the children she had lost.

For the surviving members of the Young family, the prosperity that came to others in the forties and fifties passed them by. Charles Young, a grandson, recalls that as a seven-year-old he visited his grandfather, who was then living in a dingy apartment over a coal company. The man he called "Grandpa" was frail and thin and nearly blind. The poverty that Chester and his wife endured did not end with them. Decades later, their son Alvah was buried in one of Canton's pauper graves. Five of Chester and Nancy Ellen's grandchildren also endured turbulent and impoverished childhoods. Charles Young remembers that in 1956, following his parents' divorce, he and his brothers and sisters were placed in the Fairmount Children's home, an orphanage, for a year and eight days.

The saga of the Young family would have struck home with Sam Stone. Though he never spoke of it, he too had lost a sibling in infancy—perhaps more than one—and in later years, the grandchildren of his brother were found so malnourished and living in such squalor that they had to be rescued by city workers. But that too was a story I would discover only later.

Bad Company

The Youngs suffered in silence, praying for better times. But for others, want fueled resentment and desperation. Many who had lived an exemplary life—hard work, family, and church—went hungry. Living by the rules offered few tangible rewards. Prohibition came to an end on December 5, 1933—two weeks before Sam Stone placed his ad in the paper. But long before that event and long after, many in Canton had surrendered themselves to corruption.

Neither the law nor city officials were held in high esteem in those days. Canton's police crowed about their "Goon Car," a four-ton bulletproof vehicle, more a tank than a car, with portholes for tommy guns. It was always ready to battle mobsters, though it was seen more as a departmental trophy than a vehicle of enforcement. Too many police were in the pocket of those they were supposed to be locking up. The city was rife with speakeasies, numbers rackets, loan sharks, and prostitution. It was impossible for a man to walk down some of Canton's streets without being propositioned from entire rows of nearby windows. Public corruption was widespread. Many in the trough of the Depression secretly cheered on the likes of Bonnie Parker, Clyde Barrow, and John Dillinger.

The banks, they reasoned, had it coming to them.

For the ordinary fellow, out of work and unable to put bread on the table for his wife and children, there was the ever-present lure of crime—not the great heist, but a petty score to see a family through the worst of it. These were not hardened criminals looking for an easy score, but men who had exhausted every legal way, who were willing to take any job, who had stood in endless lines, filled out countless applications, walked themselves out of their shoes, and still came up empty-handed. The crowded Mansfield Reformatory that served Canton was living proof that good men had their limits. The vice-ridden culture of Canton, the complicity of city officials and police, and the near total absence of either work or public relief collectively created an environment in which crime became, for some, the last and only option.

Sam was not a man to judge others. He had made his own mistakes, and understood that nothing was more precious than a second chance. As B. Virdot he was only too ready to help those who, like himself, had strayed. He might even have felt a tinge of envy for those who had "paid their debt to society." At least now they could put it behind them. His actions were such that the most severe punishment that would be meted out was his own decades-long dread of being discovered.

Among the letters that came to him as B. Virdot

was one from Alverna Wright. Today she is best remembered by her grandson, fifty-eight-year-old Joseph Watters. He had spent much of his early life with her and his grandfather, Noble Wright. They were loving people, doting grandparents, and generous to a fault. And though they didn't talk about it, he knew they had endured much during the Depression. "I knew my grandfather very well," Joseph Watters told me, speaking on a cell phone as he drove along a highway in Medina County, south of Cleveland. "My grandfather was a very decent, gentle person." But before I read him the letter his grandmother Alverna had written to B. Virdot on December 18, 1933, I felt obliged to warn him that it might not be easy for him to hear its contents. It contained what I suspected would be a painful secret and he would do well to ready himself. This he did.

"Dear Sir," the letter began,

Considering your spirit of giving I will not be afraid to write to you because I know you have real charity. I have felt like I would like to do just what you are doing but I have not been so favored.

The depression has affected me from the very beginning. Work not being steady, then no work at all. We were too proud to ask for help but went on from day to day saying tomorrow we will ask for help. My husband said he was able bodied and willing to work and didn't want charity.

Becoming restless my husband went from place to place looking for work. Some times walking for miles always in hope of finding work. We were very unfortunate as none of our relation could help us at all.

Finally after every effort was exhausted he fell in with some bad company and finally landed in the Mansfield reformatory where is listed as a depression inmate.

This left me to look after my little girl alone. Where we were living and couldn't pay the rent in furnished rooms, we had lost all our furniture because we couldn't pay the storage bill. The water was shut off, the gas turned off, and then the city came to my rescue. I receive $6.00 every two months from the state out of which I buy some groceries & the rest shoes & necessaries.

My husband has been transferred to Applecreek with some of the trusted inmates but I do not know definitely when he will be home.

This letter finds me without any money at all to get anything for my little girl for

Christmas. I am not asking for myself but I would appreciate it if I would have the pleasure of giving even $5.00 worth of useful things to my little girl and husband and mother & mother-in-law who have been unfortunate too. My mother-in-law lost her home & is seventy years old.

Even if you do not consider me worthy of your kindness I want to say that you will be rewarded at least three times for your charity in some way for as the saying is:

"He who gives himself with his alms feeds three,
  Himself, his hungering
  Neighbor and Me. (meaning God)"

SINCERELY YOURS,
MRS. A. WRIGHT
1527 FRAZER AVE.NW

Joseph Watters was at a loss for words. He had not known that his grandfather had done time in prison, nor the depths of his grandparents' anguish. I understood well what he was feeling, having only recently discovered that my grandfather too had crossed the line. His grandmother, Alverna Coombs Wright, was thirty-one when she wrote the letter, the mother of a single child, Miriam, then seven. She lived with her seventy-two-year-old mother, Sarah, a widow; an older sister, Anna Belle; and a boarder named Frank Grissard.

A decade earlier, in June 1923, she had married Noble Ebenezer Wright, a man who could build anything with his hands. But even such talent as his was no shield from the Depression. All around him honest and industrious neighbors failed, engulfed in a misery seemingly oblivious to skills or virtue. Decent men and women not otherwise predisposed to a life of crime faced choices no one should have to make.

By all accounts Noble Wright was an honorable man, but driven by need, he broke the law. State archives record that on September 20, 1932, he stole a car from a garage, a Hudson Brougham valued at $250. Noble Wright didn't make much of a criminal. He was arrested the next day and confessed to taking two other cars. He was thirty years old, stood five feet eight, weighed 152 pounds, had a sixth-grade education, and worked for a time at a dairy. All this is on his prison record, along with the fact that he had been married for nine years. His only vice—aside from stealing cars—was smoking an occasional cigar.

He was sentenced to 360 days in the Ohio State Reformatory, one mile from Mansfield, Ohio. With a prison population of some thirty-five hundred men ranging in age from sixteen to thirty, it was one of the nation's largest such facilities, a step between reform school and the penitentiary. In the depths of the Depression it became a holding tank for the desperate.

Of the 1,245 prisoners received in 1933, nearly all were there for so-called "property crimes." As the reformatory noted, "It is here that men hear the first clang of steel bars behind them; and here that they lose their identity as citizens. Here they cease to be names and become numbers." Noble Wright became inmate number 29448. It was his first time behind bars and it did not suit him. In February 1933, Noble Wright escaped. He did not get far. He was captured the next day and brought back to the reformatory, where, for his escape attempt, another 130 days were tacked onto his sentence.

On May 1, 1934, four months after his wife had written to Mr. B. Virdot, Noble Wright was paroled. When he left the facility he entered an environment no less desperate, only now he had a record. Exactly how Alverna and Noble weathered the Depression is not known, but that they did is beyond doubt. Their only child, Miriam, would marry Joseph P. Watters and have fifteen children—including two pairs of twins who died in infancy.

The Wrights' lives improved so much in the years after the Depression as to have been scarcely recognizable to them. Noble became an engineer with the Pennsylvania Railroad and crisscrossed the country delivering coal and iron ore and all manner of raw materials that helped fuel the recovery and gave rise to the great industrial boom that brought prosperity to Canton and the nation. Of course, that's not what his grandson Joseph recalls. He remembers Grandpa with his engineer's cap taking him for rides in the yard engine, the great diesel barreling down the tracks on Canton's south side. He remembers that his grandpa transformed a garage into a home with his own hands, added to it, and made it into a warm and welcoming place. They never went out to restaurants, and Grandfather Wright tended his modest garden producing tomatoes and corn and rhubarb, which he shared with the grandchildren. Joseph Watters remembers how, through that frugality that was the hallmark of Depression-era survivors, his grandparents saved enough to buy a vacation home in Melbourne, Florida, where they wintered.

Alverna, the writer of the letter, had been the first in her family to graduate from high school. As an adult, she proudly hung her diploma from McKinley High on her wall. (My grandmother Minna Adolph went to school with her.) She became president of Canton's Poetry Society, and left to her grandson notebooks of poetry she had penned that he hopes to have published someday. And in her later years she was a part of the YMCA Kitchen Comedy Club, where she and others played kazoos and washboards and took their places alongside a float in the annual Football Hall of Fame Parade.

But neither Alverna nor her husband, Noble, ever forgot the hardships they endured. Like many of their faith, they sent envelopes with offerings to Catholic missions. But they did more. A grandson, Michael, recalled the time when Noble was walking down the street in Coshocton, Ohio, and came across a nun who had a hole in her shoe. Noble insisted she come with him to a shoe store, and there he bought her a new pair.

Though their marriage was tested by adversity, they saw it through and in June 1980 celebrated their fifty-seventh anniversary. Alverna died in Florida on February 11, 1981, at age seventy-nine. Noble died seven years later, in 1988, at age eighty-six. They are buried side by side in Calvary Cemetery, between Canton and Massillon, Ohio, their simple flat gravestones flush with the grass. They are interred in the section marked "Joyful Mysteries."

Their grandchildren are a living postscript to what they endured. Daughter Miriam and her husband, Joseph Watters, inherited little but the lessons in frugality, but that was enough for them to provide a home for eleven children—four others died in infancy. They kept a journal of every expenditure right down to the penny. Not even the purchase of a three-cent stamp went unrecorded.

Miriam died on August 5, 1999, at age seventy-three, and is also buried in Calvary Cemetery.

Nearly all of Alverna and Noble's eleven

grandchildren chose to remain near Canton. Among them are a postal worker, three nurses, and a businessman. And if railroads provided Grandfather Noble Wright a way out of poverty, it also provided his family and descendants a ticket to a better life. His son-in-law, Joseph, started as a railroad brakeman and rose to superintendent. A granddaughter, Deborah, worked as a railroad stenographer; her brother Joseph helped pay for college with a railroad job; and two of Noble's grandsons work for Norfolk Southern to this day. John Watters is a locomotive conductor who, like his father and grandfather, came under the spell of train and track.

As stunned as family members were to learn of Noble Wright's criminal record, they are no less protective of his good name. Whatever Noble Wright did, they say, he did out of desperation and for those he loved. They understand that the times were punishing, and their admiration for him is undiminished. "It was probably just a survival-type mode that got him into trouble," says grandson Joseph.

Today, the dark gothic Mansfield Reformatory where Noble Ebenezer Wright was held some seventy-five years ago is familiar to many. It was where the 1994 movie *Shawshank Redemption* was filmed, and each Halloween, fright seekers pay fifteen dollars per person for a "Haunted Prison Experience" billed as "Hell on Earth."

As for the last lines of Alverna Wright's letter to Mr. B. Virdot, they are the closing to the poem "The Vision of Sir Launfal" by James Russell Lowell. In the poem, a disillusioned knight of King Arthur's Round Table searches for the Holy Grail but finds only a beggar with whom he shares his food and drink. The beggar, he discovers, is Jesus Christ.

A Lynching

I don't know if Sam was a man of great faith in any traditional sense, but he believed deeply that everyone had a right to a second chance. He'd made his own mistakes and gone on to prove that he could make something better of himself. He was proud to have risen above others' expectations of him, and his frequent references to having graduated from the "School of Hard Knocks" were a celebration of that institution, not an apology. He was eager to prove the distinction between the uneducated and the uneducable. He championed the underdog and forgave the fallen, having been both.

My mother has said he was a poor judge of character. It's true. He looked beyond a person's past to see their prospects, and in so doing ignored many a warning sign. He would never condone crime but he was slow to condemn the man, having witnessed in himself and others the lengths to which a person will go to survive. He understood that having a stain on one's record sometimes said more about the times than the man. That was doubtless how he would have seen the blemish on Noble Wright's record and how he would have viewed George Carlin, who also wrote to him. Carlin's letter began:

153

Mr. B. Virdot

Dear Sir,-

After reading your article in the Canton Repository I decided to write you.

Personally I'm very much adversed to charity in any form although I'm getting relief from the family Service since the first of this month.

Have tried every place to find employment but have not been successful, I would be very greatful if you could in some way find me a place to work.

I could use two dollars Xmas so that my wife & I could go to her home in Alliance, but as a loan.

Will add information concerning myself. Feb 23rd 1930, I was sentenced to the Reformatory at Mansfield, O. Have been home since Sept. 15, 1933 am on parole now & lots of places will not give a man a chance to work when they know it. There is just my wife & I and we will appreciate anything that you can do for us. Am 32 years old.

GEO CARLIN
921 PROSPECT AVE. SW
CANTON, OHIO

That same evening, from the same address, perhaps unknown to George Carlin, someone else was writing to Mr. B. Virdot—his mother, Florence. Her letter read:

Dear Sir-

I saw your very nice offer to help 75 poor needy familys. We are sure in need of a little help. Just now my husband got injured 2 years ago and has been unable to work since he will never be able to work any more. He had been getting compensation up till the 21 of October but they have [not] sent it yet. But we are all sure will get it in the near future we would not ask you to give it to us but just loan it to us till we receive our from Columbus we have a little girl 9 years old. she won't have any Xmas and I no you will for any one that would think of giving that much money away would be happy.

MR. MRS. L. H. CARLIN
921 PROSPECT AVE SW
CANTON, OHIO

That letter was from Lawrence Henry Carlin and Florence Maude Carlin, but most folks in Canton knew them as Henry and Maude. Today that nine-year-old daughter, Valerie—the baby in the family—is eighty-five, but she still remembers well what she got that Christmas of 1933: an orange and a little powder-blue change purse adorned with silver metallic beads that opened and closed with a drawstring. The orange was the first fresh fruit to touch her lips in memory. Both likely came from the five dollars Mr. B. Virdot sent her parents that week. But Valerie never knew of the B. Virdot letter. (Another five dollars arrived for George Carlin.)

Valerie's mother and father tried to protect her from the stresses and strains of their circumstances. "You were kind of shut out of the room when the conversations were going on," she recalls. But no amount of closed doors and whispers could conceal their dire situation. The career-ending injury to her father, Henry Carlin, was an accident in a brickyard in Bolivar, Ohio, that destroyed his back. Even years later, the only income the Carlin family could expect was the forty-nine dollars a month in workmen's compensation.

The Carlins rented a house at 921 Prospect Avenue in 1933. It was the landlady's responsibility to pay the utilities. She did not, and the power was cut off. After that, Valerie did her homework by candlelight. Some nights she went to bed both cold and hungry. Without power, the Carlins had to improvise. Emblazoned in Valerie's childhood memory is a picture of her father and brother-in-law heating a pot of beans in the coal furnace. It seemed to take forever. Bean soup was a near constant, and she swore she would never eat it again, that is, until hunger gnawed at her. To keep the furnace going, her brother-in-law was dispatched to collect coal that had fallen off the coal cars along the railroad tracks. The apartment was sparsely furnished. At nine, Valerie still slept in her parents' bedroom in her baby crib.

The Carlins were people of faith, but only Valerie went to Sunday services at the Methodist church on Dueber Avenue. "My parents never attended church," she remembers, "but they made sure that I did. I think it was because they didn't have the clothes to wear."

The Carlins were often unable to make the rent and were forced to move from place to place in what for many children of the Depression era became a nomadic, rootless life. "I went to every grade school in Canton," remembers Valerie. She attended McKinley High School and was in her second semester of her senior year when she dropped out to help support the family. She went to work at an ice cream parlor on East Tuscarawas, making sandwiches and scooping ice cream for twenty-four cents an hour. (At forty she earned her General Educational Development diploma.) The constant moving, the disruption of schooling, the early imperative to support family—

all this described Sam Stone's childhood as well.

But all was not bleak in the Carlin home. "There was always something to laugh about," recalls Valerie. And her father, despite his injuries and his struggles, remained a jolly man who always believed that "there was a light at the end of the tunnel." Some evenings, family and friends would gather to play cards by candlelight.

In the months and years thereafter, as the New Deal took shape, the Carlins, like thousands of others across the country, took advantage of the work it provided, reinvigorating the economy and transforming the nation as it slowly emerged from the Depression. One of Valerie's brothers went into the Civilian Conservation Corps. Another, James, joined the WPA and helped build dams. The toughness, the self-sacrifice, the readiness to take collective action—all hallmarks of the Depression years—later found expression in World War II and the Greatest Generation. Valerie married Robert Naef, who joined the army, was awarded a Purple Heart, and came home with shrapnel in his right foot. He made the shell fragment into a key chain for his wife. It was friendly fire and not something he talked about. In his absence, in 1943, Valerie became a true Rosie the Riveter, shooting rivets into the stabilizers of countless B-24 Liberator bombers at the Berger Aircraft plant just outside of Canton. In her sewing box, she keeps a single rivet, a token of those times.

• • •

OTHER MEMORIES OF the Carlin home come from eighty-year-old Lheeta Carlin Talbott, the Carlins' granddaughter, and one of eleven children. Her father was James, Valerie's older brother. For a time Lheeta and her family lived at the Prospect Street apartment with her grandparents. She remembers that there were times she could not go to school because she didn't have shoes. Even today that memory stings. She asks that I not mention it, then relents.

Her reluctance to speak of such remote events may be hard for some Americans today to understand. Clearly the memories remain sensitive, but the discomfort in speaking of such matters is also deeply rooted in the mores of those times. Poverty was widespread and afflicted even the most resourceful, but it was still a source of embarrassment. The closest word we have for it is *shame* but it was more than that, just as the pride ascribed to that generation was more nuanced. Both oversimplify the emotional landscape of those times. In their letter to B. Virdot, Donavon Brown, a mechanic, and his wife Mabel, wrote: "We cannot all have money, but to be honest and poor is not a disgrace, and cleanliness is something we can all have at little cost."

It was a different world, one in which the disgrace came not so much from being poor as from the implicit suggestion that the burdens of others were less onerous than one's own. To gain another's pity at the expense of self-respect was a bad bargain. Poverty was viewed not as an individual burden but a societal scourge. In such times, it was often considered self-centered to call attention to one's own predicament, as if one were oblivious to the circumstances of all those around them.

It was part of a wider communal code that applied to the individual, the family, and the community. To capitulate to self-pity or public plaints not only exposed weakness in one's own character but threatened to unravel the composure of others. It was like a team that carried a terrible load evenly distributed across many shoulders. Each looked to the other for support. To break emotional rank only added to the burden of others. It was fine to vent in a political sense, to march on Washington or rail against the banks. But it was expected that one and all would maintain a certain grit and stoicism. "When you come to the end of your rope, tie a knot and hang on," Roosevelt is said to have counseled. For some, it may have been no more than keeping up a front, but the mere ability to do even that said something about their inner reserves. So deeply ingrained was that mind-set that even three-quarters of a century later, Lheeta Carlin Talbott can barely bring herself to speak of the hardships.

In such an environment the offer by Mr. B.

Virdot presented the rarest of opportunities—someone to whom they could unburden themselves as individuals without violating the social compact. Anonymity insulated them and provided them with an emotional refuge that Sam Stone himself never had in such times. He was an intensely social being, but, out of pride or a desire not to dredge up a painful past, he compartmentalized his own years of suffering and shared them with no one. About those early years, he maintained a perfect silence. I call it secrecy, being the product of an age that promotes revelation and conflates privacy with repression. My grandfather never shared anything of his childhood. What I would come to know of it was passed on to me by others decades after he died. It is the same reluctance that Lheeta Carlin Talbott feels in revealing that there were times she could not go to school for lack of shoes.

And like Sam, Lheeta Carlin Talbott's painful memories date back even before she was old enough to go to school—back to the period when her grandparents wrote to Mr. B. Virdot. Her mother and father had bought a bedroom suite of furniture—beds and a dresser and a mirror. They had it for a time but could not keep up with the payments. Lheeta remembers men coming upstairs into the bedroom and carrying the furniture off, repossessing it. But her mother held on to one object—the mirror, convinced that after so many payments she was entitled to keep it. "They are not getting the mirror," she heard her say. Her mother apparently hid it from the men that day.

"My dad kept that mirror and it was always in our living room," says Lheeta. When her father died and his possessions were divided among the children, the one thing Lheeta's daughter, Kathryn, asked for was the mirror, knowing the story behind it. "And now," says Lheeta, "that mirror is in our daughter's house, and it makes me cry." The mirror that held her mother's image now holds for her all that she endured. Today Lheeta wonders what she and her family slept on after their beds were taken. Of this she has no recollection. For her grandparents, the Depression never really ended. Tough times dogged them to the end.

Lheeta's memories of the Depression, like those of the rest of her family, are mired in contradiction. "It was a remarkable time," she says, "but even though it wasn't, it was a better time. It was better because people were more kind."

BUT WHAT OF the Carlins' son George, and the letter he wrote that same December night in 1933? Just behind the Carlins' house, on the same lot, was a smaller cottage, and it was there that their son George Carlin lived with his wife, Irene. And it was there that he wrote his own appeal to Mr. B. Virdot.

George Carlin never did say in the letter what

landed him behind bars. For that, one must look to the state's archives of prison records. Those accounts show that George Carlin was born on August 31, 1901, in Bolivar, Ohio. One of at least six children, he had finished one year of high school, but since the age of fifteen had been largely on his own, working as a mechanic and a painter. Under "associations," meaning who he hung out with, it says simply, "Good and bad." The latter would cost him dearly.

On the evening of September 9, 1930, he and two friends drove the six miles from Canton to Louisville and held up Jonas Miller, a gas station attendant. They took the cash—about thirty-five dollars—as well as the register and divided up their take on the road. They then drove to Akron, where, that same evening, they were arrested by detectives and promptly pled guilty. George Carlin was then twenty-nine, stood five feet seven, and weighed 145 pounds.

On September 13, 1933, he was paroled into a world that was in its way as harsh and forbidding as the one he was leaving. The Depression had ravaged the economy, and not even the best of men with clean records could find work. His prospects were bleak. And yet, somehow he managed. On October 20, 1934—more than a year after being paroled—his probation officer wrote, "The man has been in no trouble since his return and is working hard every day."

George Carlin and his wife, Irene, divorced. George later met Hazel Winterhalter, or "Tootie," as he called her. Hazel, now ninety-seven, is quick-witted and protective of her late husband's good name. Born on the evening of November 5, 1912, Hazel Carlin is the daughter of the stableman who tended the horses and carriages of one of Canton's true millionaires, industrialist Frank E. Case, manufacturer of dental chairs. (Case was wiped out in the crash of 1929 and died four years later.) Hazel Carlin says her family was largely immune to the Depression, having an already modest lifestyle and but one child to feed.

George and Hazel were married on June 26, 1941, in the Zion Lutheran Church. With the coming of war, forty-year-old George Carlin was required to register for the draft. It was then that he told his new bride for the first time that he had a criminal record. "He offered to dissolve the marriage if I wasn't satisfied," she recalls. "But I loved him and it made no difference to me." I imagine that my grandmother Minna responded similarly, as Sam came to trust her enough to confide in her and tell her some, if not all, of his secrets.

The subject of prison would never again come up between George and Hazel and never again would George Carlin cross the law. "He learned," she said. The one good thing that came of his time in prison was that it was there that he learned to be a first-rate mechanic, a skill that would stand him in good stead for the rest of his life. He could repair anything.

In 1946, George and Hazel Carlin left Ohio and moved to Pima, Arizona. Lung problems eventually forced George to quit working as a mechanic, but his good nature and solid reputation in the Gila Valley of southeast Arizona led to his being offered a job managing first a movie theater and later the drive-in in Safford. Carlin was a fan of Johnny Cash, could not get enough of "The Yellow Rose of Texas," and took endless photos and slides of the family. In 1960 he purchased a new Chrysler Valiant with a push-button transmission, mostly in an effort to conserve his energy as his lungs failed. But two weeks later, he died.

George and Hazel Carlin had three children: a daughter, Jean, a social worker; a son, George, an electrician who works for the Central Arizona Project, bringing water to area farmers; and another son, Donald, a technology teacher in Henderson, Nevada. None of the children knew of their father's record, but son Donald, speaking for them all, took it in stride, his admiration for his father intact. He cannot bring himself to judge his father harshly.

For George Carlin's daughter, Jean, the revelation of her father's prison record even brought some clarity to her life. She remembered that her father was very demanding and offered morality lessons that sometimes went too far and frightened her. One of these was the story of the Haldeman brothers, who George Carlin said were hanged for rustling cattle. He suggested that the two were somehow related to the Carlin family. The story made Jean uneasy. She was nine or ten and never forgot it. It also confused her. She didn't understand why her father had told the story and with such immediacy. "Now remembering back to that incident," she says, "it makes it personal, which it wasn't then. I was thinking 'yadda, yadda, yadda . . .'

"I can only remember hearing the story once," recalls Jean Carlin, "but it left such a powerful impression that I remembered it." Years later, when she moved back to Tucson, she looked up the Haldeman hangings and discovered that they were indeed real. William and Thomas Haldeman were hanged on November 16, 1900, in Tombstone for killing a constable who tried to arrest them for shooting cattle. Perhaps the story was George Carlin's way of scaring his children into staying on the straight and narrow. Perhaps it was an oblique attempt to pass on what he had learned the hard way. Either way, it was effective. As a social worker, Jean Carlin has spent years keeping young people out of trouble.

Legacy of Lies

Sam Stone would doubtless have understood what it was that drove men like Noble Wright and George Carlin to break the law in those terrible times. Each had a single costly flirtation with crime that left them both with a sense of remorse. But there was at least one other man who wrote to Mr. B. Virdot that Christmas of 1933 who had stepped outside the law and remained there, seemingly untouched by police and the courts. His name was Allen C. Bennafield. He was African American, and, like many of Canton's blacks, had roots in the Deep South.

There are myriad conflicting versions of his early life. The one accepted by some of his descendants is this: his mother, Cora Ellington, was one of at least seven children. Born into slavery in 1863 in Georgetown, Georgia, her parents were farm laborers working the cotton fields. But her family celebrated the emancipation, naming her younger brothers who were born immediately after the Civil War Grant and Sherman in honor of those two formidable Union generals, Ulysses S. Grant and William Tecumseh Sherman. Cora too worked the fields, and married William Bennafield. It appears that he may have fathered two large families, one with Cora, the other with her sister or cousin. The confusion and enmity that ensued caused friction that passed from one generation to the next. There is a sense among his descendants that the tangled story of his origins was purposeful, that it concealed the true narrative. If so, that is something he shared with Sam Stone.

Ben and Cora's son, Allen Chester Bennafield, maintained that he was born in Jacksonville, Florida, in February 1897. In his early twenties he and a sister, Rosa Lee, migrated north to Canton, arriving about 1918, the same year Sam Stone arrived. There Bennafield ran a pool hall at 802 Cherry Avenue Southeast—one of Canton's forty-six billiard parlors. Next door on one side was the Greek-American Agency run by the Hasapis Brothers. On the other side was Friedman's Drug Store. Greek/black/Jew, side by side yet worlds apart. In 1927 Bennafield lived at 414 Ninth Street Southeast. Across the street, he looked out on the Agudas Achem Congregation, the "Hebrew Church" for Canton's Orthodox Jews.

In Canton, Bennafield met a younger woman, Emily June Johnson, and together they would have four sons, Allen Jr., Donald, David, and Paul; and a daughter, June. They apparently never married but lived as common-law husband and wife. But by 1933, the Depression weighed heavy on Bennafield and his family. On the evening of December 18, 1933, he took out a pencil and wrote to Mr. B. Virdot:

Dear Sir-

In this evening's Repository I see that you want to put a little Christmas cheer in homes where it is needed, so I am daring to write to you in the hopes that I may be one of the fortunate ones.

My name is A. C. Bennafield and I have a small dry cleaning establishment in my home at 518-8th St. S.E., but business is very poor. Every cent I make has to be paid over for bills. People put their work in, asking for it right away. I pay what little money I have to have them cleaned and then they aren't called for right away. Sometimes it's 3 or 4 weeks before I can get rid of them. So you see, in this way I haven't any chance to make anything. I have three children, the youngest 4 months old, and it is necessary that they be supplied with good wholesome food. It's rather a pull to always have bread when the others, who are 3 and 2 years old, call for it. I have been in this business for about 2 years but times have not been good enough so that I can give the kids a Xmas. Of course one good thing about it is that they are too small to know what it's all about. If business picks up I am hoping I'll be able to give them one when they are old enough to understand. Because of this little business, which just manages to keep bread on our table, the Family Service will not even give me milk for the children. I can't make them understand that business isn't any good.

Before entering this business, I was in the pool room business and made a fairly good income. While I wasn't rich, still I was comfortable and didn't have to worry about where the next meal was coming from. Then the Depression hit me and in trying to save my business I used up every cent of the little nest egg I had saved up. When I began this business I had to borrow money in order to get started and I have just recently finished paying that debt off.

So Mr. Virdot, if you think that I am deserving of your help, I will be eternally grateful to you, and for myself and my family, I thank you.

Wishing you a merry Xmas and a Happy New Year.

A. C. BENNAFIELD

A few days later, B. Virdot's check arrived in the mail. But it was not enough to hold the debtors at bay or keep bread on Bennafield's table. And as his

170

vulnerable little Monarch Tailors declined, Allen Bennafield came to realize that all his efforts would not be enough. And so he began to take in more than just dry cleaning. His son Donald says his father began to solicit bets and allowed himself to become a part of Canton's thriving gambling and numbers racket.

In time, according to son Donald, he worked for the notorious John Nickles, a Greek immigrant from Constantinople known throughout Canton as "Nick the Greek." Nick was part of the lore of Canton's thriving underworld, living large and fast—too fast. On June 22, 1953, Nick was gunned down, his body discovered in a storage garage. The next day's front-page headline declared, JOHN NICKLES, VICE LORD, SLAIN.

After that, Bennafield's son Don said his father worked for Pat Ferruccio, a racketeer with reputed ties to organized crime. (In the 1940s, before Ferruccio went to prison, he regularly raced his speedboat against my grandfather, Sam Stone, on Turkey Foot Lake. Later, the Ferruccio family lived across the street from us.)

Bennafield was never arrested but continued his numbers racket long after the Depression passed. He was never wealthy but managed to acquire at least four modest parcels of land in Canton. But on April 2, 1948, at the age of fifty-one, he dropped dead of a heart attack. He died without a will and was buried in Forest Hill Cemetery.

Just days later, Bennafield's widow and five children were hit with a second shock: Bennafield had concealed a secret marriage to a woman named Nettie Richardson. The family had known nothing of her. What they discovered in the ensuing probate struggle was that she and Allen Bennafield had married in Detroit, Michigan, on July 3, 1923—some twenty-five years before. On the marriage license, he had written that he was born in Cuba and that his mother's maiden name was Martinez. The family, disoriented from the loss and confounded by the web of lies and secrets, did not know what to believe.

And, most devastating of all, Bennafield and Richardson had never divorced. Hearing of Bennafield's death, Richardson wasted no time filing a claim against the estate. She walked away with it all, leaving Bennafield's forty-one-year-old widow, Emily, emotionally and financially devastated. Humiliated by the scandal, she retreated from Canton and moved to Cleveland to live with her son David. Emily died in Cleveland in 1988. Surprisingly, she was buried next to the man who deceived her.

In the years that followed, the Bennafield family has been plagued by tragedy and crime. As a young man, Bennafield's son Donald served time in prison. Donald's wife, Martha, was found murdered in a field in 1991. It remains an unsolved homicide. One of Donald's daughters was convicted of prostitution. Allen Bennafield's daughter, June, served in the military and died of a heart attack at twenty-nine. His son Paul found work in a steel mill. Bennafield's son David, born four months before his father wrote to Mr. B. Virdot, worked for thirty-eight years as a special delivery driver for the U.S. Postal Service in Cleveland. In March 2006, his stepson Shaun was sentenced to twelve years in federal prison for selling crack cocaine.

It is no wonder, then, that Allen C. Bennafield's oldest son and namesake, Allen C. Bennafield Jr., now eighty, has no interest in speaking of his father. He refused to even listen to the words his father had written to Mr. B. Virdot. Perhaps it was because he chose such a different path from his father. Allen Bennafield Jr. left home early, and served in the army, then the air force. Later he retired as a captain in the Washington, D.C., police department. But despite his insistence on distancing himself from his father and his clouded past, his thirty-five-year-old daughter, Leta Bennafield, has doggedly sought answers about her family's origins. She has spent years researching and trying to reconstruct the family tree, as twisted as it may be.

An information technology administrator, Leta has posted numerous entreaties on the Internet's genealogy sites seeking to fill in the gaps left by a grandfather who did what he could to obscure his own roots. To this day she continues to ask questions, and to this day her father declines to answer them—either because they dredge up unpleasant memories or because he may not know the truth. His son Damon, a former advertising executive, now lives in Atlanta, Georgia, the state where, a century and a half earlier, the Bennafields worked the cotton fields as slaves.

Mr. B. Virdot's Story: The Crossing

The more I dug into Sam's past, the more I discovered that he had something in common with each of the people he helped, and that I shared something in common with their descendants. Like the grandchildren of Noble Wright and George Carlin, I was to discover that my grandfather, for all his good-heartedness, had broken the law. And like the descendants of A. C. Bennafield, I was to learn only after his death that the man I thought I knew had concealed an earlier life unknown to us all—though it hurt no one but himself.

There were early hints that Sam Stone's life was more complex than he let on. As a young adult, my mother, Virginia, learned that Sam's name had once been "Finkelstein," meaning "shining stone." She despised the name, in part because it sounded less American than "Stone," and in part because it linked our family to what she regarded as Sam's less reputable kin. Sam had taken it upon himself in his early twenties to change his name to "Samuel J. Stone." He liked its lapidary quality and its strength. Out of that block of stone, Sam might have seen himself as a sculptor chiseling a new name and a new life for himself. "Samuel J. Stone" was a name befitting an executive, a self-made man, literally. Thereafter, the name Finkelstein was almost never uttered, and when it was, it was said in a hushed voice.

Over the next few years he persuaded his three brothers and three sisters to take the Stone name as well. Each of the brothers used the middle initial "J." It was a sign of his growing influence over the family, both as the oldest son as well as the most successful member of the clan. In time, even his mother, Hinde, changed her name, but his father did not.

The siblings understood that it was taboo to utter the old name and conspired to wipe out their own pasts. Their children would be raised as my mother was—with little or no knowledge of their early circumstances or origins. At one time or another, Sam had claimed his parents were German, Russian, Bohemian, or Romanian. I remember that when he spoke there was the slightest trace of an accent. There were just a few words he said that reminded me of the actor Bela Lugosi and brought to mind Transylvania. But it was not enough to fix it to a certain place, or even to be sure that it was foreign. It was a mere residue that only a forensic linguist could perhaps track to a crossing in steerage or time in a ghetto.

I had a copy of Sam's birth certificate from Pittsburgh but was unable to find any evidence of his birth in that city. I searched records in several surrounding cities and towns and found nothing. I began to have fundamental doubts about the veracity of Sam's sketchy account of his own early life. At that point, I expanded my search to include ships' passenger lists under the name "Finkelstein." That too seemed fruitless. But just when I was about to give up, I found them: Janne (Jacob) Finkelstein, forty-three; his son Sam, fifteen; his eldest daughter, Hana Sure (later known as Sarah), seventeen; and his son Moses (later known as Mack), eleven. Sam and Hana Sure were listed as "laborers," and Janne as a "private dealer." They sailed from Le Havre in France aboard the *La Champagne* and arrived in New York on October 6, 1902. They listed their final destination as Pittsburgh. Their nationality was "Roumanian," their home village, Dorohoi. It was the first I'd ever heard of Dorohoi. It meant nothing to me. It was also the first time I heard that my family's roots went back to Romania.

But why all the secrecy, I wondered. There was no shame in being an immigrant. Why had Sam and his family taken such elaborate measures to conceal from their neighbors and even their own descendants the truth of their origins? He had sworn falsely under oath, violated federal laws, fabricated documents, and lied to his own children and grandchildren about his origin and their heritage. I needed to understand why. I suspected that in finding an answer I would also understand far better what it was that motivated him to take on the guise of B. Virdot.

But first, there was a more immediate mystery: how and when the rest of Sam's family came to America. These too I eventually found in the passenger lists. Sam's mother and four other siblings followed a year after Sam aboard the SS *Ivernia*. They sailed from Liverpool, England, and arrived in Boston in September 1903. Listed in steerage was Hinde Finkelstein, forty; an eleven-year-old daughter, Gusta (later known as Gussie); another daughter, Tina (later known as Esther), nine; a son David, four; and a son Isadore (later known as Al), nine. On the list, Hinde Finkelstein declared that she and the children were bound for Pittsburgh to join her husband, Jacob, and a brother-in-law, Hersh Eger, a dry-goods peddler already living in the Jewish ghetto of Pittsburgh's Hill District.

On May 11, 1954, fifty-two years after boarding the *La Champagne* in Le Havre, France, for a crossing in steerage, Sam Stone returned to that port—this time with his wife, Minna, aboard the luxury liner *Isle de France*. But in all the intervening years, he did not speak to anyone of what it was that had driven his family from Romania or why it was he was so intent upon keeping it a secret.

. . .

IN YIDDISH, THE word for troubles is *tsuris*—the cumulative measure of a soul's burdens; not the routine setbacks life deals out to one and all, but the true body blows to heart and will. Sam Stone knew the word though he would never say it. Yiddish was his native tongue, but it was a language he refused to speak almost from the moment he stepped off the gangplank in 1902.

On the passenger manifest Sam's father, Jacob, and mother, Hinde, had both listed their home as Dorohoi. With some effort, I found it on a map. In my grandfather's day, as today, it was a shtetl in northeast Romania that sat along the Jijia River. In 1899, some sixty-eight hundred Jews made their home there, a little more than half the town. Jews had lived there for centuries and in relative peace. By 1895, it had its own secular Jewish school.

All that changed during Sam Finkelstein's boyhood. Increasingly Jews were singled out and marked by law as "foreigners" and "aliens," targeted by the state, and ostracized by the community. Sam was born in 1888 in a country that year by year tightened an economic noose around its Jews. Laws barred them from working as peddlers or shop owners and made it illegal for them to sell sugar, flour, or other staples. In 1898, when Sam was eleven, new laws imposed a quota on the number of "aliens"—Jews—allowed to attend schools. (That word, *alien,* would haunt Sam throughout his life.)

Jews could neither vote nor obtain licenses. Crop failures and economic reversals turned their Gentile neighbors against them. They became targets for popular discontent and scapegoats of the state. In 1900, a new set of decrees was passed designed to starve the Jews or drive them into exile. They were forbidden from owning land or cultivating it, barred from living in rural areas, and even working as laborers, subject to a quota that required that two Romanians be hired for every "unprotected alien," a thinly veiled reference to Jews. They faced homelessness, hunger, and depression. An influx of Jewish refugees from neighboring Russia and Galicia, nearly all of them destitute, triggered further repressive measures. The Romanian government declared the Jews "a nation apart," separated by culture, faith, and dietary restrictions. As such, they were entitled to none of the civil rights accorded to those considered true Romanians.

Reading the grim history of Dorohoi, I caught my first glimpse of Sam's early years and adolescence. The physical hardships that he and his family—and all of his faith—endured in those years could be read in the decrees of the state. But the psychological and emotional toll of such oppression on a childhood like Sam's was only beginning to dawn on me. The notion that one's homeland could turn on him, treat him and his family as trespassers, the subject of constant public suspicion, hostility, and harassment, made me see what Sam had been so eager to escape, why he had never spoken of it, and even why he had gone to such lengths to bury that past in the fabrication of a less nightmarish childhood.

As a child, he was pushed to the margins of his own society. The insecurities of a more ordinary adolescence pale beside what he faced. The tensions with which he grew up—the constant threat of violence and pogroms, the shame and degradation—were the defining features of his childhood, and they go a long way in explaining the man he was to become. The bleakness of Canton during the Great Depression, the specter of so many unable to scratch out a living, the sight of immigrant families pushed to the edge with no one to come to their rescue—all this must surely have triggered in Sam Stone recollections of his own bitter youth. The letters to B. Virdot from children and teenagers must have brought back to him memories of his own escape, the crossing, and the turbulent arrival. Turning his back on them, knowing what he had endured, would have been all but impossible. I do not have the benefit of Sam's own story, but the historical record of what befell the Romanian Jews of his time fills much of the gap and explains why he was loath to speak of it.

For the Finkelstein family, remaining in Dorohoi was not an option. They faced what many Romanian Jews faced—extinction. U.S. Secretary of State John Hay described the plight of these Jews this way: "by the cumulative effect of successive restrictions, the Jews of Romania have become reduced to a state of wretched misery. Shut out from nearly every avenue of self-support which is open to the poor of other lands, and ground down by poverty as the natural result of their discriminatory treatment, they are rendered incapable of lifting themselves from the enforced degradation they endure."

Those Romanian Jews who fled the country became known as the Fusgeyers, or "foot-walkers." It was a mass exodus. By the thousands they walked across Europe, only to be rejected by one country after another. One account of the conditions they endured appears in the *Jewish Criterion* of Pittsburgh, published on August 30, 1900:

The Rumanian Jews possess, for the greater part, nothing but the few rags upon their bodies. The poorest among them do not travel in wagons or in ships, but drag themselves upon their wounded feet from one frontier to another. At home they leave nothing but the bones of their fathers in their graves, constituted the only ownership in the soil of their native land. They had to carry with them nothing else but the wanderer's staff and the unendurable burden of their memories and their fears. . . .

The Rumanian Jews have no goals, they wander planless about like a horde of Northern water-rats endeavoring to elude the grasp of the birds of prey, and who, as they pass, pounce upon and devour their victim. No one desires them, everybody sends them farther on from their own district, and when they ask in despair, "Where are we to go, what is to become of us?" the only reply they receive is a shrug of the shoulder and a turn of the hand, mercilessly pointing to the distance further on into the unknown, unto the blue away, far away.

The suffering of Romania's 400,000 Jews caught America's attention. On September 17, 1902—nine days before Sam Finkelstein boarded the SS *La Champagne*—Secretary of State Hay protested Romania's inhumane treatment of the Jews and pressured Romania to relent.

Nineteen years earlier, the poet Emma Lazarus had penned her poem "The New Colossus," but it was not until 1903, the year Sam's mother and four younger siblings arrived in America, that the now famous lines were added to the pedestal of the Statue of Liberty:

Give me your tired, your poor,
Your huddled masses yearning to breathe free,
The wretched refuse of your teeming shore.
Send these, the homeless, tempest-tost to me,
I lift my lamp beside the golden door!

In America, Sam Finkelstein and his family hoped to melt into the mass of ten million foreign-born in a country of seventy-six million. But thousands of Romanian Jews had preceded the Finkelsteins and found their welcome tentative at best. Americans made no secret of their displeasure at being a dumping ground for Romanian Jews. Secretary of State Hay said as much in his appeal to European heads of state. The *New York Times* article about his appeal was headlined, ASKS THAT ROUMANIA STOP OPPRESSING JEWS, and the subhead under it read, "Says Present Harsh Treatment Breeds Men Who Are Not Desirable Immigrants to This Country."

His language reflected a deep antagonism toward these refugees. "The pauper, the criminal, the contagiously or incurably diseased are excluded from the benefits of immigration only when they are likely to become a source of danger or a burden upon the community," declared Hay.

Immigrants like my grandfather and his family were seen as defective and future wards of the state. "Removal under such conditions," warned Secretary Hay, "is not and cannot be the healthy intelligent emigration of a free and self-reliant being. It must be, in most cases, the mere transplantation of an artificially produced diseased growth to a new place."

"Diseased growth" was a far cry from the "golden door" Emma Lazarus had envisioned. Even many American Jews looked down upon the Romanians. In the pecking order of new immigrants, they were considered, especially by some of German descent, an embarrassment, impoverished, uncultured, and barely literate. Fifteen-year-old Sam and his family were used to no better.

Though he carried almost nothing when he stepped off the *La Champagne*, Sam was determined to rid himself of all baggage and begin anew. Reviled in the Old World, a pariah in the New, he wasted no time reinventing himself. But escaping the past, its sorrows and shame, would prove more difficult than he imagined. He could leave his Yiddish on the boat and master English; he could cast off the Orthodox Jewish rituals and embrace a secular America; he could erase his childhood and fabricate an American birth. But whether he uttered the word or not, the tsuris would remain a part of him. And it was that which helped give birth to Mr. B. Virdot.

The Canton to which Sam Stone eventually found his way was a city of well-established pioneer stock that faced a swelling population of foreigners, each of whom, like Sam, wanted nothing more than to blend in and become whatever it meant to be an American. Germans, Greeks, Hungarians, Slavs, Spaniards, Italians, Syrians, Croats, Danes, and Jews had all found their way to this midwestern town, drawn by the promise of work and the vision of a life free of the Old World's political and religious persecution, the endless wars, the decaying monarchies, and the grinding poverty. In those early years it made for an uneasy and watchful peace. The *New York Times* in July 1926 wrote: "Half of Canton's population are either foreign born or negro. The other half accuses this foreign and negro group of being the source of all their troubles; but, when pressed, admit that most of the foreigners and negroes are honest and decent."

Like Sam, many among this wave of newcomers to Canton had endured their own exoduses. And like him, they yearned for nothing more than the chance to fit in. That was all Sam really wanted— to be accepted, to find a home, to feel that he belonged. For Sam, and for many who reached out to B. Virdot, Canton was such a place, even in the most dire of times.

SO COMPLETE WAS Sam's break from his youth in Dorohoi that it seemed no link remained. He virtually erased all traces of his first fifteen years, concealed the circumstances of his escape and arrival—perhaps the defining experience of his life—and then filled the void with a new story, supported by bogus documents, dates, signatures, and elliptical references to his childhood in Pittsburgh. He simply inserted himself into a seamless narrative of his own design, drawing together real people and places to lend credence to his fiction.

Having interviewed hundreds of former covert officers of the Central Intelligence Agency for my first book, I knew how exhausting it must have been for him to maintain that cover story for an entire lifetime. Like a spy, he could never risk letting his guard down or letting slip a word or reference that might betray him. Family, friends, and community had all come to know him by the fictitious life story he had woven. The threat of exposure and the temptation to come clean were all around him. In 1933, a neighbor who lived two doors away was a Romanian immigrant, and yet, it appears he never reached out to him as a fellow countryman. How many times, I wondered, did he yearn to confide in someone, to open up and reveal himself? And was he still emotionally attached to the land of his birth? Again and again, I sorted through his stories, the papers in the suitcase, and the meager possessions he left to us, hoping to stumble upon a clue some twenty-five years after his death.

Among the objects of my renewed attention was

the bronze sculpture *The Jumper*, which had followed him from home to home. I examined it in greater detail and for the first time noticed the name of the sculptor inscribed on the base: "D. H. Chiparus." The full name was "Demetre Haralamb Chiparus." He was one of the foremost Art Deco sculptors. His studio was in Paris and his work is highly prized today. A sculpture expert at Sotheby's auction house found the exact piece listed among the sculptor's works. Some of Chiparus's pieces, especially those of dancers with ivory inlays, fetch hundreds of thousands of dollars at auction. Sam's piece was an original. In all likelihood, he was the first and only owner, dating back to the 1920s. Perhaps he bought it in Paris during one of his trips abroad. But why had this piece meant so much to him?

Something about Sam's attachment to the sculpture drew me to it. I began to research the sculptor. I discovered that, like Sam, Chiparus was Romanian by birth. Indeed, he and Chiparus were both born in the same tiny town of Dorohoi— Chiparus in 1886, Sam in 1888. It was entirely possible that the two boys might have known each other, even been childhood friends. At the very least, my grandfather felt an obvious kinship to him, one that he secretly could take pleasure in without compromising the American identity he had so carefully forged. Here, at last, I'd found a link to his past, perhaps the only one with which he had felt safe. How and when he acquired it I will likely never know, but why he so treasured it was no longer such a mystery.

IN DECEMBER 1933, less than two weeks after Sam Stone made his offer as B. Virdot, Ion Duca, the newly appointed prime minister of Romania and a liberal who opposed fascism and that country's virulently anti-Semitic Iron Guard movement, was assassinated. For the Jews of Dorohoi and Romania at large it was but one more sign of trouble to come. Today Dorohoi no longer has a single functioning temple. The last Jews left a decade ago. Anti-Semitism, Nazism, communism, relentless poverty, and the allure of Israel all fed the Diaspora. Over the years, Sam Stone returned to Romania several times, always alone. On one such trip he took pictures. Communist dictator Nicolae Ceausescu was still in power. When Sam returned to the United States he discovered that the film had been removed from his camera. He had nothing to document his visit—which, in its way, mirrored how he had lived.

For Sam, the escape from Dorohoi was never complete. The town would remain a part of him. It was that way too with those who endured the depths of the Depression, defining their needs and aspirations, even giving rise to its own brand of dark humor, as trauma often does. One of Sam's favorite jokes was about two men traveling on a train across Europe. One was Russian, the other Jewish.

"We have no Jews in our village," boasted the Russian.

"That's why it's just a village," responded the Jew.

In the edgy way Sam said it, it was less a joke than a verdict of history. More than a century ago the Jews of Dorohoi shared with the other citizens of Dorohoi a modest but decent standard of living. Today the town of forty thousand—half the size of Canton—is one of the poorest in one of Europe's poorest countries. Several charities that provide relief to Dorohoi report an unemployment rate in excess of 50 percent. It is a town in the depths of its own relentless Hard Times.

IV.
If I Would Accept Charity

Oppression

Even before the Finkelstein family boarded the ship to America, they knew their new home would be Pittsburgh. There, Jacob Finkelstein had a brother-in-law. The family also knew Samuel Sheffler, the most prominent of Pittsburgh's Romanian Jews. Sheffler was head of a cigar factory and active in relief organizations that helped bring Romanian Jews to the city and watched over them once they arrived. By 1902, thanks to Sheffler and others like him, Pittsburgh had become a haven for thousands of Romanian Jews. Already the city boasted two Romanian synagogues and a thriving Jewish life in what was known as the Hill District, where Jews from across Europe had settled. In 1905 there were fifteen thousand Jews in Pittsburgh. Seven years later the number was thirty-five thousand.

It was much the same in Canton, where early immigrants paved the way for their countrymen and extended families to follow, and assisted them with housing and jobs. Others, like John Jacob, whose family would later purchase Bender's tavern, set up a profitable travel business arranging for the passage of immigrants—Germans, Italians, and Hungarians among them—chartering railroad cars that brought them from Ellis Island directly to Canton, their tickets prepaid by relatives. Many, if not most, were illiterate. By 1890, Canton's illiteracy rate ranked fourth from the bottom among cities of twenty-five thousand or more. Several of the city's wards were enclaves of the Old World—the Germans concentrated in the second and the fifth, the Greeks and Italians in the fourth.

All of them were drawn by the promise of America. But if fifteen-year-old Sam Finkelstein imagined after arriving in Pittsburgh that he too was now free to participate in that new life, he was mistaken. He had traded a shtetl for a ghetto. Sam spoke no English, and the prospect of going to school, first denied him by the laws of Romania, was now denied him by his own father, who hid his shoes so that he could not attend. Instead he was forced to spend his days rolling cigars along with his brothers and sisters. (Even so, there were days when Sam Stone went to school barefoot—even in the snow—he later told his niece Shirley.) Their cramped white frame house at 51 Rowley Street became as much a sweatshop as a home. Cut off by language, physically isolated by the ghetto, and marooned in his own home, Sam's first taste of America was anything but liberating. What he saw of America in 1902 as a fifteen-year-old boy stayed with him. And when, years later, in the depths of the Depression, he became B. Virdot to many, he could not help but remember what it was like growing up in such circumstances.

So often the parents put B. Virdot's gift toward buying shoes for their children so they could go to school. How close to home, literally, that must have struck my grandfather, who, more than anything else, wanted to go to school in this new land but could not because his shoes were denied him. And for many of those who wrote to B. Virdot, more than a lack of shoes stood in the way of going to school. Lottie Allen wrote on behalf of her daughters, Louise and Isabel: "They do not ask for anything but clothes, so that they can go to school." Three years earlier her husband, James, an Irish immigrant and out-of-work stonecutter, had died after a long illness. His last vision of America, so stark and impoverished, was not the one that had drawn him to this new land, any more than that which greeted Sam Stone upon his arrival in Pittsburgh.

Up and down Pittsburgh's Hill District were home-based cigar "factories," mostly mothers and fathers and children in attics working over benches and rolling tables, with poor ventilation, terrible hours, and a dulling tedium that in some smothered ambition and in others kindled it. The air was thick with tobacco, and young backs, stooped for hours over benches, ached like those of old men. Pittsburgh had a hundred such cigar factories. It became the nation's leading maker of stogies, or "tobies," as they were called. They were the cheaper, smaller version of the cigar. Such readily available work was a way to survive, but also an economic trap that held many in its grip for a lifetime.

For some few, it was a ticket to wealth. William Marsh became the millionaire "Stogie King." Before Oscar Hammerstein—grandfather of the famed lyricist Oscar Hammerstein II—was a theatrical producer, he was a cigar maker whose invention of a device on which cigar wrappers were cut helped make Pittsburgh's Standard Cigar Factory the largest stogie maker in the world. (In reaction to abuses, the labor movement found fertile ground in the industry. Samuel Gompers, a Jewish immigrant and cigar maker, would become a dominant figure in the upstart labor movement.)

In 1913, cigar workers went on strike against the larger manufacturers. One of the Pittsburgh brands struck was Dry Slitz, in whose factories child workers were forbidden from speaking. The union slogan was "You smoke the blood of children if you smoke Dry Slitz."

Sam and his siblings hated the work, Sam enough to declare himself a socialist, a stand he repudiated years later. One of Sam's brothers, Al, would recall feeling so confined by the routine of rolling cigars that he could not even stretch his legs. He would nervously rub the ball of one shoe against the other until he had worn clean through the leather. But the cigar business provided one advantage to the Finkelsteins and other Jews: it allowed them to set their own hours of work, enabling them to honor the Sabbath.

There was little laughter in the Finkelstein home, and fewer expressions of affection. In her Jewish faith and keeping kosher, Sam's mother, Hinde (she later went by the name "Hilda"), was more than strict. She was fanatical. She was also the consummate nag. But with age, she apparently mellowed. My mother only remembers sitting on her lap while she sang the 1907 song "School Days." My aunt Dorothy recalls passing her room and being frightened at the sight of her swaying and mumbling as she davened (the Yiddish word for praying while rocking slowly forward and back).

Sam's father, Jacob, was distant and demanding, steeped in faith and the exigencies of feeding his family. A tyrannical figure, he was obeyed but not loved. The hardships of Romania, the trek across Europe, the inescapable sweatshop in their home, all made his father's emotional distance that much harder to bear. Only Sam, the oldest son, had the courage to stand up to him. There is a story passed down that when Sam was a young boy he was sent to pick cherries, and he fell from a tree, broke his leg, and limped home. There he received neither sympathy nor help. The hardness to which Sam was exposed in his youth made him appreciate compassion all the more. He saw what his father was. He saw emotional wreckage all around him and he wanted no part of it. He had escaped the cruelty of the state, and was no less determined to put the callousness of his home life behind him.

Sam was unwilling to fritter away his days in an attic rolling tobacco leaves. He began to eye the door and plot his getaway. In Pittsburgh, he found work as a peddler, then a salesman, and finally a window dresser in a millinery shop. Along the way he taught himself English, suppressed his accent, and learned to dress in the fashion of the day and carry himself with pride. He became a student of advertising, merchandising, and window dressing. He implicitly understood how dependent the world's judgment was upon the visual. His new life could be affected as simply as a costume change. Like so many immigrants, he had something to prove—to the world, but also to himself. The limits and doubts and foreshortened horizons with which he had grown up were still there to be tested. His was an ambition fueled less by what he longed to acquire than by what he hoped to shed.

In 1920, nearly two decades after arriving in America, his father, fifty-eight-year-old Jacob, and his sons David, Isador, and Moses were all still living at 51 Rowley Street, still answering to the name Finkelstein, and still rolling stogies. And there the sons might well have spent their entire lives if Sam hadn't rescued them with the promise of a new job, a new name, and a new life in

Canton, Ohio. It was a kind of Pittsburgh in miniature, a gritty midwestern steel town of diverse immigrants and ample opportunity for the willing.

Rarely did Sam speak of his years in Pittsburgh. There are no pictures of him from that period, and none of his father. "Sam Finkelstein" virtually vanished in 1918, when he first arrived in Canton. In his place was Sam Stone—eager, tireless, and, by his own account, native-born. To thoroughly reinvent himself he had to leave Pittsburgh and find a place where no one knew him or his family. He had traveled thousands of miles from Romania to Pittsburgh, and yet much of the grimness of his life had followed him every step of the way. In Canton he could truly begin again.

But the earlier years, the years of rolling cigars, had left their mark. A whiff of tobacco sickened him. Long before it was fashionable, he supported antismoking campaigns, and there was nothing he reviled more than a cigar. (That his future father-in-law would be a cigar salesman did not endear him to Sam.)

The education that was denied him also left its mark. He never learned to write in cursive. His siblings too suffered from a lack of schooling. As a young woman, his sister Gussie could neither read nor write. In later years, her daughter, Shirley, then six or seven, would return from school and teach her the alphabet and how to read. One of

Gussie's proudest moments was being able to sign her own name as she opened up a meager bank account. On Saturdays—Shabbat, the seventh day of the Jewish week and the day of rest—Gussie would take her daughter to the homes of Jewish immigrants newly arrived in Pittsburgh and have her teach them as well. Often they would offer little Shirley food as payment, but she had been instructed in advance to decline, saying she was not hungry even if she was. If she forgot, her mother would remind her with a pinch. She knew to politely decline even an offer of a few pennies.

It was a way for a proud mother to show off her daughter, the American. But it was also a mitzvah, a Hebrew word meaning "commandment," but one that has come to mean an act of human kindness—not something to be tainted by money. The truest and highest form of giving is that in which the giver expected and got nothing in return. It was a commandment that was ingrained in each of the children and consummated in Sam's reaching out to those in need that Christmas of 1933.

Sooner Starve

Sam and many of his generation entered the Depression clinging to a stubborn individualism that bordered on social Darwinism. They had made it, so others could too. Those who did not share their good fortune had their own network to fall back on. It was called family, the church, or, at its most extended reach, the community. But one in distress did not generally look to government. In 1933, government was still seen as distant and removed, and, given the experience of many immigrants in the Old World, so much the better.

In 1933, the notion of individual responsibility and the role of the state were both being sorely tested. Across the sea, the Soviet Union was creating a society that, as hard as times were here, was seen by many as toxic to individualism. That nation was mired in its own Hard Times, one that made America's pale by comparison. By some estimates, more than seven million people starved to death there between 1932 and 1933.

Still, American confidence had been shaken, and its revulsion to Marxism was not universal. Had the New Deal not struck some middle ground between laissez-faire capitalism and unfettered socialism, had it not moved to resuscitate the nation, the outcome might have been different. There reached a point here where misery was so widespread and opportunities so few that many came to believe individual action alone could not address the catastrophe they faced. Resistance to government aid would soften, and expectations of the role it should play underwent profound change, for better or worse. (That debate continues.)

It is difficult for Americans today to grasp the stigma that attached to government "handouts" in 1933. By February 2010, thirty-eight million Americans—one in eight—were on food stamps. But in those early years of the Depression, the people of Canton, and those of the nation, would have recoiled at the idea of such a program. The seismic shift in public attitudes toward welfare and public relief programs, indeed toward government as a whole, that followed the Hard Times was as fundamental and far-reaching as any in our history. But in 1933, antagonism to public aid was still deeply ingrained. That fierce individualism can be heard in many of the letters to B. Virdot. Among these was the one written by Joseph P. Rogers, a once successful insurance agent who for six months of the previous year could not say whether he would be able to feed himself, his wife, and his daughters, Carolyn and Eleanor. "I cannot go to the Welfare for help," he wrote. "I can't even express myself in writing this letter. It hurts. Something within me rebels."

Merely being identified as one in want was more than many could bear. In one case in particular, the writer's anguish in reaching out to B. Virdot was so intense and her fear of being identified so deep that even three-quarters of a century later I cannot bring myself to identify her by anything more than her first name—Mrs. Bessie A. She wrote:

> I am a poor woman with a sick girl trying to work and help keep home for a crippled sister and myself. We are one of the thousands of unfortunate familys who had seen better days, now to Proud to ask charity . . . This is one of the poorest xmases I ever had. If I thought this would be printed in the papers I would rather die of hunger first as I haven't been a begger all ways. Hope for better days for my family and the others like us. . . .

The woman who wrote those words was a fifty-five-year-old mother and former phone operator for Western Union. She had emigrated from Ireland in 1880 hoping for "better days," words that surely would have resonated with the immigrant in Sam Stone. But instead, she found only more of the same. Bessie A.'s words to B. Virdot, particularly her revulsion to accepting charity, are repeated almost verbatim in other letters. Both those born into poverty and those born into privilege viewed the dole with equal distaste. "I believe Mr. Zerby would starve before he would ask for help," wrote Catherine Zerby of her husband, George. The daughter of esteemed photographer Jacob S. Wissler, she was not accustomed to such hardship. "We cannot afford the newspaper," her letter began, written on personal stationery with a gold embossed letter Z.

For many today it is difficult to understand the stigma attached to going on the dole or accepting charity. For men like my grandfather, who took such pride in escaping poverty and in providing for himself and his family, charity represented the final act of capitulation. It was not seen as a stop-gap measure to tide one over, but the repudiation of a lifetime rooted in self-reliance. The shame of poverty was tolerable—so many were in distress that Christmas of 1933—but the loss of face that came of publicly applying for relief, of claiming that one's needs were equal to or superior to another's, of enduring the gauntlet of probing questions, of surrendering one's dignity and privacy, for many was too much to ask. They had already been stripped of so much. Self-respect was all they had left.

In her letter to Mr. B. Virdot, Stella Waidman wrote that her husband, Albert, an out-of-work toolmaker, had had surgery and that to pay for the doctors, nurses, and hospital bills, they had sold their home, which was almost paid for. "We could have kept that home if we would have accepted charity," she wrote, "but we thought it best for Mr.

Waidman's name and for the childrens sake to pay off our bills and sacrifice our home, and build up again." Her aversion to charity surfaced again near the end of her letter when she wrote, "Please do not send us anything out of pity . . ." The B. Virdot check arrived days later.

American notions of accepting charity were riddled with contradictions. Giving was the Christian thing to do, contributing alms in church and recognizing that we are our brother's keeper. To give to charity was ennobling, but to accept it was degrading. That was, at least in part, why Sam Stone insisted on his own anonymity and pledged confidentiality to those who wrote to him. They were the only terms under which people, as proud as they were destitute, would come forward. They were the only terms under which Sam himself might have reached out to others.

Many resisted the dole with a mix of defiance and faith. Among those who wrote to Mr. B. Virdot was Roy Rhoads. His December 18, 1933, letter begins:

> I saw your kind letter and offer to help the unfortunate to at least one day of happiness. I am like many others. You will not find my name on the Family Services I have been fighting it out and trusting in the Lord and believe me Brother he helps. My name is Roy

Rhoads—1124 Clev. Ave. N.W. am 58 years old, wife and our Boy. He has been out of work over 2 years and I worked at Hoover Co. 11 years was laid off 3 years ago and have Battled ever since. I get out and sell razor blades and my wife cares for tourists and people looking for a room and does washing for others. We are back with our rent 4 or 5 months. I hate to admit all this as I worked all my life and would work at any honest work if I could get it. I worked a few days for the city and cleaned snow from people's sidewalks. That is all the work I have found. I signed up at Y.M.C.A. last Aug. but have never been called. Not for my sake but for the wife and brighten one home, if you could help it would be appreciated.

> YOURS RES.
> ROY RHOADS
> 1124 CLEV. AVE. N.W.
> CANTON, OHIO

Roy Rhoads and his wife, Margaret, did indeed survive the Depression. In the years after, as the economy improved, Rhoads found work at the Hoover Company and later Timken Roller Bearing. The years of trauma and desperation behind him, he again learned to enjoy life and gained a reputation as a master of the French horn, an instrument he played in several area groups, including the 135th Field Artillery Band. Hard work and frugality eventually allowed him to retire. His granddaughter Kathleen remembers him as a quiet man with wire-rimmed glasses, sitting in a rocking chair, smoking his pipe. He died in 1950 at age seventy-three.

Dandelions and Pencils

What Roy Rhoads and so many others faced in the depths of the Depression was an utter absence of jobs. No matter how willing one was to work, no matter how humble the wages one would accept, there was still often no work to be found. The Depression pitted one unthinkable against another—the stigma of the handout against the sight of one's loved ones going to bed hungry and cold. It forced many to the edge between personal honor and false pride. Howard Sommers's letter to B. Virdot described the desperate straits that many faced but also the determination not to seek charity. On December 18, 1933, he wrote:

Dear Friend, B. Virdot

As I picked up the evening paper I saw your most generous offer to worthy people. I count myself & my wife most worthy as for the last four years I have only had a few days work here and there. But I will go ahead and state the jobs my wife & I have had to do before we would ask for Charity. Picking berries in season and selling them as late as 12 oclock at night, picking cherries on the share and selling our share, My wife had to climb to the tops of the highest trees as I am lame and cannot climb. We have started as early as February to gather dandelions to sell and sold them till May or till people would not buy them any longer as they to tough to eat. Our winter time job is gathering Sassafras which is a lot of hard work and not much money in it. The last 6 or 8 months I have been selling Liquid Solder, Pills & Styrtie pencils in and about Canton for about 10 miles around at nearby towns but I found that selling house to house is a hard job as scarce as money was. As far as clothes is concerned I have had to buy a few things for myself as I had to meet the public, but my wife has not had a coat in 7 yrs. and her last pair of shoes were bought in 1929. The coat is not fit to wear. We have always kept an old car which was the only way we had to get our wood & coal and take us to country to pick our berries & etc.

Well I think this is enough said, but I could sit here and write for hours, but 3 pages is enough.

After you have read it over and you are the gudge and you don't feel that we are worthy of your donation, secretly as you promised then, please destroy this letter so no one will know but you & I.

So Good-bye & Good Luck, and we are living in hopes that good luck comes our way.

FROM MR. & MRS. HOWARD
SOMMERS.

Sommers's reference to gathering cherries and being lame would likely have triggered Sam's own childhood memory of being sent to pick cherries and breaking his leg. Howard E. Sommers was the son of Franklin and Phebe Sommers, farmers who worked the land outside Canton in Jackson Township. Despite the weary tone of the letter, Howard Sommers was only twenty-eight when he wrote it. Almost nothing is known of the turns the Sommerses' lives took after writing to Mr. B. Virdot. Howard Sommers died at fifty-seven; his wife, Mary, died before him. His July 9, 1962, obituary in the *Canton Repository* notes only that he worked as a handyman, that he had been under a doctor's care for a heart condition, and that neighbors who had not seen him for days discovered his body in his home. No survivors were listed. It would appear that his letter to B. Virdot is all that survived him.

Shame

Over time, the Depression had a slow, grinding effect on the spirit. On one level, some of those who wrote to Mr. B. Virdot knew not to take their hardships personally, that so many around them were enduring much the same, but the universality of their suffering did not keep their babies warm, pay for medicine, or save them from eviction. Husbands often took to the road in search of jobs and did not return for months or even years. Before the Depression, John Boyer had had his own service station, and he, his wife, Margaret, and five children lived in a home that he owned. The Depression undid all that. When Margaret wrote to B. Virdot in 1933, John Boyer was in Florida looking for work. The family was left behind, having been forced to give up their home. Circumstances were bleak. "The conditions under which my children are now living," she wrote, "would seem unbearable."

Four years into the Depression, the sense of personal failure stole into their lives. Shame and self-reproach took many forms—alcoholism, spousal abuse, depression. The children of Roy Teis remembered their father walking in back alleys and going blocks out of his way to reach their home, all in an effort to avoid a neighbor's glance or questions. His wife called it his "shame-face." But it was being at home, seeing the suffering of little ones, that was often the hardest part. The letters to B. Virdot are filled with such anguish.

One of those to write B. Virdot was thirty-three-year-old Hilda Criswell, a mother of four and wife of Reuben Criswell, an out-of-work painter. The daughter of Danish immigrants, she had married at sixteen. She knew how to make do on little, but her resourcefulness had its limits. She had always made her children's clothes, but now there was no more material. Her twin ten-year-old daughters, Virginia and Vivian, had worn clear through their shoes. "I am ashamed to face my children anymore," she wrote. Sam would have had a soft spot for her. She shared his mother's name, Hilda, and one of her daughters shared his firstborn daughter's, Virginia. And any letter that spoke of the need for shoes—and there were many—would have rekindled personal memories.

Until then, it seemed to some that poverty afflicted only a particular class—those born into hardship . . . It was a kind of negative inheritance, not something that randomly befell the frugal and hardworking. But Mrs. Bessie King, a forty-three-year-old widow and mother of a ten-year-old boy, was caught in the same vortex of poverty that held those she had always viewed as apart from if not below her. Suddenly she found herself applying for assistance. "Oh how it goes against the grain," she wrote, "to have to go up and sit among the foreign element, and Negroes from 1 to 2 hours, sit there and wait for your turn just like a barber shop . . ."

There was still among some a lingering illusion that poverty was associated with a lack of character or sloth. Mrs. Edna Schaub, hoping to put B. Virdot's check toward an overcoat for her husband, felt compelled to explain that her thirty-three-year-old husband—out of a job for four years but once an employee in one of Canton's steel mills—"has always been a good worker and provides, but when there is no work to be had he can't work. Now we are not the kind of people who are shiftless poor." Schaub's letter reflects a pre-Depression prejudice that was sorely tested in those years. Before the Depression, there was less sympathy for the chronically out of work. The employed were sometimes hasty to dismiss them as "shiftless," suggesting they had brought their circumstances upon themselves. The Hard Times forced people to take a second look, to not be so cavalier in their dismissal of "the kind of people" that were out of work. It ushered in a sea change in societal attitudes toward the needy, lifting some of the blame from the victims and directing some of the remedial responsibility to government and society at large.

Many of the letters were written without the knowledge of other members of the family. Often it was the wife who wrote the letter, not wanting to run afoul of the husband's pride. George Saal had been one of the leading salesmen in the local office of the Metropolitan Insurance Company, then lost everything during the Depression. He did not object to his wife, Fern, writing to B. Virdot, but he was not privy to the note on the back of her letter: "Mr. Saal read this," she wrote, "but what he doesn't know is that today I went to D. Grigsby to get $5.00 on my engagement ring." David Grigsby was a pawnbroker. It appears that Fern Saal used the B. Virdot money to purchase bread or, more likely, to pay off a debt for such past purchases. The check is endorsed to Nickles Bakery.

The Seeds of Resentment

In some cases it was a wife writing without the knowledge of her husband, who was unwilling to admit his inability to provide for the family. Myrna Jury, wife of Donald Jury, was such a case:

B. VIRDOT
CANTON, OHIO
GENERAL DELIVERY
CANTON, OHIO

Dear Sir

I read your add in todays paper and I talked it over with my husband and he decided that we would not write and therefore some other family would get help. But I feel we need a few things.

My husband was out of work almost three years (prior to July 11,1933.) Since then he had been employed at Timken Roller Bearing Co. At present he is making 40 cents and we're in debt and are trying hard to get out. Our money doesn't reach from one pay to the other. Of course if we could let our bills go for a while we could get along fairly well. The only reason I am writing this is to get warm clothes for the children for this winter. We have the following children, Virginia aged 9 Charles 7 Alvin 3, Helen 1. They all need shoes and clothes and Charles needs an overcoat. My husband will not let me go to see the Family Service bout clothes. We were on the Family Service list 17 months and he was so glad to get away from there that he doesn't want to go back. He said that "we will get along somehow" — But it is awful hard sometimes. My husband lived in Canton since 1915. We have been married almost 11 years. I would and I know my husband would be very glad for anything you could do for us. Whether you help us or not I think you are doing a wonderful and noble deed. Wishing you a Merry Xmas and a happy New Year.

I remain Yours Truly, Mrs. Donald R. Jury P.S. I decided to write without telling my husband. I tried to write our circumstances hoping that you will see fit to help us- Mrs. Jury

MRS. DONALD R. JURY
1326 44TH ST N.E.
CANTON. OHIO

IT IS CHRISTMAS Eve, 2008—nearly seventy-five years to the day that Mrs. Jury wrote that letter—

when I finally track down one of her descendants. I read her the letter. In Jury's letter, Charles's mother had said he was in need of an overcoat. But there was more to the story than that. Though Charles was only seven at the time, as the eldest son it often fell to him to contribute food for the family. His father, Donald, refused all outside help. So, Charles was dispatched to find food for the table. With each passing month, as circumstances grew more desperate, his responsibilities increased.

He routinely brought with him a 16-gauge shotgun and a .22-caliber pistol, boarded a city bus, paid the five cents (except when the driver took pity and let him ride for free), and rode the bus to the end of the line and out into the countryside. There he scoured the fields and woods for rabbits and pheasants. But the cost of the shells and bullets was so dear that he dared not miss. Every shot had to produce a kill. Whatever he brought down became the meal that day. And the overcoat? It was to keep him warm so that he might stay out longer and kill more game—a success upon which the lives of others might depend.

When the state offered the Jury family a packet of seeds for their vegetable garden, Donald refused to accept, even though son Charles pleaded with him to do so. But Charles found other ways to keep the family fed. He was not above stealing vegetables from neighbors' gardens, and each time he did, his father scolded him. Over time, Charles came to bear a deep and abiding resentment toward his father, and to loathe his pride—obstinacy, it seemed to him—and his refusals to reach out for help. That pride, he felt, added to the family's misery and created a chasm between father and son that would linger throughout their lives. We know this today because Charles's son, Charles Jr., and his sister, Elizabeth, recall their father telling them of the constant conflict between Donald and Charles over whether to accept outside help.

The scarcity of meat in the Jury household and the memories of hunger left their mark on Charles. As an adult he insisted on having a table full of food at every meal and he often would have steak two and even three nights in a row, perhaps to remind himself that he was now a safe distance from the past. He often talked about the Depression as if it were a parable with a lesson. He told and retold the story of his mother making a birthday cake and the two precious eggs rolling onto the floor and breaking. His mother knelt and wept at the sight.

The legacy of the Great Depression and what the Jury family endured continues to play out. "Even third generation, it's funny how things follow you," says Donald Jury's granddaughter, Elizabeth, now fifty-eight and a systems analyst in Illinois. "Though I do shop, sometimes I feel so wasteful, that we indulge ourselves a lot. You don't really need it. I have this guilt feeling about Christmas."

After the Depression, Donald Jury found work as a cabinetmaker at the Walker Lumber Company in Canton. One of the lessons he learned from the Depression was the need for labor to organize. He became president of the Carpenter's Local 2092 and did not retire until 1968. He died two years later, at seventy. Donald Jury's son Charles—the boy who hunted—left Canton at nineteen and headed for Florida, where he dived for seashells (another kind of hunting) in the Keys off Seven Mile Bridge and created one of the largest seashell businesses in Florida. Later, he made and lost a small fortune in the roofing business during Florida's midfifties housing boom. Charles is buried in the Dominican Republic. His grave overlooks the sea. His son, Charles Jr., now runs the family's seashell business.

When Myrna Jury wrote to B. Virdot in December 1933, she referred to her husband's disdain for Family Services. In this he was hardly alone. Across Canton, those who wrote to Mr. Virdot shared that feeling.

It was made all the worse by the often degrading circumstances that awaited those who could bring themselves to swallow their pride and apply to Family Services. The agency was woefully underfunded and unable to provide aid to all who were eligible for relief. To winnow down the pool of deserving applicants, the review process got longer and ever more intrusive. The worse things got, the more hoops the desperate were asked to jump through, and the less was left of their self-esteem.

For many, it appeared that was precisely the intention of the process—to frighten away would-be applicants and reduce the numbers facing a bureaucracy that was, like an overcrowded lifeboat, already swamped. By then, it had gained a nasty reputation, its screening process so invasive that many said they would sooner die than face such indignities. Some administrators were deeply resented. They were seen as imperious and arbitrarily wielding the power over the decision as to who ate and who starved. In the midst of such economic turbulence, they alone seemed to enjoy the sinecure of a secure position. It was a combustible mix, made all the more so by the perception that these bureaucrats were untouched by the plight of so many. More likely, it was a necessary professional distance they maintained, lest they become overwhelmed by the suffering all around them.

But for some, unable to watch their loved ones waste away, there was no choice but to run the gauntlet of Family Services. A commissary and a network of Canton merchants and grocers of all ethnic backgrounds—Italian, Jewish, Anglo-

Saxon—were affiliated with Family Services and offered the agency goods at a deep discount. Those items were then provided free to Canton's neediest, or at least those who had endured the screening process.

In 1931, grocer Felicia DiGianantonio offered Family Services a loaf of bread for ten cents; Charles Strasser of Canton Poultry sold the agency a pound of lard for nineteen cents; Joseph W. Farwick & Sons sold them navy beans for twelve cents a pound; Wagner Provision offered them soup meat for nineteen cents a pound. Similarly, Family Services had outlets providing clothing, shoes, and coal. The week of Christmas 1933, recipients, often mothers and their small children, could be seen trudging through the snowy streets of Canton, stooped beneath the load provided by Family Services.

The list of foods available at the Family Services "Community Store" reflected the influx of foreigners and African Americans drawn by the city's once-expanding industrial base. There was hominy and turnips, sauerkraut and spaghetti. But among the African American population of Canton, as among all Cantonians, there was a strong preference for making it on their own. During the Depression, the city's Urban League borrowed some fifty-two acres north of Canton, which was used as a vegetable garden for the African American community. In 1932, a coalition of dairies built six cheese factories to process their surplus milk. Everyone who was able had a private vegetable garden, but with mixed results.

Compounding their misery, the growers of 1932 discovered that more than half of the area's wheat production was infested with the Hessian flies, whose greenish-white maggots concealed themselves under the sheaths of the leaves. Prices for farm produce in 1930 fell to levels not seen since 1910, and over the next three years plummeted to lows last reached in 1900. Farm foreclosures accelerated, and hunger spread.

On December 7, 1932, the year before B. Virdot's gift, some three thousand "hunger marchers" gathered in Washington, D.C., to call attention to their plight. Among them were two from Canton, Mr. and Mrs. C. W. Austin. They were discovered in an unheated and vacant two-room house, hungry and suffering from influenza. A Washington rescue squad raced them to Gallinger Hospital. Their discovery and that of two dozen others in the abandoned house triggered a single paragraph in the *Washington Post* that ran under the headline, HORRIFIED.

In the forty years leading up to 1933, Canton's population quadrupled, but its capacity to provide for the needy had not kept pace. When the Depression struck, Family Services was hit by a tsunami. In December 1929 it provided relief to 188 families. In 1930, the number was 1,324. In

1931, it was 3,128. By 1932, it had risen to 3,511. The number could have soared far higher but resources were exhausted.

In August 1933, the once-private Family Services, no longer able to cope with the demands made upon it, became a public agency under the Stark County Relief Administration, and in 1935 came under the Federal Emergency Relief Administration, or FERA. But no change of administration could overcome the reluctance of Donald Jury or thousands of other Cantonians raised to believe that a man who could not support his family was not a man at all. That was in part the genius of Roosevelt's New Deal, that it understood and took stock of how down-and-out Americans were feeling, offering them the three things they hungered for most—a job, self-esteem, and a second chance. The hope that Roosevelt kindled was reflected in the names of some of Canton's businesses: The New Deal Lunch, New Deal Oil Company, and New Deal Tavern.

In the fall of 1933, the Roosevelt administration created the Civil Works Administration, or CWA. It was the first of the New Deal's public jobs programs, and though it lasted only until the following spring, it led the way for Americans to both provide for their loved ones and preserve their sense of self-worth. Letter after letter to B. Virdot refers to the CWA and the hope that it might come through with a job.

Charles Minor, a father of five, was out of work and in dire need when his wife, Mary, wrote to B. Virdot. "While a steeple jack by trade not turning down digging a ditch. While some of the children needing shoes others needing clothes and unless some Good Person sends us a dinner haven't got a thing in sight. In the past three weeks had many meals on bread and coffee." But this was not the first such letter she'd written. Earlier she had written Harry Hopkins, Roosevelt's federal relief administrator, hoping he might persuade the CWA to find her husband a job. His response had arrived in that morning's mail: "said he would try to take it up with head of the CWA here but don't know when that will be." Still, it offered a glint of hope.

In its brief time, the CWA put some four million Americans to work, and is credited with building some half a million miles of roads, as well as work on thousands of schools, playgrounds, airports, and other public facilities in which individual workers and entire communities could take pride. Its successor agencies, like the Works Progress Administration (WPA), understood that to restart America, it must offer a hand up, not a handout.

The County Poorhouse, which took in the homeless from Canton and the surrounding area, like Family Services, underwent a succession of names, each reflecting an attitudinal shift—from County Poorhouse in 1837 to County Infirmary in 1850 to County Home in 1924. Its purpose remained largely unchanged. But during the Depression its meager capacity to hold a few hundred homeless men and women was no match for the numbers in need. Ironically, it provided shelter and sustenance in another, less direct way: one of the jobs the WPA came up with for the unemployed was archiving the records of the poorhouse.

But for many in need that December of 1933, Roosevelt and the promises of a New Deal were still just that, mere promises. The day the B. Virdot offer appeared in the *Canton Repository*, Roosevelt amended yet again an executive order related to the National Emergency Council. To the hungry in Canton who even bothered to follow such bureaucratic minutiae, such news only fed their suspicions that help was still a ways off. Frank Walker, a wealthy lawyer for Anaconda Copper, was named acting executive director of the council, and *Time* magazine on December 18, 1933, noted wryly: "To outsiders this looked like a new title for an old job. . . . On a nation-wide scale his Council's representatives were to steer befuddled citizens through the fog of new Washington agencies to the particular bureau that could supply the relief needed."

Compared to such shuffling and reshuffling of the bureaucratic deck and the growing proliferation of agencies and boards, there was something utterly refreshing about B. Virdot's offer. It was direct, free of politics, and immediate.

Left Behind

It was an intense source of pride among even the neediest that winter of 1933 that they had not given in and sought help from Family Services. As long as they had the strength to resist that temptation they could claim that they were not yet defeated. For some, even Sam Stone's anonymous offer of help was too close to a handout. What they wanted was work.

George Hensel wrote, "We have asked for no charity all through the depression. . . . I would like to have work for a Christmas present for I have no shoes. You may think I have nerve writing this, but if you have been in need as long as my wife and I have you know how it feels to eat only one meal a day. . . . I walk so much every day and come home hungry and not much to eat. It makes you feel pretty bad. . . ." In a postscript he added, "There will be no Xmas for us."

Before the Depression, Hensel had worked for years in a steel mill. Now he was going door-to-door peddling his wife's doughnuts and cupcakes, but almost no one had any money to buy them. It was all made that much more uncomfortable wearing a pair of shoes he'd long since worn out. In the fierce competition for jobs, employers often looked to hire those who most needed work, but need was defined in ways that disadvantaged the likes of George Hensel, who had only his wife and himself to support. That put him at the back of every line. "We have no children," he wrote, "and folks thinks we do not have to live."

Such triaging for work was common during the Depression. Alwyn C. McCort, who had long worked on Canton's streetcars and in a steel mill, had been out of work for three years and was trying to provide some support to his aging parents, Henry and Anna. From B. Virdot, he wanted only a job. "Now I am not asking for charity," he wrote, "but thought since you are interested in unfortunate people you might be able to help me get a job. I get turned down again and again because I am single but my parents need my help very badly and I would like to be able to help them and know once more what money looks like."

But it was the women, married, widowed, and unmarried alike, who often had the most difficult time during the Depression. Employers large and small presumed, often wrongly, that men were the principal supporters of families and women merely supplemented their incomes. But many of the letters to B. Virdot were from women who had no other support than whatever they earned, and on whom others—fatherless children, aging parents, and disabled spouses—counted for their survival.

Catherine Miller, the mother of two children, a daughter aged seven and a son aged four, faced the bleakest of holidays. "I have to support myself and they are both in school," she wrote to B. Virdot. "They have never known what Christmas is. My husband is in a penal institution at present in York Pa. The children are both in need of clothing and I don't get any help from any Society." Days later, her check from B. Virdot arrived.

Wrote another woman, intent upon not throwing herself on the mercies of charity, "I am a widow with an only child, a daughter, and have been struggling to send her to school, and feed her and myself, and often I have gone with nothing to eat, as long as she, who is growing gets it, for she needs it worse than I do. As long as I know my little girl is not hungry it's all right even though I am."

These women shared the men's disdain for charity and the dole. They were no less proud. But in the depths of the Depression, they had fewer options than men. Unlike their male counterparts, few had served apprenticeships or acquired the skills sought by Canton's mills and factories. They were the first to lose their jobs, as companies, assuming that men were the families' primary breadwinners, furloughed en masse all married women. It was a sign of how different the times were that there were no uprisings or challenges to such edicts and that these measures were generally greeted as prudent under the circumstances. For these women, such decisions were devastating.

Those who made their way through the Depression on their own without recourse to charity or Family Services were a special breed—tough, resourceful, and resilient. B. Virdot's offer was addressed not only to the men of Canton but to the families that allowed for women too to come forward, and they did.

My grandmother Minna would not have had it any other way. As a teenager and an only child, she provided essential support to her mother and father, a veteran of the Spanish-American War who returned with a disabling case of malaria. Minna would never have allowed Sam to ignore the appeals of women, even if he were inclined to do so, and he was not. Sam had known nothing but strong and independent-minded women in his family. His mother was not to be trifled with, and two of his three sisters had wrenching struggles with poverty. Minna was a feminist with a fierce social conscience whose influence over Sam in such matters could not be overstated. She would have read every incoming letter, doubtless helped him triage the worthiest from the rest, and championed the case of the women. She knew exactly what they were up against.

Years later, in World War II, as men marched off to war, women like the much-celebrated "Rosie the Riveter" filled the industrial ranks. But it was not for lack of ambition or need that the women of the Depression eyed those same positions. Given half a chance, the generation of Rosie's mother would gladly have rolled up their sleeves in Canton's mills and factories, and no one thought less of those who were able to do so. In Canton, the fortunate found work as nurses, secretaries, shopgirls, and maids, and did piecework in factories. But as the Depression deepened, they were the first to be let go.

A photo from the 1920s taken at the Hoover vacuum plant shows a vast room filled with women sitting row upon row at sewing machines. But in March 1931, the order went out—all married women must go. No inquiry was made as to whether their husbands had jobs or whether they were their family's sole support. The next year, Hoover launched a national ad campaign "based on the powerful appeal that the Hoover was the one possession which enabled the women of modern means to enjoy equal luxury with their wealthier sisters." The appeal fell flat. In 1933 the company began a marketing drive built around the slogan "Elmer is the key to '33." The idea was that in Hard Times, Hoover's sales force should concentrate on the husbands—the "Elmers"—who alone had the authority to purchase costly items like sweepers. Sales sank even further. The company had failed to show women due respect, either as employees or as consumers.

Gumption

For many women the Great Depression represented a bewildering descent into poverty. Many had been working even before they reached puberty. Their struggles echoed those of their mothers, whose hardships became templates for their own lives. Childhoods, such as they were, had been cut short by the demands of family and their own survival. In Canton, as across the country, there was nothing novel about the idea that a woman would have to support herself and others, but opportunities were rare.

So it was with Rachel DeHoff, who was among those who reached out to B. Virdot. She never enjoyed any delusions that life was going to be easy. The daughter of William and Elizabeth Davis, she was born in August 1897. Her father, William, the son of Welsh immigrants, was a gritty-faced coal miner, a veteran of the Civil War who was born in 1836, already sixty-one when daughter Rachel was born. Her mother was a Scottish immigrant, twenty-nine years younger than her husband. Their bare-bones home in the rural coal-mining village of Somerdale, Ohio, relied on an outside pump, an outhouse, and a crudely dug-out fruit cellar. In 1905 her father died, leaving Elizabeth, then a forty-one-year-old widow, to house and feed her three daughters on her husband's meager Civil War pension.

School was a luxury Rachel DeHoff could not afford. After the fourth grade, she had to look for work. Not long after her elder sister Esther moved to Canton, Rachel joined her. At thirteen she was working in Canton's massive Dueber-Hampden watch factory, one of three thousand employees in what was then one of the world's largest makers of pocket watches. Since the plant's arrival in Canton in 1888, it had been a magnet for labor and one of the driving forces in Canton's rapid growth. The sprawling industrial edifice, with its turrets, clock towers, formal gardens, and fortresslike presence, dwarfed the little girl from the village of Somerdale. Three years later, at sixteen, she married Howard DeHoff, who would become a machinist with Timken Roller Bearing Company, another of Canton's gargantuan employers. The couple saved and built a new home in 1927, had two sons, and appeared well on their way to living out the American dream. Then the bottom dropped out of Rachel DeHoff s world.

First came the Depression. Then, in 1932, Howard fell ill. His urine turned dark and smoky-colored, his back ached, and he was feverish. Something was wrong with his kidneys. Returning by train from the Mayo Clinic, he crawled into bed. Two days later, on March 1, 1932, he died. They said it was Bright's disease. Howard DeHoff was forty-two. Into the hands of the Great

Depression fell his thirty-five-year-old widow, Rachel, and two sons, along with a crushing mortgage and little or no savings. For Rachel, history had repeated itself.

Less than two years later, as Christmas 1933 approached, Rachel DeHoff noticed the B. Virdot ad in the *Canton Repository*. She waited a day to respond. On December 19, she took up a fountain pen and, across a small pad of lined manila paper, wrote these words:

Dear Mr. B. Virdot

I saw in last nights paper the most human thing I have ever seen in print before. Instead of giving to some church or organization to have your name mentioned over the pulpit, or in the news paper, you have chose the silent way of celebrating Christs birth, which you surely will be repaid. No wonder prosperity has returned to you, and yours. May it never look dark again for you is my prayers—Well I will write a few things about my circumstances. You mentioned men—but I am not a man but I am taking the Responsibility of a man. As Father + Mother. My husband died 2 yrs ago this March left me with 2 Boys to support one in McKinley High another 9 yrs old -I have worked every day at Real Estate, and you know what a uphill job that has been, but I have been able to keep my home & Boys with food & clothing by the effort I have put forth. It looks pretty dark sometimes but we still hold on to that ray of hope—that this terrible depression will soon be over—and I want to state that I have never received charity of any kind or have never complained to anyone before but after I read your letter I made up my mind to write to you, not asking, just telling you my circumstances, but if you think I am deserving of part of your Xmas cheer that you are giving I assure you it will be greatly appreciated & spent for the right kind of things for my boys & myself.

May God Bless you & Wishing you a Merry Xmas & a prosperious new years- I remain—

> MRS. R. DEHOFF
> 3039 9TH ST SW
> CANTON

Days later, she received a check for five dollars signed by B. Virdot. To what use she put the money is not known, but there was little reason to fret for Rachel DeHoff. She was hell-bent on

234

providing for her small family. In the months before her husband died, she had begun to study for the real estate test and to prepare herself for a career. She was one of the first women in the state to become a real estate agent and she shrewdly navigated the harshest of markets. In those dire times, few homes were sold. Many had been foreclosed on and were owned by the banks, which feared nothing as much as vandals in the empty houses. DeHoff understood that and initially focused on renting the houses, thereby assuring the bank that someone was there to watch the property. She arranged to take half the first month's rent in such homes, giving her an income stream that allowed her to hold on to her own house even as she provided other families with at least temporary housing. She was tough and tireless and, notwithstanding a mere four years of schooling, deft at running numbers, calculating mortgages, and projecting her financial needs.

And she was compassionate. Just as her sister had taken her in, so she took others into her home. One of these was a childhood friend in need of shelter. Nola Walters would live with the family for years, and in return for cooking and cleaning she was given not merely lodging but a family to call her own. Christian spirit or not, no one got something for nothing. That was the singular axiom of the Great Depression. Hoboes would come to Rachel DeHoff's back door, as they did to so many homes, and offer to shovel coal or, in winter, clear the sidewalk, and in return they received a sandwich they would eat on the back porch—a scene repeated hundreds of thousands of times across the nation. And such generosity was repaid in kind by neighbors and shop owners.

In her field, Rachel DeHoff would prove herself the equal of any man. She made a name for herself in the industry, paid off her mortgage, vacationed in Cuba, and eventually became successful enough to open another real estate office in Phoenix, Arizona, where she wintered. She was always frugal, but the Hard Times she had twice endured—once as a child and later as a widow—were forever behind her.

But it was her sons, Howard Ellsworth and Harold, upon whom she lavished the most attention and for whom she sacrificed much. Rachel DeHoff endowed them with an appreciation for education and a keen sense of service to community and country. Like so many children of the Depression, they were grateful for the sacrifices made on their behalf but grateful too to the nation that provided them with prospects brighter than any their parents could have imagined. The fusion of sacrifice and gratitude was later put to the test on the battlefield.

DeHoff's sons both served in World War II. Howard was a second lieutenant in the Army Air Forces. Harold became an infantry platoon sergeant, fought in the Battle of the Bulge, and crossed the Rhine at Remagan. He came away with a Bronze Star and two Purple Hearts. Both men not only finished high school but got college degrees. Howard had a long and solid career with Hoover.

Son Harold got a law degree, and became the city prosecutor and then a distinguished judge on the Common Pleas Court. His life intersected with much of Canton's history. As a prosecutor in the late 1950s, he helped shut down the city's teeming trade in prostitution, padlocking some nineteen brothels and bringing to an end a decades-long stain on the city's reputation. Today, at eighty-four, he is a last living link to what was. He remembers well the city's corruption.

To outsiders vice and graft may have smacked of hypocrisy, but in Canton, corruption was seen as something of a homegrown industry, not unlike Timken, Hoover, or Diebold. They may have been the wages of sin, but they were still wages. The furniture stores furnished the brothels' waiting parlors and sold them hundreds of mattresses, the doctors examined the girls and collected their fees, the laundry gathered their soiled sheets, and the police took their cut of the action in envelopes in exchange for keeping out-of-town girls from encroaching and making sure the johns and ladies carried on their business safely.

Decades later, a well-known madam married a vice-squad cop without raising an eyebrow. A mayor had been dismissed for "inefficiency," a polite word for graft, and, as the *New York Times* duly noted, Canton's police chief had been suspended amid accusations that he had sold protection to gangsters.

Such corruption went way back. In September 1905, William S. Couch wrote in the *Cleveland Plain Dealer*: "For a lurid little city, commend me to Canton." He described Canton as a "monument to present day Ohio politics built by the present day Ohio politicians, who have piled gambling hells [*sic*] and Parisian music halls on a foundation of other iniquities in their effort to attain such immortality of memory as may be derived from public office and political power. . . . Fluttering, tawdry rags, faded tinsel, leering faces and satyrs' figures, a frieze of poker decks and roulette wheels, these predominate in the design and decoration of the other memorial [President McKinley's monument], the flimsy whole lit with red lights by night and covered from sight by day." Whiskey Alley, then one of Canton's more notorious sections, was "lined with gambling dens, each located above a saloon. During a moment's quiet, when the music machines are still, the rattle of ivory chips reaches the ear on the street." And for half a century, Canton's brothels operated with a brazenness that attracted patrons, gawkers, would-be soul savers, and, of course, fallen women.

238

Rachel DeHoff's son Harold, both as prosecutor and as judge, was one of those who helped put an end to all that, or at least reduce it to a scale befitting Canton's size. He was too young to remember when in 1926 the mob gunned down Don Mellett, the city's corruption-fighting editor, but he remembers when, as prosecutor thirty years later, two trustees from the Ohio State Penitentiary delivered his prison-made desk. One of the two men was a former Canton police detective who was convicted for his role in Mellett's murder.

Service continues to run in the DeHoff family. Rachel's granddaughter Rachelle Martin became a commander in the U.S. Navy, retired as a deputy inspector general, joined the gubernatorial administration of George W. Bush as commissioner of a regulatory agency in Texas, and later headed a rape crisis center in New Bern, North Carolina. She remembers her grandmother Rachel DeHoff helping her with college tuition and making it clear that nothing would be allowed to stand in the way of her getting an education. Today she has her grandmother's fine Haviland china, a mark of the better times she came to know. Granddaughter Rebecca J. Canoyer also pursued a career of service, first with the Red Cross, then as an oral interpreter for the deaf, and today as a management and program analyst for the Department of Homeland Security in Washington, D.C.

She too feels a close affinity to her grandmother. To her two sons, Rachel DeHoff passed on what Rebecca calls "a tremendous feeling of patriotism for the country and a need to give back." They in turn passed that feeling on to the grandchildren. I read her Rachel DeHoff's letter from 1933. She cried. Later that day Rebecca and her fourteen-year-old son were to volunteer at a shelter.

Many of the landmarks of Rachel DeHoff's life are now gone or unrecognizable. Dueber-Hampden, the giant watch factory that first employed her as a young girl, went out of business in the late 1920s, largely a casualty of the advent of the wristwatch. In March 1930, industrialist Armand Hammer sold the watchmaking machines to the Soviet Union. They were loaded onto twenty-eight railroad cars and transported to Moscow, where they became the First State Watch Factory.

Along with the equipment went twenty-three of Canton's finest watchmakers and engravers, who, under contract, worked in Moscow for a year or more, setting up the plant and training Russian workers. There were, after all, no jobs to be had for them in America in 1930. Each of the workers received passage aboard the SS *Aquitania*, a Moscow apartment, a cook, and a waiter. They were paid a daily wage and, at the completion of their contract, a princely five thousand dollars a year to be deposited in a New York bank. Well into the twentieth century, the equipment from Canton was used at the now renamed First Moscow Watch Factory and continued to turn out as many as now renamed six million watches a year. One of those watches was reportedly given by Soviet leader Mikhail S. Gorbachev to President Ronald Reagan. Some of the Canton machinery was even spotted in China in the mid-1980s.

The twenty-acre industrial site in Canton fell to weeds and broken glass. As a child I remember them taking down the massive Dueber-Hampden factory in 1958 to make way for Interstate 77. The site is also home to the Trinity Gospel Temple. But before the buildings were torn down, workers vacuumed under the floors to retrieve the gold shavings that had accumulated over the decades. Today, Rachel DeHoff's son Harold still has the Dueber-Hampden gold watch his mother wore around her neck. To her, it symbolized the distance she had come.

As for Somerdale, Ohio, where she grew up, it bears little resemblance to the place Rachel DeHoff knew. It was swept away by the Great Depression—literally. In the 1930s, as part of the Works Progress Administration, the Dover Dam was built upstream across the Tuscarawas River. Somerdale was moved in its entirety from what became known as "The Bottoms"—periodically washed out as a flood-control area—to higher ground. Even Somerdale Cemetery, where Rachel

DeHoff's parents were buried, was dug up and relocated above the flood plain. Today the population stands at 242, the sole business is a bar, and the coal shafts that Rachel DeHoff's father, William, once worked are now exposed to the skies and reworked as strip mines.

Rachel DeHoff died on January 27, 1974, at the age of seventy-six. She is buried in Forest Hill Cemetery, among so many others who weathered the Great Depression. She lies not far from the graves of James Brownlee, Allen Bennafield, and others who, that dark Christmas of 1933, reached out to B. Virdot.

So Little for Women

R achel DeHoff's life was a testament not only to the virtues of hard work but to the promise and reality of social mobility that had drawn so many to America. She had lifted herself out of the ranks of the poverty-stricken, where she had been born, and provided her children with lives of promise. As a woman, her achievements were all the more noteworthy, having overcome not only a lack of formal education, the Depression, and widowhood, but the many societal obstacles placed before her gender. But for every Rachel DeHoff there were many more women, no less intelligent or industrious, who could not surmount the barriers before them, barriers made all the more formidable by the Depression and the scramble for jobs and scarce resources.

Many of these women, talented and willing to work long hours under wretched circumstances, came to resent the unfairness of an economic system that was rigged against them. For a woman to succeed it was not enough for her to be a man's equal. She must be better than him—or find another way around the system. Many of the women who wrote to B. Virdot faced just such a challenge.

Edith Marie Saunders, like Rachel DeHoff, was a woman of great determination, not someone who was looking for, or willing to take, a handout. She was born on May 12, 1909. Her early life was fraught with emotional and financial setbacks that toughened her up but also left her resentful. Her parents divorced when she was a child. She dropped out of school and at sixteen entered into a miserable marriage that lasted only a few months—just long enough for her to contract a venereal disease that left her unable to have children. She was struck by a car, which broke her collarbone and so damaged her leg that the doctor told her she would never walk again. She proved him wrong.

Edith was the oldest of three children and the only girl. Her childhood was briefer than most. Following her parents' divorce, she found herself burdened with adult responsibilities. Something of a tomboy, she played ball with her brothers in the alley, but books were her refuge and her salvation, as they were for her mother, Minna. After the divorce, Minna sold the children's literature series "My Book House" door-to-door. Minna Saunders wrote of her own childhood, "I used to go into the apple orchard, put apples in my pockets, and climb a tree and read Grimm's Fairy Tales."

She passed that passion on to her daughter, Edith. "I loved to read and always had books hidden in my room," Edith Saunders wrote years later. "When I thought everyone was asleep, I would turn my light on and read for a long time."

Independent, strong-willed, and miffed that what few breaks there were in this life favored men over women, Edith Saunders steered her own course. In 1932, as the Depression deepened, she left New York City and returned to Canton to help support her mother and younger brother, Jim. She invested her savings in a small mom-and-pop grocery store and for a time did well enough. The three of them lived in an apartment in the rear of the store. But the Depression caught up with them. At the time she wrote to B. Virdot, Edith Saunders had nothing.

504 NEWTON AVE. NW
CANTON, OHIO
DEC. 18, 1933

Dear Mr. Virdot:

I think that what you are doing this Christmas is a very beautiful and fine thing. It is something I had often wished I could do too.

It isn't very easy to tell anyone about one's misfortunes, except in just the manner you have suggested.

Of course, I may not be considered as a businessman, but I have had to bear all the responsibilities of a man during the greater part of this depression. Anyway — may I tell you about myself?

Over a year ago, I was living in New York City and was earning quite good money. Just about that time everything began to go wrong for my family here in Canton, my two brothers and mother.

I knew that I could not possibly support a family in New York on the salary I was making.

But I had saved some money and I returned to Canton and invested it in a small business.

My youngest brother worked with me, and together we managed to build up our business to the point where it was supporting all of us.

But just when everything was progressing beautifully, I lost my little business through the unscrupulous methods of another business man here in town. I was only twenty-three years of age and of course, too I tried it again but eventually lost everything except for about $50.

It broke up my family. One brother is in Michigan, the other in St. Louis Missouri. They are practically living on charity, and earn so little there is nothing to give to help mother and I.

But both mother and myself have always worked at direct selling, and together we have managed to scrape up a few dollars on commissions now and then, but always such a constant strain I fear that sometimes it becomes almost too great for us to bear.

We do not own a home here, nor furniture, tho we once did, like many others and we have no relations — only each other. Recently we were unable to pay any rent for five weeks and were ordered to move. A friend gave me money to pay a week's rent at the address given but my new landlord found out about what happened, and I have been asked to move again.

It seems strange to think that probably some of the money I brought to Canton and invested or some of the money which passed through my hands while I was in business may have found its way into the pockets of the same landlord.

So much is done for men — so little for women who need it often worse than a man.

Many girls might have drifted into dreadful things to keep from starving — even suicide perhaps.

But that is such an ugly thing to do.

Tho I confess often I have thought how sweet it would be to lie down to rest, and feel my work was done, and that I never need face another day of fear again.

But that is dramatic and I am not a bit like that really. Only just once in a while, deep inside me. I have usually managed to find some humor in this tragedy.

I wonder what ten dollars would do for me—it has been such a long time since I had that much.

Pay rent for two weeks—or one week and buy food with the rest, or stockings, those pesky things that will wear out no matter how neatly one tries to keep them darned. And it does make a girl look so poor. Thank heaven I have decent enough clothes otherwise—and so do my brothers and mother.

Or best of all I could buy some gifts for those who are dear to me and whom I have always managed to remember—until this Xmas.

Perhaps you think I am not too deserving. It isn't my nature to weep. Even in this letter I could not describe how dreadful things are not knowing from day to day whether we shall find ourselves homeless—and nowhere to go—and no money to go there.

This sounds like the adventures of "Tish" does it not? But whether some morning I shall find a grand surprise or not — I still [think] that what you are doing is fine and splendid, for nothing builds morale and inspires self confidence and courage like money in one's purse. I should long to be able to say "It is a pleasure" to the person who could think of such a fine thing to do. However I must move by Wednesday so my landlord says — but where or how I don't know. But shall leave change of address for postman. But remember — I won't miss what I never had — so unless you feel I deserve it — give to the others. Most sincerely, Edith M. Saunders.

Two days later, Sam mailed a check for five dollars to Edith Saunders. It was forwarded and caught up with her a few days later.

In the letter, Saunders obliquely compares herself to "Tish," an apparent reference to the redoubtable spinster Letitia "Tish" Carberry, the heroine of the popular mystery novels of Mary Roberts Rinehart. It was Rinehart who said of life, "a little work, a little sleep, a little love and it's all over." At the time Saunders wrote her letter, she was twenty-four, stooped beneath the weight of the Depression, and suppressing the yearning for it to be "all over."

But Edith Saunders's life was just beginning.

The themes she touched on in her 1933 letter to B. Virdot would resonate throughout her long life. Whether because of her parents' divorce, her own disastrous first marriage, the unscrupulous man who cost her a fledgling business, or her justifiable perception that men were given an unfair advantage, Edith Saunders sought and held the upper hand over most of the men in her life.

She married five times and in each divorce emerged with that much more of a treasury. Her exes did not fare so well. Among them was a senior engineer at Chrysler, Steven Lazorshak, husband number four. Edith Saunders would settle in the exclusive Bloomfield Hills suburb of Detroit and live in an expansive brick house with a manicured courtyard and a pool. (She would later marry the gardener, Paul Lemieux, husband number five.)

"Nothing," she had written in 1933, "builds morale and inspires self confidence and courage like money in one's purse." Edith Saunders became a bona fide millionaire, perhaps not entirely self-made, but a millionaire nonetheless.

But it was not just about money. She had also been determined to make up for the educational deficit of her youth. "I had never finished high school and regretted that very much," she wrote decades later. So, in her midfifties, she studied for six weeks and earned her General Educational Development diploma, or GED. She then went on to earn a bachelor's and a master's degree in English. She taught English literature in high school for years.

Edith Saunders died in 1999 with a long string of men's names after her own and a sizable estate. But even in death, she left behind a legacy that reflected what stirred her to write to B. Virdot in 1933. To her two brothers, Robert and James, she left only one thousand dollars each and a hand-written note in the codicil to her will suggesting it was more than they deserved. Ten years after her death, there is still property from her estate unclaimed in the hands of the state of Michigan, which is seeking her heirs.

And finally, perhaps stung by the shady businessman who cost her a business in 1933, she endowed the Oppenheimer-Mancuso (Lazorshak) Award at Central Michigan University, established in 2000. A member of the class of 1965, she funded it from her estate. The one-thousand-dollar prize goes to "a senior philosophy major who submits an outstanding essay on the subject of the necessity for teaching ethics and/or character development in the elementary grades."

As a twenty-three-year-old woman, Edith Saunders had hoped to better her position in life through business, but the Depression and a predatory businessman scuttled that dream. One after another, her marriages failed or ended, but each provided her another rung toward financial stability and social ascendancy. Five marriages later, she was a millionaire, had acquired the education long denied her, and found a profession that gave her a measure of autonomy and pride.

She was hardly the first to recognize that marriage could act as a kind of social elevator that could carry one either up or down. Her first marriage, brief but defining, had taken her into the depths; the subsequent ones were more to her advantage. B. Virdot—Sam Stone—was no less aware of the role marriage could play in one's social and financial fortunes. His mother, Hilda, had often pointed out that she had married beneath her in accepting Jacob's hand, and that had she done otherwise, she might have averted much of the heartache and hardship that followed. That lesson was not lost on Sam. In marrying Minna, he took a major step upward, and won for himself social acceptance in circles that until then had been beyond his ken. It did not mean he did not love her, but to win such position with a ring and to gain a lifelong tutor in the finer things of life—literature, music, and manners—made the union all the richer. What Minna got in the bargain was a man of great heart and a student eager to improve himself.

Mr. B. Virdot's Story:
A Foreigner No Longer

Those efforts at self-improvement did not begin in Canton but were fully realized there. Exactly why Sam Stone first came to the town is not known. More than a dozen years of his life are largely unaccounted for. From Pittsburgh, he wandered from state to state, boardinghouse to boardinghouse. A niece says he spent time in West Virginia. It was there that he likely did his unpleasant work in the coal mines. In 1914, then twenty-six years old, he was living in Kenosha, Wisconsin, working as a salesman in Block Brothers department store—the Block Brothers were themselves Jewish immigrants. Two years later, he was managing S & J Gottlieb Dry Goods in the same city. From those years only a single scrap of paper survives, a sheet of stationery from a shoe store on which Sam had copied a poem by the Cleveland, Ohio, poet Edmund Vance Cooke. It is titled "How Did You Die?" The first stanza reads:

Did you tackle that trouble that came your way
With a resolute heart and cheerful?
Or hide your face from the light of day
With a craven soul and fearful?

Oh, a trouble's a ton, or a trouble's an ounce,
Or a trouble is what you make it.
And it isn't the fact that you're hurt that counts.
But only how did you take it?

By 1917 Sam was in Chicago, briefly working for a millinery shop. On June 5 of that year he registered for the military, one of twenty-four million American men to do so. He listed his name as "Samuel J. Stone," his date of birth as March 2, 1888, and his birthplace as Bucharest, Rumania. It was one of the last times he acknowledged that he was an alien.

Years later, Sam told me he received his military training on the fields of Gettysburg. He never went overseas but he did see death. One afternoon, while his tentmate was cleaning his rifle, he was struck by lightning and was killed instantly. The body was blackened and Sam was close enough to have his own brows singed. I have a black-and-white picture of him standing in front of a field tent holding his bolt-action rifle affixed with bayonet. Underneath, in his unmistakable pen, Sam wrote "THE UNDECIDED SOLDIER." Doubtless he enlisted because he had to. But he must have felt considerable ambivalence, torn between his desire to serve his adopted land and his apprehension about wading into the interminable disputes of the Old World from which he had hoped to forever distance himself.

A year later, he was living in Canton, a boarder in the home of a local Jewish merchant. On January 9, 1920, he told a U.S. Census enumerator that he and his family had emigrated from Germany in 1900. He also claimed to have been naturalized as an American citizen. The lifelong lie was beginning to take shape. But as I later unwound the skein of lies, I came to at least understand, if not his reasons, then at least his fears.

It was no later than 1920 that he invented the story of his birth in Pittsburgh. For the next sixty years, he would hold fast to that account, risking everything. But why suddenly invent such a story? Perhaps it was because he was now beginning to establish himself in Canton as a businessman and he yearned for the social acceptance he imagined came with being native-born. He was admittedly impatient and yearned to be American in every sense of the word.

But something else was happening in the country then that had to frighten him. Across the nation, there was growing xenophobia and suspicion of leftists, anarchists, labor organizers, and Eastern European immigrants. A rash of bombings in major cities heightened tensions. Thousands of immigrants were rounded up and put in jail. Hundreds were deported in the middle of the night. Much of the suspicion centered on the foreign-born. Jewish refugees in particular came under scrutiny, linked in the minds of many to the sort of internationalism and labor activism that was behind the radical assault on America. Provoked in part by the Bolshevik Revolution, the bombings and unrest triggered a hysteria that Sam would have seen as a direct threat to him.

It reached a crescendo in January 1920 when U.S. Attorney General A. Mitchell Palmer and his special assistant, a young firebrand named John Edgar Hoover, arrested some six thousand people and held them without trial. The discriminatory residue of the Red Scare soon found expression in the nation's ever-more-restrictive immigration policies, which took aim at excluding refugees from those countries suspected of carrying the contagion of radicalism. Technically the quotas were set as a percentage of each of those country's immigrants and offspring already in the United States, but the baseline was set to 1890—before the great influx of Eastern Europeans—and was designed to reduce that immigration to a trickle. A 1924 law allowed a mere 794 immigrants from Romania. In such an environment, it is easy to imagine Sam's eagerness to conceal his origins.

The governmental crackdowns and growing public apprehension raised the specter of anti-Semitism and even deportation. There was nothing that Sam Stone and his siblings dreaded more than the prospect of losing their place in America and being forced to return to the doleful landscape of their youth. It was something they talked about among themselves and it was an insecurity that several passed along to their children. That fear, that the Old World could somehow, even after two decades, reach out and seize him, was kindled anew by America's midnight roundups of immigrants. Once already, in Romania, he and his family had been stripped of all the rights of citizenship. To "Sam Stone, the American," falsely claiming to be native-born may at the time have seemed to offer a safe haven. Ironically, it was precisely that action that would later put him in fear of prison or deportation.

Amid so many contradictions in Sam's life, there was also this: as intent as he was upon concealing his past, he was always true to it. He constantly drew upon it as a reservoir of acquired wisdom and never dreamed of apologizing for the humbleness of his beginnings, the rough edges, the gaps in his education. He may have reinvented himself—by changing his name, his country of origin, his date of birth—but he never attempted to be anything other than who he was, a self-made man who had grown up in Hard Times and who, even in his most prosperous days, identified with those who struggled. In that way, as in so many others, he shared a common bond with many in Canton who straddled two very different worlds.

Sam's documents may have been fraudulent, but he was no fraud. He never put on airs, pretended to be high-born, or said an unkind word of those who were forced to scratch out a living. To the end, they were his people. The vulnerabilities he shared with them trumped any differences of religion, race, or gender, and if he fit in with those of privilege it was because they recognized in him something authentic, and not because he pretended to be one of them. So it was with Mr. B. Virdot. It was a made-up name, a pseudonym, but one that allowed him to express his truest self. That was the only contradiction in the man, that to be himself he had first to be someone else.

Such an act of prevarication would have found an understanding audience in Depression-era Canton, and well beyond. A lie that liberated one from encumbrances past and over which one had no control and bore no responsibility was still a lie in the eyes of the law, but if it moved a man and his family closer to their dream, if it distanced him from ancient prejudices, if it merely allowed him to be judged on the merits of his work, most, I would wager, would have withheld judgment. Canton was a place that had drawn its share of immigrants from countries deemed undesirable by the town's longer-established upper crust, those same people who used the laws to close the door behind them. Being unwanted by others was something many in Canton had in common, that and the need to be valued, if not for who they were, then at least for who they or their children might become. For them, emancipation was more than a simple matter of emigration. Back then, many did not speak of the past, and some, like Sam, chose to fictionalize it. No one thought the less of them for it. Canton had summoned them all with the promise of a second chance.

V.
Families
The Crisis That Brought Them Closer

For Sam Stone, the real and final break with the past did not come until 7:45 Sunday evening, March 14, 1926. That was when his father, Jacob Finkelstein, died at Montefiore Hospital in Pittsburgh's predominately Jewish Hill District. The cause of death was a cerebral hemorrhage. He was sixty-five and determined to the end to honor the old ways. He died as "Finkelstein," not "Stone," and in the medical care of Jacob Grekin, a Russian Jewish doctor who emigrated the same year Jacob did—1902—and whose native tongue, like Jacob's, was Yiddish. He was laid to rest in the New Light Cemetery in Millvale, just outside Pittsburgh, across the Allegheny River.

His obituary in Pittsburgh's *Jewish Criterion* lists his surviving children. The sons are named "Samuel J., Max, David and Albert Finkelstein, all of Canton, Ohio and one brother." Restoring the name Finkelstein to the sons, albeit in an obituary, was perhaps a last nod and concession to the old man, for by then all four sons had long since adopted the name Stone. If the boys had come to despise the baggage that went with their birth name, their father reviled its bastardization. But, in one final act of defiance, my grandfather signed his father's death certificate "Sam J. Stone," not "Sam J. Finkelstein."

Eighty-three years later, in May 2009, I went in search of the cemetery of Sam Stone's parents, Jacob and Hilda. I found their graves just below the summit of a steep hill in the crowded New Light Cemetery, just outside Pittsburgh. In death, as in life, the American experience seemed to have touched them little. There is no "Stone" buried here, only "Finkelstein." Jacob's stone is a pillar of granite with an acorn for a crown. The acorn symbolizes birth, strength, and fertility. On the stone is written, in Hebrew, "Yakov ben Moshe Shmuel Finkelstein" and the dates of his birth and death. The Hebrew side of the stone has been worn down by the wind and is hard to read. The English, on the back side, shielded from the elements, is clear:

Jacob Finkelstein
Died
March 14, 1926
Aged
67 Years
Father

The word *Father* at the base makes me uncomfortable, knowing what I know of him. Still, as is the Jewish custom, I placed two pebbles on the marker, one in Sam's name and one in my own. Sam's mother's orthodoxy, which had smothered my grandfather in life, continued in death. Hilda died on September 17, 1939, and, in accordance with Orthodox tenets, was buried in a casket free of all metal ("earth to earth"). Her grave is not beside Jacob, nor at his feet, but catty-corner. She is buried between one Sophie Klapper and one Bessie Mandelbaum. The undertaker suggested that some Orthodox women would not risk being laid to rest beside another man, and so preferred to be placed between two women, even if not contiguous with her husband's grave. (Her death certificate lists her maiden name as "Bacall," and so it seems plausible that what Sam once told me was true, that he was related to the actress Lauren Bacall, whose mother was born in Romania and was Jewish.)

Hilda Stone's obituary was itself, at best, a half-truth. It said she "was a native of Rumania and had lived in this country 50 years." That would have meant she came to America in 1889—fourteen years earlier than her arrival as recorded by passenger lists. Doubtless it was Sam who placed the obituary in the newspaper, and, in fabricating the date, avoided any public inconsistencies with his own fictionalized account of being born in America.

JACOB HAD BEEN more than Sam's father (or less, if affection is a requisite of fatherhood). He had been a living symbol of the duress of the past. Sam had not one picture of him. His father's passing brought a change over Sam, who was then thirty-eight, single, successful, and something of a playboy. After that, he seemed to take stock of himself. The succession of sleek convertibles, women, and trips abroad had not filled the void within.

Not long after Jacob Finkelstein died, Sam found himself at a dance in Canton. He noticed a shy, dark-haired girl sitting in the dim light of the dance hall. He walked over and introduced himself. Her name was Minna Cecilia Adolph. He asked if she would care to join him on the dance floor. She accepted, but was a little tentative in her steps, having removed her glasses before the dance. They danced through the evening, said their good-byes, and parted. Sam came away with the address of the law office where she worked.

The next day, Minna Adolph, then a stenographer for Judge Harvey Francis Ake, was at her desk when an elderly gentleman—elderly at least by her standards—approached and greeted her warmly. Minna had no idea who he was. "Sam Stone," he said, his ego deflated to have been so quickly forgotten. But now, in the full light of day, nineteen-year-old Minna had her glasses on. She eyed the fatherly figure before her. He was, by his own count, thirty-five. (Actually, he was at least thirty-eight, and quite possible forty—twice her age.) Even the twenty years that separated them did not do justice to the experiential divide between them. He stood all of five feet five, his hair thinning, his face far older than she had imagined it. He invited her to dinner. Only reluctantly did she accept.

Before long, they were courting. But Minna was of a different social stratum than Sam was accustomed to, and his wily ways of winning women lacked a certain refinement. The last week of July 1926, Minna Adolph splurged and treated herself to a stay at the Chautauqua Institution in New York, drawn by its music, arts, and literary salons. When she checked into her room there was a new set of golf clubs waiting for her and a note from Sam. She was thrilled, but her parents were less so. She was ordered to promptly—but graciously—return the gift. It was deemed inappropriate. Minna's parents, Al and Rosa Adolph, had something better in mind for their only child, someone with less wear and fewer rough edges.

But something about Sam's wild side appealed to Minna. On their first date, he had been pulled over for speeding. Minna liked that.

Sam, though more worldly, was insecure in Minna's company, and keenly aware of his lack of education. To him she seemed a nearly unattainable prize. She was everything he was not. On August 5, 1926, Minna received a letter from him. The postmark was from the Ambassador Hotel in Atlantic City, New Jersey. It began:

Dear Minna:

I can write a book filled to capacity with reasonable explanations "why the delayed writing" but the fact will remain unchanged so please excuse me. I promise it will not happen again.

Do you remember the first night I met you—and do you recall one of my remarks that I was semi-interesting; so again I will say: I am not a waste of English and many a time I possess wonderfull thoughts but no ability to express them . . . so this is my predicament . . . wonderful thoughts, unsurpassed sentiments . . . but no command of English to convey them.

. . . It is 3:30 AM. I have just returned from a local time killing event; a dance at the Ritz . . . and early morning lunch served a la Grabo [sic] a wild ride out in the country and here I am writing to Minna: So you see no matter of time or circumstances, I am always thinking of you and I shall continue to do so. . . . I look forward to hearing from you soon . . . until then I miss you beyond words. Yours, Sam

If the letter was a testament to his deep feelings for her, it was also a measure of his insecurity and the ends to which he would go to conceal his inadequacies. It is almost certain that Sam did not write the letter. They may be his words, but they are not written in his hand. The cursive strokes are elegant and the words almost free of spelling errors. Sam could not write cursively and his spelling was atrocious. But he did not yet feel confident enough with her to risk revealing how little education he had.

In Minna, he had more than met his match. From the beginning, she could see his foibles and his roguish ways, but they only made her feel that much more alive.

Minna and Sam became a pair, though a more unlikely pair would have been hard to find. Minna was a bookish virgin, he far from it. She had skipped the second, fifth, and seventh grades and graduated from high school in 1923 with the highest honors, at fifteen, the youngest graduate in McKinley High's history. Her picture was featured on the front page of the *Canton Repository* under the headline, MCKINLEY HIGH GIRL HAS UNUSUAL SCHOOL RECORD. "Although still a little girl in years and in many of her mannerisms," the article began, "Miss Minna Adolph, 15 years-old . . . finds real fun in solving problems in higher mathematics and conquers experiments in chemistry with the ease of professionals."

She matriculated with a 99 percent average, was so smart that she was never asked to take an exam (according to the *Repository*), had more credits than she knew what to do with, and in her spare time had been active in half a dozen clubs, excelling in debate, while working part-time. She was also an able golfer, a talented tennis player, and an intellectual who liked nothing better than to debate the affairs of the day, from civil rights to the place of women in society.

All of this was new for Sam, and thrilling. He was shrewd and intuitive—no one doubted that—but had little formal education. He tried mightily to smooth out his rough edges, not yet sensing that they were a part of his appeal.

Minna came from a fine family, German Jews with deep roots in America. In 1861, her grandfather Isaac had enlisted in Company D of the 5th Pennsylvania Regiment in the Civil War, and had left the Army of the Republic in 1864 as a captain. Her father, Elias, or "Al," was a tall, broad-shouldered figure who had served in the Spanish-American War as a private in the 28th Company, United States Coast Artillery, and had returned from the Philippines with a case of malaria that would dog him to his final days. While Sam's father rolled cigars in Pittsburgh's Jewish ghetto, in nearby Jeannette, Pennsylvania, Minna's father, Al, and mother, Rosa, ran a hotel, overseeing a staff of cooks, clerks, and chambermaids.

In 1912 the Adolph family settled in Canton, where they were soon accepted well beyond the confines of their faith. Al Adolph would hunt with Ed Bender, founder of Bender's restaurant. Al Adolph had been a liquor salesman and later sold cigars, something Sam would just have to get over. (Al Adolph probably would have agreed that tobacco was cursed after his dentist discovered cancer in his mouth.)

The Adolphs were a family of considerable class but modest means. Disabled by malaria, Al Adolph in 1933—the year of B. Virdot's gift—was living on a meager sixty dollars a month from his military pension. But Minna had been raised properly; she carried herself with squared shoulders and head erect, her words enunciated clearly, her command of the language dazzling. She knew where the salad fork went—and how to tackle an artichoke. She aspired to be a lawyer, and was already clerking for one of the city's most esteemed attorneys. She had turned down a college scholarship to help support her parents.

Sam was an immigrant, untutored and determined to conceal his foreign birth. In Minna Adolph, he found social acceptance, legitimacy, and the kind of love that had long eluded him. She was the door to a whole new life, someone who could introduce him to all that he had missed. She was a prize, someone to tutor him and fill in the massive gaps in his education, someone of such dignity and intellect that some of it was bound to rub off on him. His own mother had married beneath her, to the consternation of the family. A union such as that between Sam Stone and Minna Adolph signaled to the world that Sam Stone had risen beyond all expectation, that he possessed not only property but something even more elusive—class.

In the Canton of that day, it was rare that one would cross a social divide as wide as the one that separated Sam and Minna. Class lines were well marked and, more often than not, respected. In Canton, they were defined less by wealth than by the intangibles of culture, manners, and breeding. The chasm that separated Minna and Sam by education and age further complicated matters. It was a crushing disappointment to Minna's parents, who had hoped for someone more refined, and it raised eyebrows in social circles where this parvenu was viewed with suspicion. But these very differences made for a mutual fascination that fueled their attraction to each other, and what Sam lacked in polish he more than made up for in charm.

They were married on April 24, 1927—not in a temple, but in the backyard of the Adolphs' modest home on Canton's Oxford Street. Even on the marriage license, Sam once more attempted to distance himself from his past, swearing that he was born in Pittsburgh, and fudging his birth date by four years, claiming to be thirty-five, not thirty-nine.

Sam's father, Jacob, was now dead, and a new life lay before him. None of his six siblings was invited to the wedding, though some lived just minutes away. Sam feared they might embarrass him with their crude comments and common manners or inadvertently reveal too much about his own past. But if Sam thought he was free of the Old World, he was mistaken. His mother refused to attend the wedding. Minna was a Reform Jew who did not speak Yiddish, did not keep kosher, and did not observe the Sabbath. In Hilda's eyes, it was worse than if her firstborn son had married a gentile. Minna was not allowed to set foot in Hilda's home. It was not until more than a year later, after the birth of their first child, a daughter named Virginia—my mother—that the two actually met. It would remain a frosty relationship. Minna, who rarely said an unkind word of anyone, would tell me years later that Sam's mother was a captive of her faith and Old World superstitions. Her mother-in-law, she said, was "dumb."

It is almost certain that in 1933, six years into their marriage, Minna played a key role in the administration if not the conception of B. Virdot's gift. It is her signature on each check that went out that Christmas. She was a woman of conscience, a social activist whose heart went out to the needy, and she was a skillful organizer. Many of the documents associated with the B. Virdot gifts—the ledgers, the retention of canceled checks, the very preservation of those records—bear her imprint.

She had endured her own Hard Times, having had to help support her family from an early age. Minna did not know the meaning of prejudice. She cared only about character and had no tolerance for bigots or snobs. She worshipped Eleanor Roosevelt, and on the afternoon of January 20, 1938, as a delegate to the Cause and Cure of War Conference, had tea with her in the White House. (In a letter home that afternoon, she wrote to her three daughters that she slipped a number of White House cookies into her purse and was bringing them home for them.)

She saw Christmas as a secular holiday, a celebration of giving and sharing in which she took great delight. She was proud of being Jewish but wholly ecumenical in outlook. The notion of Jews as "the Chosen People" made her squirm. All faiths, she would say, were "Chosen." She was president of the temple and temple sisterhood but was equally comfortable trimming the towering Christmas tree that Sam dragged into the house each year. The tree was clearly visible to every passerby, Jew and Gentile alike. Lighting the Chanukah candles paled by comparison.

Sam was beyond Reform. The old ways reminded him of the orthodoxy in which he was raised. He openly rebelled against them. He rarely went to temple, thought nothing of working on the Sabbath, and even went to the office on the holiest of Jewish holidays, Yom Kippur. He was not ashamed of being Jewish, but he drew a line between faith and practice, the latter being inextricably linked to bitter memories of Romanian and parental oppression.

It is easy to imagine how Minna's upbringing would have brought her to Sam's side in devising the B. Virdot gift. In her high school autograph book classmates and friends inscribed notes. But the first entry is from her mother, dated January 21, 1923:

> *Dearest Minna*
> *Question not but live and labor*
> *Till your goal be won*
> *Helping every feeble neighbor*
> *Seeking help from none.*
> *Life is mostly froth and bubble,*
> *Two things stand like stone,*
> *Kindness in another's trouble,*
> *Courage in your own.*
> YOUR DEVOTED MOTHER

MINNA, AN ONLY child, had come from a tightly knit family, held together by love and common respect. Sam's family had been held together by the brute strength of his father's will. But by the week of Christmas 1933, Sam and Minna had created their own family with three daughters, Virginia, five years old; Dorothy, four; and

Barbara, one. That week, as Sam and Minna Stone prepared for their own holidays, they also oversaw the gifts that were to go out under the name "B. Virdot." That Christmas, above all others, they must have been mindful of the misery all around them. Even in their neighborhood of relative privilege, there were homes vacated under duress, family businesses failing, and worry on the faces of neighbors like George Plover, a Hoover executive who watched as the company's sales plummeted and workers were furloughed en masse.

"As Good as the Best"

A s the letters addressed to B. Virdot began to pour into the post office, it was clear to Sam and to Minna just how fortunate they were. Christmas 1933 put enormous strains on families. But, as is often the case in crises, those very strains, for some, helped define and clarify the importance of family. Mothers and fathers who had little for themselves wrote to B. Virdot hoping that they might have something to give their children for Christmas. So it was with Mattie Richards, wife of Joseph Richards.

Kind Sir, am writing to you in regards to your statement i read in the paper. i did not know if it would be alright or not but here is the true facts of our circumstance. you are welcome to come visit our home. i live in an apartment of 3 rooms- 917 4st SW but we each furnish our own coal, lights, gas. my husband is working a little but it does not mean a thing in the way of Xmas. He only makes 37 cents an hour just part time. we have 3 little children, 2 undernourished, the baby has been sick every since she was 3 weeks old. we lost 2 little boys one 11 years old, one 7 months. we are just simply up against it in plain words for clothes and anything in the way of Xmas. he only makes $12-14 a week when our rent gas coal and just the cheapest of food is bought we have nothing left. if you care to take this letter in consideration I am sure it will be apperecated i don't care for myself but i would love to see the children made Happy at Xmas for we have had so much bad luck. last year they had no Xmas- the oldest Mary 8 years Betty 5 years. Emma 21 months they each wrote a letter to Santa Claus and are expecting a great time a Xmas but i am afraid they will be dissipointed unless someone is kind enough to take them on thair heart I have never ask any one or told them our needs for i did not think it would do any good. i can not write very good but mayby you can read it. if you care to come to the house i can talk better than i can write.

May the Lord Bless you.

And prosper you, in every thing you undertake. Wishing you a Mery Xmas a Happy and proserous new year.

RESP.
MRS. J. RICHARDS
917 4TH ST. SW
NORTH SIDE APT

At the time she wrote the letter, Mattie Richards was thirty. She was part Native American, a descendant of the Wyandot, or Huron, tribe, as it is sometimes called. Mattie Wogan had married Joseph "Joe" Richards when she was twenty-one. His parents were Welsh immigrants. His father was a miner. They had settled in Glouster, the coal country of southern Ohio. By six, little Joe Richards was himself working full-time in the mines, carrying the tools and fetching water for the miners. He had no education and could write and recognize only his own name. Mattie went as far as elementary school. "Since my father was totally uneducated," said Kenneth Richards, "my mother had to explain a lot of things but my father never took that as debasing—he understood she was trying to help him."

They were a couple of few words and were not given to displays of affection. But the children knew how they felt about each other and about them. They were the centers of their hardscrabble lives. "He believed in taking care of his own and he did it with the sweat of his brow and the muscles in his back," recalls his son Kenneth. "Family was everything. It was their life. My parents had a lot of love to give. They showed it by what they did."

At mealtime, the children ate first. After they were put to bed, Joe and Mattie would eat whatever was left, whatever they could find. Joe was a hunter and would sometimes return with a rabbit or pheasant for supper. Daughter Beverly wore gaily decorated print dresses her mother had made for her from the feed sacks of the pigs and chickens they kept. "Daddy built us a house," says Beverly. "We lived in the garage until the basement was built, then we moved into the basement until the house was built." The house in East Canton still stands. The Richardses had an acre that they planted. Joe butchered the pigs, Mattie canned the fruits and vegetables. Nothing was wasted.

The Richardses were a deeply religious family, Pentecostals who read the Bible and gave thanks for whatever they had. Whatever they lacked they could live without. Joe and Mattie were determined not to let the hardships cloud their children's lives. "My mother was very religious and spared us from most things," says Beverly. "She didn't want us to know how bad things were."

The Richardses were strict, but on Friday nights the children were permitted to read and swap comic books with the other children in the neighborhood. Kenneth was allowed to hunt, but had to conserve on shells, and if he missed, his father put the gun up for a week. "I taught you better than that," Joe Richards would say. And he did. Kenneth would later become a crack shot as a sniper in Special Forces. (Kenneth retired in 2003 after forty-one years as a long-haul trucker carrying Canton's steel across the country.)

But there was no hiding the heartache in the Richards family. Joe Richards's namesake, Joseph Richards Jr., was born in October 1927. Seven months later he died of acute gastroenteritis. In September 1932, a year before Mattie wrote her letter to Mr. B. Virdot, they lost son Donald Dale Richards, a student at Canton's Wells Elementary School. He was eleven. He had long suffered from rheumatic heart disease and ultimately fell to septicemia. And then there was the reference in the letter to the baby who had been sick ever since she was three weeks old. That was Erma June Richards, born on March 16, 1932. Less than fourteen months after writing the letter, on February 16, 1935, Erma too died. The cause: bronchopneumonia. She was two years and eleven months old.

During the Depression, Joe Richards took work wherever he could find it. If that meant filling up buckets of glass on the railroad track, so be it. He never complained. In the years after, he drove a forklift at Republic Steel and, to supplement their income, held a second job in a junkyard and worked weekends. Mattie too would work, at Republic Steel's roundhouse and at the Fame Penn Laundry. But though their work was menial and their education limited, the Richardses always held their heads high. "We are as good as the best and better than the rest," Joe Richards would tell his children.

But the years exacted a toll on Joe and Mattie Richards. They looked much older than their ages. Their son Kenneth was somewhat uncomfortable having his friends meet them. "At first I would disassociate myself from them," he recalls. "I would tell my friends my parents were killed in a car accident and that I was being raised by my grandparents."

But as the years passed, Kenneth came to respect his parents, who they were and what sacrifices they had made on behalf of the family. "Listening at the crack of the door, I learned a lot about them and I learned to understand them," he says. "The first part of my life I always feared I'd grow up to be like my dad, and the second part, I knew I could never be like him, not the man he was. You would have had to know him to appreciate him."

Decades later, as an adult, son Kenneth accompanied his mother to Forest Hill Cemetery to help her find the graves of her little ones, those who had died in childhood. She carried a pad of paper and a pencil with notes to help her find the graves. Hours passed and she had been able to find only two of them. Mattie told her son she had to rest. She sat down under a tree and sobbed. "It was the most emotion I ever saw from her," says Kenneth. Eventually they found the third grave.

"She never mentioned that again. She knew where her children were. She was at peace."

Joe Richards died in 1982 at the age of eighty-four. Mattie died at home twelve years later. She was ninety-one. They are buried where their little ones are buried, in Forest Hill Cemetery.

To their living children, they didn't leave much in the way of material possessions. But what they hoped to pass along they did. "I think we got their strength, their determination," says their daughter Beverly. "They just never gave up."

That indomitability and self-sacrifice became the hallmarks of that generation. The Richardses were hardly alone in placing family above self. It is one of the grace notes of the Depression that the worse things got, the less some people worried about themselves and the more they fretted for their loved ones. Many of those who appealed to B. Virdot that week of Christmas 1933 made their pleas on behalf of others who were too proud to do so for themselves. And so it fell to loved ones to make the appeals for them.

The Pump

Among the many who asked for nothing for themselves was Ruby Blythe. Her letter on behalf of a "veary Dear friend" was simple and to the point:

> CANTON OHIO
> DEC. 18TH 33

Dear Sir:

Read your announcement in this evenings Repository, saying you would help for the answering of the announcement. Now I am not asking for myself even though I want to have a happy Christmas myself. But I have a veary Dear friend that can't afford to get a paper to even see your add. As she never gets a paper unless we take her them.

This family lived in town 1 year ago but Mr. Long got layed off where he was making a small income at the Kholers Shovel shop on East Tusc. He is 52 yrs. of age or somewhere near that, if not over. Well they would not take him on at another shop on account of his age anyhow.

So things got worse than ever for them. They had to coax for a little off of his boss that layed him off. They were good friends before he went to work there. You might know this boss at Kholer's Shovel Factory, Paul Holms. Well, this Mrs. Long's father gave Mrs. Long enough to move out on a small farm, but after they did move, they never got enough to plant gardens. They have a daughter living in Akron Ohio that helped them a little, kept them in eats, only just plain stuff. But guess she is getting low on money too. And he has tried to work a little on farms but only takes eats. They need clothes to send their 3 children to school. I got a letter a few days ago from Mrs. Long saying she'd be lucky to have bread for her Christmas dinner. Now it will be nice of someone to help them and if you can send them a little I know they will be glad and will feel like carring on. Mrs. Long never has had a very happy Christmas since I met her 18 yrs. ago. They have tried hard to save, but what little he did save was lost in the American Exchange Bank. They put it in the bank instead of having nice things like most people want, but they knew they were getting old. And their three children needed the savings after they were gone. But it done either of them any good, as they never got any of it yet. I hope my writing you will let you know your money will be needed for them. I cannot help as I just can get what clothes I need and eats myself. Mr. Blythe is working. But he don't only make veary little and if you will help this family which I hope I have plainly told you of it will make me as happy if I got it myself. As I always share what I can and whenever I can with them and others, but as I am poor myself I can't help them much.

I hope this help out of the city will not make any difference. This family lives just a small ways out of Middle Branch, Ohio.

YOURS TRULY,
MRS. RUBY BLYTHE
2104 EAST TUSC. CANTON, O.

Just mail the money to address on opposite side. Address of folks in need—

MR. MRS. DAVID LONG
MIDDLE BRANCH OHIO
R.F.D. #1

Days later, Mr. B. Virdot sent a check for five dollars to the Long family.

But there was something Ruby Blythe neglected to mention in her letter to Mr. B. Virdot: Mr. and Mrs. Long—her "very good friends"—were in fact her mother and father, David and Nellie Long. Everything else Ruby Blythe said of them was true. They were indeed hurting and the Blythes were in no position to help. The Longs had raised eleven children and three of them were still at home. Why Ruby Blythe concealed the truth of her relationship to her own parents is not clear. Perhaps she feared that Mr. B. Virdot would expect family to take care of family and not seek outside help. That was a common enough presumption during the Depression. There was also the very real possibility that had the Longs known that their daughter played a role in securing the gift, they would not have accepted it, any more than if they had written to B. Virdot themselves. As it was, it appears that they never did learn of their daughter's appeal on their behalf.

Just as their daughter Ruby Blythe had said, David and Nellie Long had moved out of Canton to a farm outside of town. Their home had neither indoor plumbing nor electricity. Grandpa Long, as he was known to the children, plowed the field using a Model A Ford. He read by kerosene lamp. The path to the outhouse was made of rubber—a worn-out belt from a grain elevator. The sole source of water was a hand pump and the cold water that issued forth flowed into a trough that served as the Longs' refrigerator. Long's grandson Richard will never forget that pump. While playing tag with his cousin, he rounded the corner a little too close, grabbed the pump handle to steady himself, and it broke off in his hand. He was ten or eleven years old. For that his father, Clarence, took the strop to him. "I couldn't sit down for a while," recalls Richard.

The pump had to be fixed if Grandpa Long were to have water. So Clarence Blythe and his son Richard drove into town and loaded a small forge onto their car and returned to the farm, where they melted a brass coat hanger and used it to reattach the pump handle. During the Depression, there was little money for others to provide a fix. You did it yourself, or you did without.

But for the Long family and the Blythes as well, the Great Depression did not come to a neat end with the New Deal, or even with World War II. As it was with many families, the Longs and Blythes would know nothing else but hardship for at least another generation. Those who toiled in the shadow of that Depression were barely aware that there was another way to live because despite the emerging prosperity for many, little had changed for them. David Long's farm never did get electricity, not even in the 1950s.

In 1944, his daughter Ruby and son-in-law

Clarence, together with their four sons, moved to a tiny farm outside Canton. Son Richard was six. Among his jobs, Clarence Blythe drove a truck and hauled coal to the Firestone plant. Their humble frame house was constructed of wood planks scavenged from homes that had burned down, and the boards still showed the char marks of their earlier use. The kitchen, such as it was, was in the basement on wooden boards that rested atop a clay floor. It was there that water drawn from a well was set in a big galvanized washtub to heat for baths. "That was Saturdays only," recalls Richard. "The rest of the time you sponged off or just stank."

Nor was a bath anything to look forward to. This was coal country, and the water from the well was yellow and smelled of sulfur. It made all their clothes smell of sulfur and turned them yellow. Years later, when things were better, the family put in a concrete basement and dug a well four hundred feet deep to get to the good water.

This was the house in East Canton that the Blythe family called home for fifty years. And for all its shortcomings, it was indeed a home, a place where family counted for much and comforts were neither missed nor coveted. It is strange to hear the Longs' grandson say of the Depression, "I have no knowledge of what they went through," given that his own early years were little different.

As with many families of that day, children

looked after their parents. Two years after she wrote to Mr. B. Virdot, Ruby's mother, Nellie, died. When Grandpa Long became a widower unable to care for himself, he moved into a trailer in the rear of Ruby's home. David Long died on September 15, 1968. He was eighty-five, and, as his obituary in the *Repository* noted, he left behind, in addition to his three surviving daughters and six sons, some twenty-six grandchildren, forty great-grandchildren, and one great-great-grandchild. When, as a widow, Ruby could no longer care for herself, she moved in with her son Richard. Ruby Blythe passed away on February 5, 1997, in Florida at age eighty-seven.

If there was love in the Long house, there was also some conflict. During the Depression, David Long's son Melvin left home at age ten and found himself living the life of a hobo, riding the rails and sharing the fires and stews of other men in search of a job, food, and adventure. At twenty-one, he found that adventure for a time out West, working in 1933 on a bridge that was to span a scenic bay. The Golden Gate Bridge, it was called. Later Melvin Long returned to Canton, settled down, and worked for Hercules Motors and Timken. His son Marvin would work in the junk business and for car dealerships.

Marvin's thirty-seven-year-old son, Jason—great-grandson of David Long—grew up hearing little of the Great Depression, and he failed to heed his father's words "Neither a borrower nor a lender be." He spent ten years in customer relations with Chase Manhattan in the credit card division. That job and his own credit problems gave him a sobering insight into the American character and what he believes led the nation into the recession of 2008 and 2009. "Greed got us here," he says. "Nobody ever wants to say no. Basically 'no' is not even in the culture. The hole in the heart will never be filled no matter how much crap you have." In the difficult months that followed, as the Great Recession claimed more jobs, upended retirement plans, and altered the economic landscape, many Americans said they were reviewing their priorities and finding that materialism no longer held so central a place in their lives. As Jason Long had suggested, self-restraint and discipline were slowly making a comeback, both in his own life and in that of the nation.

Ruby Blythe's son Richard and his wife raised two boys and a daughter. Richard made a decent living, working for the Marriott Corporation and managing a Big Boy restaurant. "You always want your kids to have it better than you do," he says. "Some of us made it . . . you still got to watch your pennies—you don't know what's down the road."

Today, Richard Blythe lives in Lakeland, Florida. He and his wife, Sandra, retired in 2003 and traveled the country in a motor home. She died in January 2009. But Richard's life bears little resemblance to his poverty-stricken childhood. He lives beside an orange grove, and has a private swimming pool and a Jacuzzi, a far cry from the outhouse and sulfurous bath he knew as a boy.

Still, there is something to remind him of that earlier life. In the 1980s, he returned repeatedly to walk the land that was his grandfather's farm. He was searching for something in particular—that old pump, the one whose handle had cost him so dearly. He found it in a field and paid twenty dollars to the Mennonite farmer who now owns the property. It was a large ungainly pump, but he loaded it into his car and drove it off. Later, he converted it into a lamp for his home in Canton. And when he moved to Florida, he took it with him. Today, once again, water courses through that old pump, only now it has been made into a fountain in his garden of bromeliads and spider lilies. For my grandfather, it was the sculpture of the Jumper that linked him to his dark past. For Richard Blythe, it was a pump. For Lheeta Carlin Talbott, it was a mirror that was hidden from the repo men. Hard as their early lives had been, they each held on to some token of their past, a tribute perhaps to sacrifices made, or a reminder not to take anything for granted.

Plantation

The Blythes were not alone in appealing to B. Virdot for help for other family members in distress. Though she had little herself, Maude Burnbrier did just that:

Dear Sir:

I wonder if in your endeavor to help someone in need, that you would consider an out of town party? This family lives in Kentucky, and is oh so desperately in need. I have always sent them a box on Xmas, but now, since I myself have such depleted funds that I scarcely know how to turn I will not be able to send them even a small gift. They have not always been this way. Only the last two or three years, but this is the very _worst_ winter of their lives. The father is a splendid salesman,—one out of the ordinary,—but because of such depressing times has been out of work only at intervals. He came of a prosperous southern family, pioneer Georgia Planters. The wife, the sweetest dearest saint like woman whose whole heart is given to her family and religious work. Five lovely children ages, —16 -13- twins 6 -3. Proud, well educated and refined hers has been a hard lot. A ten dollar gift would mean _so_ much. W. L. Brigham is the name, but please if you feel like you can, make it to Mrs. Mary E. Brigham. I wish I could tell you what it would mean to her and those adorable children. She is my sister. Her prayers will certainly call down an unusual blessing upon you, and I myself will thank you. I know God does not overlook such kindness as yours, —its of the heart, and it makes me feel so good to know so many people will be made happy by you. Would to God I could do likewise.

SINCERELY,
(MRS.) MAUDE BURNBRIER
3207 6TH ST. S.W.

Mrs. Brigham is well known among the members of Dueber Ave. Church, having lived here [Canton] seven years ago. The address is London, Ky. Box 108.

Maude Burnbrier was then forty-one, the wife of Carl Joseph Burnbrier, a plumber, and parents of three children. Maude and Mary, on whose behalf the letter was written, were not only sisters but inseparable friends. Mary was the older by three years. They had grown up in rural London, Kentucky, where the family had a farm—no indoor plumbing, no electricity. At fifteen, their mother, Sallie, had married a twenty-seven-year-old English immigrant whose visit to America was meant to have been only a brief apprenticeship as a stonecutter, but he fell in love and stayed. His name was Thomas Dennison, a devout believer and much in demand for the delicate angels and lambs he carved to adorn gravestones. He hand-cut the stone pillars that to this day mark the entrance to London, Kentucky. The Dennison home put a premium on education, and the girls, Mary and Maude, were raised to value both reading and the Christian spirit of giving to others in need.

Maude had been named after the John Greenleaf Whittier poem "Maud Muller," which begins:

Maud Muller on a summer's day
Raked the meadow sweet with hay.
Beneath her torn hat glowed the wealth
Of simple beauty and rustic health.

It was as good a description as any of the girls' rural upbringing. Together, they attended a private Methodist preparatory institution in their hometown, a school that took in children from Kentucky's backwoods and mountains and turned out more than its share of preachers, missionaries, teachers, and lawyers. When daughter Mary was young she contracted diphtheria. The fever turned her hair white. Sister Maude married an Ohio man who worked with his hands, Carl Joseph "Joe" Burnbrier. He was short, bald, incapable of sitting still, and rarely without a stogie. He tended twin boilers as the maintenance man at Canton's cavernous Masonic Temple. Maude and Joe's daughter Virginia learned to ride her bike in the dining room of the Masonic Temple. When people asked him how old his daughter was he would answer, "She was born the year before The Crash." From the way it was said and how it was received, little Virginia Burnbrier assumed it had been a spectacular auto accident.

In 1916, Mary married William Lewis Brigham, a portly figure of distinguished lineage—"a Southern gentleman" by all accounts—whose prospects for a comfortable life seemed assured. He was known as "Lewis." A photo from the year they were married features Mary sitting on a porch in Georgia holding the top to a shipping barrel that contained her wedding china, newly arrived by boat on the Savannah River at Brigham's Landing. Lewis Brigham was five years her junior, polished and, to some in blue-collar Canton, a little taken with himself. There's a story that when he was driving through a small town he was stopped by a policeman and issued a ticket for speeding. Brigham told the judge he would be happy to pay not merely for the one ticket but for two, as he planned to speed through town again on his return in a few hours.

He could trace his roots back to *the* Brighams of New England two centuries earlier. Before the Civil War, his grandfather William Brigham had purchased a plantation named "Stanley," and throughout his life Lewis Brigham proudly spoke of how high the cotton grew there. There's a picture of him at about age fourteen in a buggy with a team of horses. His daughter holds a mental picture of him as a man in a white suit on a horse. The book *Men of Mark in Georgia* devotes a chapter to one of his distinguished forebears.

Brigham's father, Charles, was a flamboyant man who also owned a three-story department store that had everything the people of Girard could imagine. When there were sales, the local paper reported, he would stand on the balcony tossing coins to the crowds below. But it was the land that Lewis Brigham knew to be his birthright that figured into all his calculations of the years ahead.

But if on paper his prospects seemed enviable, his reality was not. He was two when his mother, Ada Mariah, then twenty-four, died of an unidentified disease, leaving him in the care of a governess, and later, a no-nonsense boarding school. "I think there was always a longing there," said Brigham's daughter Doris. He was nine when his sister Sarah died of disease. His father's marriage to a "Miss Minnie" further confounded his destiny. His father died a gruesome death. It began with the removal of a corn from his toe and progressed to gangrene, which led to the amputation of his leg and, finally, his death in 1915, when Brigham was twenty. After that, the farm and its future rested exclusively in the hands of Miss Minnie, Lewis Brigham's stepmother, and she had little use for him.

A year later, in 1916, Lewis Brigham married Mary Dennison—sister of Maude Burnbrier, who wrote the letter to Mr. B. Virdot.

For Lewis Brigham, ownership of the plantation hung like a mirage on the horizon, but until the plantation was his, he had to find work elsewhere. By 1926 he was as far from his Georgia dreams as was humanly possible—in a gritty Canton, Ohio, steel mill. There a crane loaded with steel somehow ran amok and pinned him against the wall, crushing his ribs. Lewis Brigham's tenure at the mill was just a few days shy of the time needed to be eligible for benefits. He would spend a long and painful period in bed convalescing, his prospects spiraling downward.

Then, on May 11, 1927, Mary and Maude's father, Thomas Dennison, died of "apoplexy." Lewis Brigham's wife, Mary, was pregnant. She was huge and feeling sick. Still coping with Lewis's injuries and struggling financially, the

Brigham family retreated from Canton and moved to London, Kentucky, where Mary's widowed mother lived and where they could try to piece their lives together. In June of that year, twins Doris Jean and Kathleen were born to Mary. Then came the Depression.

Maude would come to the aid of her sister, Mary, and her husband, Lewis, the scion of Southern privilege. In the letter to B. Virdot, Maude spoke of the boxes she would routinely send to the Brigham family. Maude's daughter, Virginia, still remembers those boxes. "My mother would say 'Aunt Mary needs help' whenever she was getting a box ready. 'The girls need clothes,'" she would say, referring to the Brighams' twins, who were a year older than Maude's daughter, Virginia. Maude Burnbrier would then go through Virginia's clothes. "I was kind of chubby," says Virginia, "and if anything was the least bit tight it went into the box. One year she put in a dress I liked and I saw it and cried and she said, 'Shame on you, I can make you another.'"

Maude's caring went beyond family. When homeless and hungry strangers showed up at her back door, she shared with them food from her table, recalls Virginia. "I remember she had cornbread and it was hot out of the oven and this gentleman couldn't believe he was having hot buttered cornbread."

Joe Burnbrier too cared about others. Each day

he would look in on an old man, an invalid unable to raise himself out of bed.

The Burnbriers were people of faith, and at least once it seemed that Providence repaid them for their kindness. In 1933, the year the B. Virdot letter was written, their decrepit icebox (a box that literally held ice) sprung one leak after another. "Joe," Maude Burnbrier implored her husband, "you've got to do something with this icebox. It's leaking again." Time and again, he would tack a sheet of tin to the box, but not long after, a rivulet of water would snake its way across the floor.

"I can remember my dad sighing," recalls Virginia. But there was no money for a new icebox. Then one day a delivery truck pulled up to the Burnbrier house and workmen unloaded a dazzling new GE refrigerator with a circular motor on the top. "I can remember my mother screaming and starting to cry that they had a real refrigerator," says Virginia. Her father, Joe, had won the appliance in a drawing at the local Kroger grocery store.

But for Lewis and Mary Brigham, the Hard Times continued. "My mother named me 'Bill' because I arrived on the first of the month," their son would laugh. It was years before the Brighams got on their feet. But if Mary was disappointed in her man or the road chosen for them, she never let on. "Mama was never one to put Daddy down for anything," says daughter Doris, the surviving twin.

"He worked so hard. My mother always held Daddy up to the children. She could serve grits and a fried egg for an evening meal with as much grace and glory as if it had been a banquet, whatever it was. And it was never discussed as being enough. I wondered how she did it."

Throughout the Depression, Lewis Brigham was on the road, selling insurance, venturing into mountain hollows seen by few salesmen. Three years running, he was named the state's outstanding insurance salesman. But there were times when Brigham had to accept vegetables in lieu of cash for insurance, and when the family would dine on green beans and potatoes for the week. "Whatever we had, we ate, and nobody felt sorry for anybody," said Doris. "They did not sit and pick at what had happened in their lives—the bad part. We never knew the bad part. I just thought everything was perfect as a little girl. I didn't realize we were in hard times."

There was one Christmas that stood out. Doris remembers it because it was when she got long stockings and a dollar doll—a fat little baby—and her older sister Caroline made the clothes for it. That, she now believes, was 1933, the Christmas the family received B. Virdot's gift.

By all accounts, Lewis Brigham was a man of good heart, a keen sense of humor, and a willingness to follow the work wherever it took him. In the years after the first bout of Hard Times,

301

he was known by his three-piece suit, his felt hat, and his Dutch Masters cigars—but not for his luck.

On October 31, 1936, three years after his sister-in-law Maude wrote her letter to Mr. B. Virdot, William Lewis Brigham was driving through south Georgia between sales calls. A man beside the road flagged him down asking for a ride. Brigham could not bring himself to pass a fellow traveler.

"Where you goin'?" Brigham asked.

"Anywhere I want," said the man, brandishing a pistol in Brigham's face. From out of nowhere, two other men jumped into the car—escapees from a prison road gang in Treutlen, Georgia. Brigham had been kidnapped. For the next eighty-six miles they held a gun to his head and ordered him to make for the Florida line. He knew they had no intention of letting him go, at least not alive. When he entered Waycross, Georgia, he opened the door and jumped, rolling to freedom behind a pyramid of oil cans stacked in front of a filling station. The convicts got off two shots, but Brigham was unharmed—except for the bruises that came from tumbling onto the pavement.

Some months later, after the prisoners had been caught, Brigham visited them in jail. He wanted to know what had happened to his summer and winter clothes, his keepsakes, and, most of all, the family Bible he had had since he was a boy. All that had been in the car. The convicts just laughed at him.

After that, Brigham seldom went anywhere without a Smith & Wesson .38. He kept it in the glove compartment and dropped it into his valise before entering the hotel each night.

By 1950, the family was living in Girard, Georgia, in a frame house with a front yard and a picket fence—no plantation, to be sure, but a long way from the depths of the Depression. The plantation was still in the hands of his stepmother, Miss Minnie, but he was determined to prove to her that he was worthy of his birthright, that the farm should be his. For three years he tirelessly worked that land, oversaw its operations, and tended to whatever needed tending. And for three years, she paid him nothing. Miss Minnie died in 1953, but Brigham had already resolved to move on with his life. The plantation would pass to her blood kin. Brigham retained an attorney, but, as he confided in his grandson, he knew the farm was lost to him forever.

Lewis Brigham and wife, Mary; daughter, Caroline, recently widowed; and two sons moved to Roswell, New Mexico. Lewis Brigham was now a paint salesman in charge of an expansive western sales territory. Among the brands of paint he sold was one labeled "Plantation."

Brigham had developed a bad heart, and the frequent changes in altitude aggravated his condition. He had his fifteen-year-old grandson, Brigham "Brig" Knight, drive for him. Brig did not yet have a license, so Brigham propped him up on a pillow and set a man's hat on his head to make him look more mature behind the wheel of his huge black 1958 Buick Roadmaster. Wherever Lewis Brigham went, so too did the oxygen tank and the Smith & Wesson.

Over time Brigham and a partner built up a formidable business—the Southland Paint Company. Its products were sold in twenty states and afforded the Brighams a measure of comfort. But by then the demands of life on the road were taking their toll.

"He wanted to keep working," grandson Brig recalls. But all hint of smugness was long gone. "He was a little cocky, but I think he had it all rather cruelly taken out of him," says Brig. "I don't think he had it coming." His wife at one time had every reason to expect a more gentrified life, but both Mary and Lewis Brigham adapted over time. "Nobody was going around licking their wounds or feeling sorry for themselves," says grandson Brig. "But there was always a sense our economic situation was temporary. It was as though we were the same as the people that had money but we temporarily didn't have it—but we would have it again. Lewis always carried himself and looked like a man of means—he might not have had two pennies to rub together in his pocket."

Mary Brigham died in 1960. Then, late Sunday afternoon of March 2, 1964, Lewis Brigham sat in a rocking chair in the living room of his daughter's Roswell, New Mexico, house, let out a groan, and died.

The Brigham children referred to in the letter to B. Virdot would go on to live lives of public service and faith, guided by lessons learned during the Depression. Son William Lewis Brigham— "Bill," as he was known, and thirteen when the letter was written—became a decorated paratrooper with the 82nd Airborne in World War II. During the invasion of Normandy in June 1944, he helped liberate the town of Sainte-Mère-Eglise, one of the war's most celebrated battles. He earned a Purple Heart in France when a bomb went off near him, damaging his aorta. Ten years later he dropped dead of a heart attack at age thirty-four.

But even after three-quarters of a century, the Depression is neither remote nor abstract for the descendants of the Brigham and Burnbrier families, linked by blood and love and hardship. Sixty-eight-year-old Thomas Burnbrier, grandson of Maude, still remembers the Depression-era lessons passed down to him by example. He remembers his grandmother saving rubber bands on the doorknobs, and his grandfather removing the screws before discarding scraps of wood. That too is a legacy of the Great Depression.

"I am still one of those guys," he says, "who goes room to room and turns the lights out. I learned to make do with what I have. I have never forgotten. That's how I was raised." But Thomas Burnbrier can afford to leave the lights on if he so chooses. A former financial planner and broker, he employed some forty workers in his insurance business before selling it to Wells Fargo and retiring in 1997 at fifty-seven. "I did very well," he says. Thomas Burnbrier says there was no secret to how his grandparents survived the Great Depression. "They just outlasted it."

Carl Joseph Burnbrier died on January 31, 1958. A year later, on May 4, 1959, Maude Burnbrier died.

William Lewis and Mary Brigham are buried side by side in the Georgia soil he so loved, at the Bethany United Methodist Church Cemetery, a couple of miles down the road from his ancestral farm, Stanley—as close he would ever get to returning to it. The plantation has long since been divided up and sold off. Lewis Brigham's lone surviving child, the twin Doris Jean, finds it difficult to speak of what has become of that cherished tract of Georgia soil. A part of it is now a row of apartments, low-income government housing. Once called "the plantation," it is now known locally as "the projects."

Asylum

The bond between sisters Maude and Mary had moved the Burnbriers to help the Brigham family that Christmas of 1933. Others were moved by parental instinct to write to B. Virdot. And in at least one case, it appears that only that single-minded determination to provide for the children rescued the parent, pulling him back from the abyss of depression and self-pity.

John Gissiner wrote his letter on December 18, 1933, from his home at 816 Marion Avenue Southeast. Gissiner enjoyed a reputation as an honest and generous man. He had put on the roofs of many of Canton's public schools and until the Depression had prospered. Coming from humble roots in rural Tennessee, he had made something of himself. But as his letter makes clear, he was now a triple casualty of the Depression, losing his money, his wife, and, for a time, his mind.

MR. B. VIRDOT

Dear Sir, having read of your wonderful way of spreading Christmas cheer and after a short outline of my misfortune if you feel as though I am worthy of your help no one would appreciate it more than myself and may god bless you in your endeavors to make others happy. Oct -11 -1931 I had a nervous breakdown from over work. Although I blame no one but myself having had many reverses in business. November 10-1931 while I was in Massillon hospital my wife died. I was only in that hospital two months but shortly after being away I began to hemorrhage so I went to Molly Stark San [Sanitarium]—I have come back home but am not able to take care of my business in my line which is sheet metal work. I have two small sons, one thirteen &, one eight. I am trying to keep them in school. At present we are keeping a bachelors hall and trying to keep the home fires burning. You are at liberty to look up my past record. I am a member of Dueber Ave—M.E. Church and the faithful Man Bible Class. Have been having lived in Canton for the past twenty two years and have always payed my debts & have not and enemy. Never played the stock market. Not a drinking man. Just another victim with to much real estate dealing and uncollectibal book accounts. Hoping this letter meets with favor. And wishing you a Merry Xmas & a prospris new Years.

RESCTFULLY YOURS
J. S. GISSINER

John S. Gissiner and his wife, Evelyn, were the parents of one daughter and four sons, the youngest then but three years old. John was a small man, starting to lose his hair. He wore glasses and spoke softly, never raising his voice and never swearing. They were both homebodies—"gentle and meek" is how their ninety-seven-year-old former daughter-in-law Betty remembers them.

Gissiner had no history of mental illness or emotional imbalance. One day he just snapped. He leaned against his bedroom wall and refused to let his wife enter. From there, he was taken to a mental hospital. What set him off, recalls Betty, was a trip to the Dime Savings Bank on Walnut and East Tuscarawas. In that bank, Gissiner had his account, representing years of roofing and tin work. It was an opulent structure with Italian marble floors inlaid with green and gold. Its doors first opened in January 1895, and its motto, "Safety for Canton Savers," had persuaded many to entrust the bank with their life's savings. A 1928 county history notes, "It's like a government bond—it assures the highest degree of security for their many patrons. Experienced management and conservative loaning policy are major safeguards for the funds entrusted to The Dime Savings Bank."

But when Gissiner arrived at the bank, standing beside its Doric columns, he discovered that, without any warning, it had simply closed and locked its doors. Betty remembers Gissiner's shock. Her own father made the same grim discovery that day at the doors of the Dime Savings Bank. On October 5, 1931, the story made the front page of the *Canton Repository*. The headline said it all: DIRECTORS PLACE DIME SAVINGS BANK IN HANDS OF STATE: ACTION TAKEN FOR PROTECTION OF DEPOSITORS. Just six days later, John Gissiner had his nervous breakdown. Across the nation, it was no better. In the first two months of 1933, 4,004 banks closed their doors. By then, Gissiner was one of millions of Americans who had lost their savings.

While Gissiner was in a mental ward, tragedy struck again. His daughter-in-law Betty was in the living room with Gissiner's four sons and forty-eight-year-old wife, Evelyn, who was sitting in a chair. One minute she was knitting and talking, and the next, she was dead. Now her husband, still hospitalized with a breakdown and mourning the loss of his life's savings, had to be told that he had also lost his wife.

But John Gissiner could not let himself unravel. He had his three-year-old son, Merle, to think of, and the other boys. As soon as he returned from the hospital, he set about preparing meals for his sons. As a single parent, his new duties taxed him, but also perhaps rescued him from plunging into depression. From the endorsement on the back of the check, it appears that he used the B. Virdot gift to pay off the Canton Pure Milk Company.

For all his own worries, he never ceased to extend a hand to others. His son Karl's family was invited to move into the other half of Gissiner's duplex, rent-free. Later, when his son's father-in-law lost his job, that family too moved into the duplex, again, rent-free. Gissiner had long made a living putting roofs over people's heads, and now, in the worst of times, he had put a roof over the heads of his extended family.

Gissiner was also a peaceful man. Throughout the thirties he struggled to keep his roofing business going, but the advent of war brought other opportunities. He was offered a job with DuPont working on the construction of a munitions plant. He declined, apparently uncomfortable with the idea of contributing to the armaments industry. Instead, he and his son Karl went to work on a massive new construction project in Tennessee, Gissiner's native state. Gissiner worked on the air-conditioning system. Then, one day, Karl returned to Canton and told his wife, Betty, that he had been given the month off, that he had been exposed to some toxic fumes or substance and had been advised to rest and make sure he was okay. Not even he knew the purpose of the facility he was working on, though he knew its location—Oak Ridge. Only after the war did Gissiner learn that the facility, called the Oak Ridge National Laboratory, made the enriched uranium that powered the atomic bomb that leveled Hiroshima on August 6, 1945. So much for Gissiner's reservations about working with munitions.

Years later Gissiner and his sons moved to Florida. There, at age ninety, John Gissiner died. He is buried in Canton's West Lawn Cemetery—not far from the grave of his long ago benefactor, Sam Stone.

There was a certain paradox to the lesson of John Gissiner's life and that of his family. He worked so hard it nearly killed him. But it was hard work that pulled his daughter-in-law Betty through those most difficult years. All around her others were laid off, but she had made herself indispensable. There was also some luck involved. At Stark Dry Goods, she worked from eight to six, six days a week. Her salary: eight dollars a week. "I was the only one they kept," she said. Later she went into real estate and excelled as a salesperson.

Even John Gissiner's great-grandchildren got the message about taking pride in one's work. Among them is his fifty-four-year-old great-grandson Jeffrey Gissiner, who today is senior vice president of Key Bank, the successor to the George D. Harter Bank, located where it was when my grandfather opened the account in the name of B. Virdot that week before Christmas, 1933.

The Harter Bank had been closed from October 1931 until August 24, 1932. On that day, aided by the Reconstruction Finance Corporation, the bank began releasing some $750,000 to fourteen thousand depositors. The money went first to children with school savings accounts, holders of Christmas savings accounts, and account holders of less than fifty dollars each. Checking accounts were limited to a 10 percent withdrawal. The rest would have to make do for the time with certificates pledging to honor 85 percent of account values at some future date.

That was then. Today, with a staff of 120 people reporting to him, Jeffrey Gissiner heads the Direct Loan Center, overseeing all lending to consumers. In December 2008, Key Bank asked for and received some $2.5 billion from the Troubled Assets Recovery Program, or TARP, one of many banks around the nation intent upon not letting history repeat itself.

GRIM AS THE Great Depression was, Gissiner's indefatigable daughter-in-law, Betty, was determined not to let it get her down. Through the entirety of the Hard Times, she not only held on to her job but also enjoyed herself. She knew

Marjorie Gray, the lovely daughter of "Gray the Painter." They were classmates at McKinley High. More than that, Betty wooed Marjorie's boyfriend away from her. She was tall with dark hair, high cheekbones, and a knack for finding a good time even in the worst of times.

In 1933, the year her father-in-law wrote to Mr. B. Virdot, Betty was twenty-one. She and her husband, Karl, refused to surrender themselves to the economic pall. They were young and full of life, the Depression be damned. On weekends, she and Karl and a merry band of friends took the trolley to Canton's Meyers Lake Park with its celebrated Moonlight Ballroom and rides. Laffing Sal was one of the park's star attractions, a ride in the dark where lovers cuddled in two-seated cars and stole kisses as it careened around one steep curve after another, all to the ceaseless cackling of a woman's laugh.

Misery and entertainment converged on the floor of the park's Moonlight Ballroom, where those whose backs were against the wall competed in the notorious marathon dance, a dance-till-you-drop elimination in which the last couples standing won cash prizes. The marathon of 1933 began on June 7 with seventy-seven couples. The jobless, teenagers out of school and unable to find work, and professional marathoners all took to the floor that day in the midst of a record heat wave. They were given five-minute breaks every fifteen minutes, twenty-four hours a day. For the surviving three couples, the purse was a kingly fourteen hundred dollars. Spectators paid ten cents during the day, thirty cents in the evening, and forty cents on weekends to watch the ordeal.

Betty Gissiner, her husband, and their friends would show up around midnight and stay until three in the morning, taking a forty-cent seat in the spectators' gallery. "Those dancers would just sort of hang on to each other, their heads on each other's shoulders, and stumble around, and we would sit there like fools and watch them. It was a crazy time," she remembers. Crazy, indeed. The ordeal went on for 3,450 hours—some 144 days. It was hailed as a world record.

In the end, three couples were left standing, and after they were declared winners, they collapsed from exhaustion within minutes of one another. Canton's mayor, James Seccombe, handed out the prize money. First place went to Bob "Popeye" Everhard and his partner, Betty Lee Doria. It was to be the last marathon dance held in the Moonlight Ballroom. Conscience and concern for the dancers ended it, a pitiable benchmark of desperation during the Great Depression.

The marathon said something of the Depression that few wished to acknowledge: that if the Hard Times produced countless examples of selflessness and compassion, like those of Mattie and Joseph Richards, or Maude Burnbrier and Mary Brigham, they also gave rise to a passivity in which the eye became increasingly accustomed to the sight of human suffering and the heart grew calloused to the anguish all around it. In a city like Canton—and there were many Cantons, factory towns where industries limped along—want became the norm, and while few were indifferent, many became inured to the pain of others and resigned to their own. In each there was a measure of altruism and courage, and in each, frustration, melancholy, and resentment.

It was not coincidental that the sight of couples too exhausted to hold their heads up was transformed into a spectator sport. The marathon competitions reflected both the best and the worst of that era—the stamina and the resignation, the cooperation and the growing isolation. Hour after hour, day after day, those on the dance floor came to represent the anguish of ordinary individuals and families propping one another up, incapable of going on and unable to quit. The marathon turned misery into entertainment and rewarded the few survivors with a handsome prize, demonstrating what one and all already feared—that the sacrifices of the rest had all been for naught. Those who paid to watch fastened their hopes onto one couple or another, cheering them on as they would have had others cheer them on. It was the truest rendering of the times in which they lived, and the cruelty of the event was not so much witnessed as experienced. Those out on the ballroom floor were proxies for a town and a nation so down on its luck that even the romance of music and dance could be transformed into a trial of will. Perhaps the marathon was banned not only because of its inhumanity to the dancers but because of the toll it took on those who watched them.

VI.
Families
The Crisis That Pulled Them Apart

Black Hand Gang

Only in hindsight could one be tempted to romanticize the Depression, to imagine it as a kind of ritualistic purification of the American soul. It is impossible to count the casualties—physical and psychological—or to assess the damage done to the individual spirit over the course of that decade. Those who survived were often of extraordinary mettle, as evidenced by the Greatest Generation. But there were also the many who might be counted among the emotionally missing in action, those who did not recover from seeing a lifetime's work erased, their possessions scattered, or their families dissolved.

That was what made the Christmas of 1933 so special and so painful for so many. Though it was a time for families to gather together, many families were disintegrating under the financial and emotional stresses. It was a story as tragic as it was common. As the numbers of children "orphaned" by poverty grew, so too did the place of Canton's orphanage, the Fairmount Home. For others, the dissolution of one family gave rise to the birth of another, as others came forward to provide for them. Often these were not people of great means, but working-class neighbors barely able to keep their own heads above water.

One need look no farther than Bender's

tavern—not the dining room that catered to Canton businessmen like my grandfather, but behind the dark oak swinging doors that separated the dining room from the kitchen—the divide between white collar and blue. There worked a man named Frank Nicholas Margo. At fifty-six, he was a devout Catholic, a member of St. John's Church, the League of the Sacred Heart, and the Altar Society.

Once, before the Hard Times, he had had his own restaurant. Now he wielded the cleaver as Bender's meat cutter, trimming prime ribs, sirloins, and flank steaks that ended up on the plates of men like my grandfather and, in better times, such distinguished diners as George Monnot and Frank Dick.

But in 1933, though Frank Margo barely had enough to feed himself, he and his wife, Louise, had taken it upon themselves to provide for others, especially orphans. But by Christmas 1933, Frank Margo was largely incapacitated by a stroke.

On the evening of December 18, 1933, Louise noticed B. Virdot's ad in the *Canton Repository*. She took up a pencil and wrote this note:

Dear Sir

I noticed in this evening's paper that you want to help unfortunate families for Christmas.

During the depression our business failed and we lost our home. Three months ago my husband had a stroke. His right arm and leg is paralyzed. His mind is also affected and he cannot talk. We are wondering will this be the last Xmas our little family will all be together. We have two adopted daughters. The youngest 11 and the other 14 . . . frequently I visit two orphan children at Fairmount Childrens home. The one girl is 14 and stayed with us one year, her little sister is 9 and I cared for her for 6 years. Last month I visited them and they asked me if I couldn't come and get them and let them spend their Xmas vacation with us. I told them if it was at all possible for me to come after them I would do so but I do not even have car fare to go after them and take them back and buy them a few little things for Xmas. It would make them so happy to be with us and in our sorrow make us happy to — to think that some kind hearted person made it possible for us to bring joy and happiness to others. God has given you a noble and good heart and I am sure he will reward you. May you continue to prosper even more so in the future that you have in the past is my earnest wish.

WILL YOU KINDLY THINK OF
US AND MAKE US HAPPY ON
THAT GREAT DAY. I REMAIN
VERY TRULY YOURS,

MRS. L. MARGO
800 9TH ST. N.W. CANTON, O.

Days later, a check for five dollars arrived in the mail signed by B. Virdot. On December 31, 1933, Louise Margo wrote again:

MR. B. VIRDOT.

Dear Sir,

Please accept my sincere thanks for the check which you sent me. The children sure are enjoying their vacation. I am taking them back tomorrow. Our little girl has been seriously ill for the past week but today made a change for the better. May God give you good health, happiness and Prosperity in the New Year and all your life. Again I thank you and will remember you in my prayers.

I REMAIN TRULY YOURS,
MRS. L. MARGO
800 9TH ST. N. W.

THREE YEARS BEFORE Louise Margo wrote her letter, the 1930 U.S. Census records that she and husband Frank owned their own restaurant. Frank was listed as proprietor, Louise as the waitress. But in the Hard Times that followed, they lost the restaurant and much more. The census shows they had not two but five children living with them at 1009 Troy Place Northwest. Eleven-year-old Mary and eight-year-old Annie were listed not as adopted children but simply as daughters. At the time, the two girls were unaware that they were adopted. The Margos had no biological children of their own.

In addition, the census records that Dorothy Shingle, age five; Bobby Shingle, age two; and Martha Shingle, an infant, lived with the Margos. They are listed as adopted. What became of the Shingle children is not known except that following Frank Margo's stroke, the Margos were no longer able to feed and clothe so large a family and took the Shingle siblings to the orphanage. There is no mention of them in subsequent Canton city directories, telephone books, marriage or probate records, or county orphanage records. They simply vanished. Perhaps they moved away. Perhaps they were adopted by another family and changed their names.

The story of how the other two daughters, Mary and Ann, came to be in the Margo home begins even before the Great Depression. Glimpses of the story can be gleaned from orphanage records and from the memories of Mary's seventy-one-year-old daughter, Shirley.

That story begins on March 29, 1910, when an eighteen-year-old farm laborer named Antonio Sabelli, from the village of Agnone in southern Italy, set out from Naples aboard the SS *Madonna* bound for America. He traveled by himself. On the manifest he listed that he was headed for Canton, Ohio, to join Gelsomina Gualfieri, who would become his wife. She would later be known as Susie. In 1922 he and Susie and their four children—Joe, Nicholas, Mary, and Ann—purchased a farm just outside Canton. Eight decades later Mary's daughter, Shirley Crew, would pass on the story as it was told to her—that Antonio Sabelli abandoned the family and returned to Italy, leaving a distraught and crazed wife to try to feed and provide for their four children.

It is undisputed that Antonio Sabelli disappeared in 1922, but the records, sealed for nearly ninety years, tell a different story. An October 13, 1932, memo from the Catholic Community League to the Fairmount Children's Home reports that no sooner had Antonio Sabelli purchased the farm than the notorious Black Hand Gang attempted to shake him down, threatening to harm him or his family if he did not make payments to them.

Coming from the region of southern Italy where Sabelli had, he was no stranger to the Mafia or its tactics. He knew the first payment to such gangsters would not be the last.

Instead of meeting their demands he secretly went to the Canton police and set up a sting operation. When the mobsters came for their money, the police were waiting. Four gang members were convicted of extortion and sentenced to twenty years in the penitentiary.

But not long after that, Antonio Sabelli disappeared. The memo speculates that he either ran away to escape the Mob or, more likely, was kidnapped and murdered. In either case, no trace of him has ever been found. In September 1923, the Catholic Community League, in a final effort to locate Sabelli, placed an ad in three Italian-language newspapers in New York soliciting information about him. There was no response.

He left behind his wife, Susie, two little girls, Mary and Ann, and two sons, Nicholas and Joe. Susie was in dire condition when the authorities found her. She had no job, spoke no English, and was found alone in a farmhouse with four hungry children living in squalor. She had retreated into her own little world, neglecting both herself and her children.

A 1932 family history written by the Catholic Community League describes the Susie Sabelli they found: "Patient is much reduced physically, probably gastric ulcer. Neglectful of personal appearance. Depressed and agitated. Talks of suicide and destruction of her children. Supposed cause of insanity is desertion of her husband, poverty and personal harm. Patient said she wished to destroy herself, did not wish to see her children live. . . . Intense abstraction exhibits much fear."

In January 1923, probate records reveal that at age twenty-nine she was judged to be mentally ill—"incurable," in the words of the court—and committed to an insane asylum. A year later, on December 19, 1923, daughters Mary and Ann were adopted by Louise and Frank Margo. It brought an end to the girls' nightmare, but even in later life Mary still remembered and spoke of the farmhouse and of waiting and hoping that someone would come to rescue her.

Seven years later, in 1930, the census finds "Susie Sabella [*sic*]" still a patient in the Massillon State Hospital for the Insane. She worked in the asylum's laundry service. She was then thirty-six.

How or when Mary learned she was adopted is not known, but it was a secret she long kept from her younger sister, Ann, afraid of how she might take the news that their mother was institutionalized. Mary had two separate birth certificates, both dated May 5, 1919. One lists the Sabellis as her parents, the other, Frank and Louise Margo.

The Depression hit the Margo home hard. Then

came Frank Margo's stroke. On July 31, 1934, seven months after Louise Margo wrote her letter to B. Virdot, Frank Margo suffered a cerebral hemorrhage and died. He was fifty-seven. Louise Margo was forced to find a job, and Mary, then fourteen, had to take on both housecleaning and much of the parenting of her younger sister.

At about this time, Mary, a freshman in high school, discovered the whereabouts of her biological mother. One day she secretly visited her in the asylum. After that, she routinely met with her mother after school and told no one. Despite the findings of the court and doctors, she was convinced her mother was not insane, just profoundly traumatized and disoriented. Unable to communicate with anyone, she had been overwhelmed by the loss of her husband, the plight of her children, and her inability to speak English. She was fated to become one of more than a thousand asylum inmates at the vast Massillon, Ohio, facility.

It was years before Mary could bring herself to tell Ann of the adoption and the story of their mother. It did not go well. Ann recoiled and refused to accept it. The topic created a decades-long rift between the two. Ann ceased speaking to her sister. Over the years the chasm only widened. Ann married and moved out of state.

Then one day years later, when Mary was at the dentist, the receptionist casually mentioned that her sister, Ann, had been in earlier that morning. Mary was stunned. Ann, now widowed, had made no attempt to contact her. Months passed before Mary reached out to her. And when they finally met again, they fell into each other's arms. Their friendship grew, but Ann still insisted that there be no public discussion of their mother, Susie. Indeed, at Ann's insistence, the rest of the world was not to know they were sisters because that would mean that Ann was adopted and Susie was her mother.

Everyone but Mary and her daughter, Shirley, believed them to be just best friends—though the family resemblance was hard to miss. Shirley was made to promise that she would never refer to Ann as her aunt. And so it would remain all their lives. Ann took her secret to the grave.

Even today Shirley declines to say where Ann is buried or under what name. Like much of Ann's life, that too is a secret. So too is the identity of the woman who lies beside her and with whom she shares a common tombstone. But Mary kept a Christmas card her long-estranged sister sent her in 1984, shortly after they got back together. It reads: "Mary, dear, The Blessing of 1984 . . . we are reunited . . . not as we would wish . . . all the way . . . but together. Thank the dear Lord that we both lived to see this day. Love and prayers . . . Always, Ann."

During all the years of Ann's living in denial, Mary had forged an ever-closer relationship with her birth mother. On Sundays after church, Mary and her family would bring Susie home for the day. "Grandma Susie," Shirley came to call her.

Susie Sabelli died on February 8, 1961. Her daughter Mary lived a simple life but not an easy one. She made no excuses for herself. In high school she worked at Wagner Fruit Stand and waited tables at the Village Restaurant, and still she excelled in the classroom. In June 1938, when she graduated from McKinley High School, she was a member of the National Honor Society.

Two years later Mary was working as a dollar-a-day-plus-tips waitress in the dining room of Canton's fashionable Hotel Onesto. On November 17, 1940, she had the pleasure of serving lunch to First Lady Eleanor Roosevelt. Mary made a note of that experience, describing how nervous she was, but wrote that Mrs. Roosevelt put her at ease.

In 1942, Mary worked as an inspector at the Timken Roller Bearing Company but lost her job two years later because she got married—company policy. From 1947 to 1957, she and her husband, William, operated a popular Canton night spot, Naples Spaghetti and Steak House, a place frequented by the likes of Cleveland Indians Hall of Fame pitchers Bob Lemon and Bob Feller, comedian Jerry Colonna, and actress Zsa Zsa Gabor, not to mention judges, mayors, and other town notables. Her biological father, Antonio Sabelli, would have beamed to know that his daughter had helped make the city of his embarkation a Canton landmark.

But Mary and her family continued to live in one of Canton's most run-down sections. The streets were riddled with drugs. Even as a widow, Mary, five feet tall and a sparrowlike ninety pounds, had little to fear from those around her. She was beloved and protected by the community. To those young neighborhood women who had infants or small children and were in need, she gave five dollars—just as Mr. B. Virdot had given to her adoptive parents. It was five dollars and not a penny more, at least until it was repaid.

"She said they had little ones in there and it was to go for bread and milk," recalls her daughter, Shirley. Given her memories of childhood, Mary was determined to protect children in any way she could. She worked into her eighties as a crossing guard.

She had a neighbor, Dennis Griffin, an African American man who was disabled, but who looked after her in her later years, and when she knew her days were few she arranged to have her house at 1517 4th Northeast pass to Griffin as a way of saying thanks. Though she lived there for sixty-one years, it wasn't much of a house. (After her death in 2005, it sold for four thousand dollars.)

But despite all she had been through, her spirits were buoyant. In nearly every picture she is smiling and clowning. One picture shows her with a baseball glove outstretched to catch an imaginary grounder.

On April 11, 1999, some 250 came to celebrate her eightieth birthday at the Bethel Temple Fellowship Hall. Among those in attendance was Canton's mayor, Richard Watkins, who read a proclamation of appreciation and honored her.

Mary and Ann remained close. Ann was suffering from emphysema. Knowing that Mary was near death with cancer, Shirley chose not to tell her mother that Ann had died on February 20, 2005. Six days later, on February 26, 2005, Mary too died. She was eighty-five and is buried in Forrest Hill Cemetery beside her biological mother, Susie Sabelli.

MOST OF THE children who were "orphaned" by the poverty of the Depression ended up at the Fairmount Children's Home. It had a long and not always lustrous history. During the Depression, many if not most of those in its charge were not true orphans but the children of families unable to provide for them. For some, the discipline and drudgery of its routine seemed a steep price for the certainty of a meal and a bed.

Opened in 1877, its children were called inmates and were expected to work the 154-acre farm. The boys tended the herd of Holstein cows, providing milk and butter; the girls were, to quote a publication of the day, "drilled in needlepoint," and supplied all necessary clothing, as well as assisting in cooking and cleaning. All of Fairmount's children had been required to attend Sabbath services, recite Scripture, and sing. The Fairmount Children's Band became a familiar sight at each year's Stark County Fair. The home was "designed to lay the groundwork of useful manhood and womanhood in the characters of those who have been deprived of their natural guardians and molders." By the time the Margos adopted the Sabelli girls, more than three thousand indigent children had passed through the institution.

It was not always remembered fondly. Chester Young was another of those to have written to Mr. B. Virdot. His grandson, Charles, was seven when he and his four siblings were placed at the Fairmount Home. He was there from September 1956 to September 1957. He recalls lining up on Saturday and Sunday mornings, with all the other children, to wax and buff the orphanage's floors. He also remembers that the penalty for wrestling with his sister was several lashes with a razor belt across his behind. Another favored punishment was placing the children on their knees with their arms aloft until they could hold them up no longer.

Two weeks before Christmas 2002, the Fairmount Children's Home fell to flames. Some one hundred firefighters poured more than 2.5 million gallons of water on the blaze but could not save the 130-year-old structure.

Louise and Frank Margo, who had adopted the Shingle and Sabelli children and written to B. Virdot that Christmas of 1933, are interred beneath modest stones in Canton's St. John's Cemetery. They left no grand estate, but there is another monument of sorts to Frank Margo. Seventy-seven years after he trimmed his last tenderloin at Bender's, the massive six-legged butcher block where his cleaver fell remains in the tavern's cellar, virtually immovable, the consummate survivor of both fire and flood.

Defeated

Having known little of my grandfather's first decades, I never knew whether he faced anything that was more than he could stand. I used to watch him hold his breath underwater for better than two minutes. I was a competitive swimmer but he could easily stay down longer. I see now that it was less a test of lungs than of will. He simply refused to come up until he had outlasted everyone around him. Whatever discomfort he endured he never showed. He was tough that way. In his seventies, he surfaced into the stinging tentacles of a Portuguese man-of-war and managed to drag himself back to his apartment. But he never could bring himself to speak of his childhood or his father. The absence of photos suggested how much it grieved him to remember.

So it is with the children of Oscar Compher. Almost nothing could have dispelled the gloom that hung over the home of Oscar and Harriet Compher that week of Christmas 1933. The letter he wrote to B. Virdot only hinted at the depth of their sorrows.

Mr. Virdot

Dear Sir, I am a man of 37 years old have held fair jobs all my life was in the

336

restaurant business for several years. I was forced into bankruptcy over three years ago. The last year an half have worked five or six months. I have held out till last week. I had to go to the family service for food. as I have 4 children one off which is sick and wife in bed under doctor weaver's care expecting child birth any minute. My past failure was do to sickness of my wife and loss of two children. I may off managed things better had I had the experience then that I have now. I only hope for another break or what ever it takes. I might ad that I have ten cents in the house for phone calls at nite. I will close hoping you investigate as I am not much of a writer

YOURS RESPECTIVELY
OSCAR B. COMPHER
500 NEWTON AVE N.W.
CANTON OHIO

The losses of the past weighed heavily on the Compher family. There was Clarence Marion Compher, the little boy born on March 30, 1924. He died just five months and seventeen days later. The doctor said he died of "malnutrition" and "non-assimilation of food." Then there was Norma J. Compher, the little girl born exactly two years after Clarence, on March 30, 1926. She died at age six months and 26 days. The cause of death: "bronchial pneumonia."

Now, as Compher wrote his letter, his wife lay in bed, about to give birth to a seventh child, a daughter, Carol. Harriet's thirty-four-year-old body was exhausted from childbirth and the stress of feeding the four surviving children—Dorothy, fourteen; Marjorie, twelve; Betty Jane, eleven; and Donald, four. It had taken a terrible toll on her, physically and mentally.

On August 13, 1935—less than two years after Oscar Compher wrote to Mr. B. Virdot—his wife, Harriet Jones Compher, died at the age of thirty-six.

A widower, Oscar now had five children, no prospect of a job, and a brood that was all but impossible to feed. With his wife's death, he came unhinged. Increasingly, he lost himself in drink. Sometimes he targeted his wrath on the youngest and most vulnerable of the children, little Carol, the child born just three weeks after he had written his letter to B. Virdot. He seemed to blame her for his wife's death, as if her tiny added weight had pushed his wife over the edge.

On May 20, 1941, six years after Harriet's death, the Compher family dissolved. Son Donald and his sister Carol were placed in the Fairmount Children's Home; the two other daughters, in the Alliance Children's Home. Both were less orphanages than holding facilities for the children of the destitute. Those institutions would become the only homes the Compher children would know.

Donald Compher was six or seven when his mother died. He entered the Fairmount home a boy of thirteen and left a man of eighteen. "I never had no problems there," said Donald. "And I got fed good." When he left the institution on June 1, 1946, he went into the air force as a member of the 414th 9th Fighter Squad, working communications. He knows little of his father, and what he does know he chooses not to speak about.

Donald Compher has led a full life—thirty years as a welder with Diebold, five with Republic Steel, and five with Goodyear Aircraft working on navy blimps. He is married and has two sons and a daughter. But he is determined not to discuss his father or his childhood, something Mr. B. Virdot himself could identify with.

What became of the other Compher siblings is less clear. In 1941, twenty-one-year old Betty Jane married eighteen-year-old Roger Humphrey, telling him she was pregnant. It was a lie. The marriage lasted four years. Oscar Compher did not even make the wedding. In fact, Roger says he met Oscar only twice, and both times it was to bail him out of the county jail. Oscar Compher had become a drunk and was so poor that he deliberately broke windows and drank in public so that he could spend the night in jail.

No one had told Oscar Compher that the Depression was over. Even in 1941, some routinely broke the law to gain access to the local jail, where a cot and three meals awaited. "Last I heard," says Roger Humphrey, "he was back in jail." Exactly what became of Oscar Compher after he left Canton is unknown. His son, Donald, says he died in Chicago of a diseased liver. Donald did not attend the funeral. The Social Security Death Index records that an Oscar Compher died in Illinois in August 1962, apparently without an obituary.

After Roger and Betty divorced, Betty placed their daughter in the same orphanage where Betty had grown up. Betty would marry several more times and move to Lady Lake, Florida, where she died on December 17, 2007, at the age of eighty-five.

But the most tragic figure of the lot is Oscar Compher's wife, Harriet. Married at sixteen, exhausted from back-to-back pregnancies, worn down by poverty and her children's early deaths, she had, over the course of some twenty years, endured more than she could bear. Her obituary said she had died "from complication of diseases." But her death certificate tells a different story. Under "Cause of death," the doctor wrote: "General Peritonitis with gangrene of uterus." The "contributing cause," it noted grimly, "self-induced abortion, catheter was used."

When he was in his twenties, Harriet's son, Donald, got out of the service and made a trip to West Lawn Cemetery to pay his respects to his mother. Only, despite what her obituary had said, Harriet Compher's grave was not to be found in Canton's hallowed West Lawn Cemetery. Instead, Donald discovered she had been buried out in the country, in a single grave beside the 162-year-old St. Jacob's Evangelical Lutheran Church. When he got there he found it was a pauper's grave. In fact, he could not find the grave at all. Half a foot of top soil had been laid over it and the flimsy marker with the number and her name lay buried beneath. A gravedigger shoveled away the dirt and exposed the marker and the grave of the woman who had given him life and who had died so young. Donald later bought a proper stone to mark her resting place.

Nomad

For the Compher children, and indeed for many of the nation's young, the Depression meant impermanence. For some it was the orphanage or a string of foster homes. For others it was being taken in by relatives or neighbors. If a single piece of paper could represent the anguish of these times, it would be the eviction notice. It could put a family on the sidewalk, their few belongings piled beside them. For many families, the Great Depression and the dreaded eviction notice were one and the same. It set a cadence to their lives, each successive notice meaning another move.

A Mrs. J. D. McCoy wrote, "Mr. Virdot our landlord came last eve and give us a three day notice to move. We have no money to pay rent as they all want it in advance. I have moved 4 times since August and now again. It is awful. No one knows only those who go through it." Her husband was a bricklayer who'd been out of work for two years. With them lived their in-laws and a ten-year-old grandson, who themselves had been evicted.

Along with such failure came uncertainty, the sort that had defined Sam Stone's own childhood—his escape from Romania, his journey across Europe, his crossing to America, his years of searching for a place to call home. He must have identified with the many who remember the Great Depression as nomadic years. Not all families survived intact. For so many, particularly the children, the constant moving left lasting scars. It meant that they could not complete their schooling, forge meaningful friendships, or find stability in their adolescent years. Many came to resent their parents for uprooting them and grew apart from their own siblings, who were often separated from them and placed in others' homes. Like Sam Stone's, their childhoods were deeply fragmented.

Ida Bailey's family, like countless others, knew no other life. In her letter to Mr. B. Virdot, she wrote:

Mr. B. Virdot Kind Friend

This Xmas is not going to be a Merry one for us, but we are trying to make the best we can of it. We want to do all we can to make the Children happy but can't do much. About 7 years ago Mr. Bailey lost his health and it has been nick & tuck every since but we thank God he is able to work again. We all work when we can make a nickel honest. Three years ago this Depression hit us and we lost all our furniture and had to separate with our Children. We have 4 of them with us again. There are three girls working for their Cloaths & Board. I do wish I could have my children all with me once again. I work by the day any place I can get work. We managed to get along on what we made until about 6 weeks ago and work was so slow that we was compeled to go to the City for help. Then Mr. Bailey got to go to work for the State so we are having enough to eat and that is about all you know the wages they get don't go very far when there is 6 to buy eats for. We only got 5 orders from the City and hated to do that. I think if there were some more people in Canton like you and open up their Hearts and share up with us poor people that does their hard work for them for almost nothing (a dollar a day) when the time comes for them to leave this world I would think they would feel better satisfied for they can't take any of it with them and they are no better than I am. I wish I could talk to you personally. There is people in this town that have a load of things stoared away that I am in need of and would do me lots of good such as Bed clothing and Rugs. We don't have bed clothing enough to keep us warm. I work for these people and I know what they have. I have got to much pride about myself to ask them for it. When my days work is done all they give me is $1 dollar and hang on to it as long as they can. We would be glad to have you call and see us or let us know and we will come to see you. We live in the Seitner Bldg. Apt #20 third floor. Our address is #229 Market Ave. S.W.

YOURS TRULY
MR. & MRS. BAILEY
WISHING A MERRY XMAS
A HAPPY NEW YEAR

Ida Bailey was forty-four when she wrote to Mr. B. Virdot. Her husband, Fred, was forty-six. When he could get work, it was as a carpenter. She hired herself out as a laundress and maid. In all they would have twelve children. Unable to provide for them, the Baileys placed many of their children in the homes of others, where they grew up. The younger ones never quite understood what had happened to them or why they could not live with their family.

The Depression marked them for life, defining not only their values but those of their children as well. Their son Denzell Bailey was born on May 1, 1919, and was thirteen when his mother wrote her letter. By then the course of his life had literally been set in stone.

The Bailey family had never owned their own home, and never settled in. By his own count, Denzell moved twenty-eight times before he was out of the sixth grade—that was twenty-eight different apartments and boardinghouses and homes and nearly an equal number of schools, some of which he entered, exited, and reentered all within the same year. He never had a chance to make friends, to settle into a routine, or to absorb class lessons. He barely had time to unpack. His clothes were all hand-me-downs from older brothers and seldom fit his slender body.

After the sixth grade, he dropped out of school and went to work. The years ahead were sometimes no less trying than the years behind. At eighteen he married Velma Lillie, a girl whose background was similar enough to his own that he did not need to explain himself. Velma had endured the Depression, lost her mother at nine, been put up for adoption, and known little stability herself.

Without an education, Denzell Bailey had few career choices. He worked for years as a bricklayer, but ill health forced him to stop.

From out of the Depression he emerged with one all-consuming certainty: his children would not endure what he had. There would be no constant moving, no rootless existence. Whatever might be out of his control, this one thing he pledged to himself and to his loved ones: that they would have a home and one home only—that they would go to school and never be asked to move until their education was complete.

But no ordinary home would do. He wanted something solid and lasting, so he set about building his own house. It would be made of stone. Nothing less permanent would suffice. He scoured the area for sandstone blocks. Some he found in an old one-room schoolhouse that had burned down. Others came from an abandoned barn. Still others came from a nearby quarry. Anywhere and everywhere that he could find sandstone, he and his son, Dan, loaded it into his truck and drove it home. During the day he worked as a bricklayer, and later as a janitor at Trump Road Elementary— his children's school. But at night, he and his son used a pick, chisel, and hammer to hew the stones to the size and shape needed.

Every evening and every weekend were spent cutting stone. A good day's work might be three or four stones cut to size. The work stretched on for months, then years, then decades, and finally a lifetime. Denzell Bailey's home took him some thirty years to complete, and though it was but a modest two-bedroom house—less than one thousand square feet—no one would or could move it, a testament to his determination.

Everyone knew of his work—his mission. And many across the town were eager to make their modest contributions to the house as it took shape.

It was a tangible investment in a dream. People brought small stones from their travels and handed them over to Denzell, who always found a place for them. The stones came from across the country and around the world. It was Denzell's house, but it belonged to everyone who had known what it was to be displaced by the Great Depression. A Methodist preacher brought a stone from the Holy Land. Another traveler brought a rock from the base of the pyramids.

And so, over time, the house at 3219 Fourth Street Southeast took shape. And there, with its one tiny bathroom and two bedrooms, the home of Denzell and Velma Bailey's four children still stands. In 1997, after both Denzell and Velma had passed, the house was sold at auction. The price was forty thousand dollars. The buyer was Denzell's son, Dan Bailey, who helped build it and who could no more let it go than see it torn down. The neighborhood has fallen on hard times and property values have declined, but the house that Denzell built is in its own way a lasting monument to the legacy of the Great Depression.

Today Dan Bailey works as a car mechanic just next door, in a garage he and his father built.

As an adult Denzell had occasionally visited his parents, Ida and Fred Bailey, but, as Deloris and the other grandchildren recall, there was little warmth between Denzell and his family. Fred, a tall, thin man, rarely said a word and resembled a scarecrow that had had the emotional stuffing taken out of him. On such visits the grandchildren were expected to sit quietly, say nothing, and ask for nothing.

Years after the Depression had lifted, it seemed that Ida and Fred Bailey were still on the move, though not by choice but out of necessity. One mark of the emotional distance that separated the grandchildren from Grandpa and Grandma Bailey—they do not know where their grandparents are buried.

But as Deloris Bailey surveys the landscape around her today in these troubled financial times, she finds it uncomfortably familiar. "I sometimes think we are ending up in the same way," she says, fretting about our inability to provide stable homes for our children. For years she has worked as a nanny helping to raise others' children. Five days and nights a week a little four-year-old girl is under her care, and has been since she was four months old. The mother, a flight attendant and single parent, can find no other job that will provide the benefits she needs. To Deloris Bailey, it feels as if history is repeating itself.

If Denzell Bailey's house was a testament to the Depression, so too was his life. He worked as a bricklayer, a janitor, a candy salesman, and, finally, he sold Den-Vel Vacuum Systems that were installed in people's homes. He worked up until a couple of months before he died at age seventy-eight, trying to ignore the stomach cancer that was consuming him. He died on November 23, 1997, surrounded by his four children, in the living room of the stone home that he had built by hand.

His obituary in the *Canton Repository* carried a picture of him, a distinguished-looking man. It spoke of his service in World War II, his membership in the United Bethany Methodist Church, his marriage of fifty-nine years, and his far-flung family, then numbering three daughters, a son, ten grandchildren, and thirteen great-grandchildren. He was laid to rest in Canton's Warstler Cemetery beneath one last block of stone.

Mr. B. Virdot's Story: Betrayal

By 1929, Sam Stone had weathered religious persecution, a frightful exodus, a home that was more like a sweatshop, a beating from union strikers and company guards, and more. But nothing prepared him for the anguish that would come at the hands of his own brothers.

It must be said that Sam was nearly impossible to work for. My own father worked for him for several years, loved him as a man, but hated him as a boss. He could be mercurial, demanding, and miserly. There is little question that the desperate days of his childhood left a mark on him, as it did on all his siblings. One minute, he could be magnanimous to family and strangers alike, and the next, stingy to the point of cruelty. There was a time in 1943 when he was so tightfisted with his own wife that she had no money whatsoever. For a time she worked as a newspaper reporter with the *Akron Beacon Journal*. Only after she threatened to leave him did he relent and grant her a modest allowance. There are other instances too where he used money as a kind of emotional weapon. He never forgave Minna's mother, Rosa, for opposing his marriage to Minna and believing him unworthy of her. When, in the 1950s, Rosa was placed in a nursing home, Sam refused to pay for her care and Minna was forced to sell off some of her jewelry.

Once, in front of other employees, he fired his own daughter, Dorothy, then in high school. He expected anyone who worked for him to give their all, and his attitude toward money reflected a kind of pathology shared by all his siblings—that it was a way of controlling others. To his siblings he was often as demanding as he was generous. He had single-handedly brought his family out of the Pittsburgh ghetto, rescued them from a life of menial labor, delivered them to Canton, found them housing, and, in a very real sense, opened the door for them to enjoy the American dream. But as a boss he had also alienated them and set them against him. Whatever gratitude they once felt for him soured into resentment. Their falling-out was sordid and ugly.

From Sam's perspective, it would have been insult enough that in the early 1930s, Al, Mack, and Dave, his brothers but also his employees, all walked away from Sam's store and turned their backs on him. It would have been the height of gumption to imagine that they would go into direct competition with him, opening a store in the same small town. That they opened that store on the same block as Sam's—just a few doors away—had to have been unbearable. But the affront did not end there.

When I was a boy, the names of Sam's brothers were never spoken in our home. But I did hear a story several times when I was older that one or more of the brothers literally backed a vehicle up to the rear of Sam's store late one night, loaded up his suits and other clothes, then placed them in their own store around the corner. I knew that families were given to exaggeration, that stories get stretched. I imagined this to be just such a tall tale.

But in 2009, Mack Stone's grandson David volunteered that the story was true in every particular. His own grandmother Edna had told him how she had backed her car to the rear of Sam's store, while her husband, Mack, carried out suit after suit, all of it bound for Stone Brothers, a few steps away from Sam's shop. Mack confirmed the story to his son. When Sam later entered his brothers' store, he instantly recognized his own merchandise.

"That's mine!" he fumed.

"Prove it," challenged Mack.

Perhaps Sam was too crushed to bring himself to prosecute his own brothers. But perhaps it was something else, something more sinister. Sam knew that Mack and the others had something on him—the knowledge that he had fraudulently obtained a passport, birth certificate, and other legal papers, that he had sworn falsely under oath before federal authorities, and that he was not, as he claimed, native-born. Sam was in no position to bring in the law.

Instead, he allowed a curtain of silence to fall between himself and his betrayers. It lasted for years. Half a century later, a residue of alienation still separated Sam's descendants from those of his brothers.

It is likely that Mack and his brothers were jealous of Sam's success and position in the community. There is evidence that Mack would have been only too willing to use Sam's mistakes against him, even if it meant sending his eldest brother to prison. In a sheaf of letters left by my grandmother is a November 30, 1932, affidavit in which a man named Ernest W. Richman, who worked for my grandfather, swore that Sam's brother Mack had come to him several times in June 1932 with a plan to blackmail Sam, and to allege that Sam had ordered Mack to torch his Buffalo, New York, store to collect the insurance. There was in fact a fire that destroyed the store, but Richman in his affidavit said "the entire story is a fabrication," that Sam had nothing to do with the fire. Sam never sought retribution against his brother Mack.

But my grandmother Minna never forgave Mack. As principled a person as ever there was, Minna recoiled from any contact with him. "Mother hated Mack like poison," said Dorothy, my mother's sister. "I think if she had a gun, she would have shot him."

Even today I cannot fathom the audacity of brother robbing brother. Perhaps to some degree it reflected the lawlessness of the city in those times.

Crimes in Canton often went unreported and unpunished. In the public's mind, many city officials and police were corrupt. In such a freewheeling environment, criminality was seen as one of the lubricants for self-advancement, particularly in the Hard Times. The crimes of Noble Wright and George Carlin had been carried out in desperation and targeted strangers against whom they meant no harm.

But there was something unmistakably personal behind this crime. It was a fraternal insurrection, a statement that the brothers would never again be content to live in the shadow of their older, more successful sibling, that no longer would they accept a supporting role. Underappreciated and underpaid, they'd had enough. Sam had done much for them, bringing them out of the ghetto, giving them jobs, providing housing, an Americanized last name, a new life. From Sam's point of view this thievery was an act of supreme ingratitude. The brothers doubtless saw it differently—it was a long-overdue comeuppance and a declaration of independence. For all the good Sam had done them, he had inadvertently taken on the same authoritarian role he so reviled in his father, and now his brothers had broken away from him. They flaunted their newfound pride and in 1931 named their new store Stone Brothers. It was almost as if they no longer considered Sam one of the brothers.

For well over a decade the two stores were bitter rivals. Even as the Depression deepened and business dwindled, they carried on their commercial feud, dueling over competing prices and promotions in the advertising pages of the *Canton Repository*. Finally, Sam bought out his siblings, and eventually, in the midfifties, sold Stone Brothers to my father. But the wound between Sam and Mack never healed. Even decades later, the brothers' names were not uttered in our house. It was as if they never existed. For much of my life, I believed my grandfather was an only child, oblivious to the fact that he had six siblings, several of whom lived a few minutes' walk from our front door.

MUCH OF SAM Stone's life—his ambitions, his appetites, his view of money as a means to help some and control others—was shaped by early hardship: the Romanian exodus, anti-Semitism, relentless poverty, a home devoid of affection. All these took their toll. The house at 51 Rowley Street in Pittsburgh was a place of crushing religious austerity and superstition. Sam and his siblings were raised with a paranoia that at any moment Old World prejudices could seize them in the New World. Even today, some of the grandchildren believe that America could be ravaged by anti-Semitism. As the eldest son, Sam was the first to distance himself from that home and its toxins, and perhaps for that reason the most successful in escaping its influences.

But those same forces defined the lives of his six siblings, who were exposed to them for the entirety of their childhoods and adolescence. Several of those lives were marked by tragedy and eccentricity. Their attitude toward money was pathological, their insecurities in the new land profound, their abilities to connect emotionally, even with their own families, damaged. From Jacob, the patriarch of the family, several inherited a kind of frozen heart unable to show affection.

As a child and a young man, I knew nothing of Sam's siblings. I knew only that there were people in town who were to be avoided and never acknowledged. I had been led to believe that they were related to us in some distant way, and that it was in our interest to maintain and expand that distance. Three of Sam's siblings lived within a few blocks of where I grew up, though I never met them, did not know their names, and was expressly told not to try to find out.

The barrier between us was erected partly to protect me from danger, real or imagined. There was also a measure of snobbery on the part of my mother and my grandmother, who viewed much of the rest of the Stone clan (though not all) as belonging to a lower social class. They were nameless specters flitting about my childhood landscape whom I came to look upon with a mix of dread and pity—and the curiosity that comes from years of stifled inquiries.

Sam had a brother David, who at twenty-three was still living at home in Pittsburgh and rolling cigars for his father's in-home factory. Sometime in the 1920s he came to Canton to work for Sam. He was a misanthrope who, like Mack, was suspected of stealing from his own brothers. It is said he bet what little money he had on the 1948 Truman-Dewey race and lost. He was suspicious of women and uncomfortable in their presence. His sister Gussie once asked him when he might marry. "Never," he replied. "Why would I want to feed a strange SOB?"

And yet for all the toughness of those words, he was never unkind to others. He was shy and socially awkward, had few friends, and preferred to bury himself in books at the public library. He is said to have been brilliant and quoted Shakespeare at length. He worked at Stone Brothers, selling clothes alongside brothers Mack and Al, but even there he did not fit in. He drank, usually alone. He died in November 1964 at the age of sixty-nine. At first, no one noticed his passing. It was the odor that led authorities to his decomposing body, found in his one-room flat above a Canton tavern. He left no will. His paltry bank account was divided among his siblings. Until a few years ago, I had never even heard his name.

Sam Stone's elder sister Sarah married an

English Jew named Jacob Berman. Her grandson, Arthur, says that one day Jacob failed to return home from work. Nothing was heard of him for years. Then he was discovered living in Pittsburgh's Jewish Home for the Aged. They speculate that he had been the victim of a mugging that had also robbed him of his memory, leaving him incapable of caring for himself. Sarah and her young daughter, Zelda, had been left nearly destitute.

In 1941, Sarah married Hyman Shapiro, a Russian immigrant who owned a barrel and bag company in Canton. On the marriage application she listed her place of birth not as Romania but "Pittsburgh, Pa." She had divorced her first husband, Jacob Berman, just one month earlier. She told her sister Gussie that she had found a man with money and that when they counted it she would hide some of it in her skirt. She lived out her final years in Santa Monica, California, overseeing the charwomen at the Shangri-La Hotel. She walked the twenty-two blocks between home and work to save the nickel bus fare. Sarah died just short of seventy on March 27, 1953, and, as evidence of her Orthodox faith, was buried that same day at two in the afternoon at the Home of Peace Cemetery in East Los Angeles.

Sarah Berman would pass on the legacy of hardship to her daughter, Zelda, who died at ninety-nine on May 17, 2009. So miserly was

Zelda that she would never buy stationery, but instead would gently open the writer's envelope, press it flat, and write her response on it. She even reused greeting cards from birthdays and holidays, taking scissors to excise the sender's salutation and signature, and sending them out again. Her sons, knowing this, sent her cards in which the greeting and signature were written on a separate piece of paper and slipped into the blank card, leaving it for Zelda to send out without need of tailoring.

Zelda washed clothes by hand in the washing machine to conserve on electricity, bought her clothes secondhand, reused turkey bones that had been cleaned off the dinner plates to make soup, and collected used Styrofoam cups from trash bins, washed them out, and put them on her shelf, some of them complete with the indentations of others' teeth.

Her husband, a onetime bookie turned real estate investor, left her millions. But she lived in constant fear of poverty and carried with her the dread that anti-Semitism would grab her and her loved ones, even in Santa Monica. She could never bring herself to trust a Gentile or to believe that she was safe in America. To the end she saw herself as "a poor little waif," says her son. "She was so afraid. The wolf was always at her door."

Zelda donated her body to the University of Southern California Medical School—apparently in part to avoid the cost of a funeral.

As for the house in Canton that I had been forbidden from stopping by on my way to and from elementary school each day, there was, I would learn five decades later, ample reason for apprehension. That was the home of Sam's brother Mack. For whatever reason, he did not apply for U.S. citizenship until 1949, half a century after coming to America. He married a woman named Edna Cook, but the marriage ended in divorce. They had a son, Don, who was in and out of trouble. Don eloped with an underage girl, for which he later went to prison. The story made the papers. "When someone was in trouble," recalls an aging cousin, "they would say, 'They had to go away for a while.'" That was what they said of Don.

Mack's ex, Edna, drank gin and became a recluse. She made the front page of the *Pittsburgh Post-Gazette* and other papers around the country on April 22, 1952, when police raided her home at 1406 Pennsylvania and discovered her with her three young grandchildren—Don's children—living in squalor amid dozens of cats and dogs. The children had not been allowed to go to school, had not bathed, had no working toilet, were malnourished, and were dressed in rags. An eight-year-old granddaughter had rarely been allowed to leave the house and had lived like the dogs, only with less to eat. The children were removed from the home and placed in the custody of the juvenile court.

It was not the last time Edna and her son would make the news in Pittsburgh. On June 21, 1970, Edna Stone, then eighty-three, thought she heard someone breaking into her garage. She and Don, then fifty-eight, went out to investigate. Edna carried a .32 pistol. Exactly what happened next is unclear, but this much is known: a twelve-year-old African American boy, Ernest Keith Caldwell, lay dead of a gunshot wound, Edna and Don faced murder charges, and the north side of Pittsburgh erupted in a race riot. Don admitted to tossing the gun into the Allegheny River, but both mother and son were ultimately acquitted of murder charges, arguing that it had been a warning shot gone awry.

But there were other goings-on in Mack's Twenty-second Street house that spelled danger and would help explain why as a child I was to treat it as a no-man's-land. Following his divorce, Mack married his brother Al's maid, a woman named Eleanor who was thirty years his junior. The marriage scandalized the family. Then, on December 17, 1957, Mack's stepson, Jack, and a brother-in-law, Richard, both twenty and both with criminal records, were shot to death on the streets of Canton. The double murder made front-page headlines. Jack Stone stumbled into a police station, blood pouring from his wounds. He died hours later. The crime was never solved. The son of one of Sam's other brothers recalls his mother bringing the newspaper up to his room the day of the murder. "This is what happens to tough guys," she said.

That was the house that I walked past on my way to school each day. It was also in that house that Sam's brother Mack was savagely beaten, allegedly by an in-law. He was discovered by his son Jeff lying in a pool of blood on the kitchen floor, an overturned table on top of him. And though he underwent extensive brain surgery, he never recovered from the beating. He died on October 10, 1961.

Sam's sister Esther married Joseph Moidell. They lived less than one minute's walk from our front door, but I never knew my grandfather even had a sister, much less that I frequently passed her house. To utter that last name, Moidell, in our home was forbidden. There was never an explanation given, and on the one occasion when I asked if they were in some way related, my question went unanswered. Their son Arnold, or "AJ," was a businessman and gambler who played the ponies and later owned racehorses. He dabbled in any number of schemes. He was a millionaire for a time, but died broke. Two of his three children didn't speak to him for decades. Though Sam was said to be fond of Esther, I heard nothing of her when I was growing up.

For years, Sam gave sporadic help to his sister Gussie. The only thing she inherited from the Finkelstein home was a coldness of heart. She was terrified of her father. She would often say things that were "cutting," remembers her daughter, Shirley. Never did she kiss her daughter or tell her she loved her. The closest she came was when, at age seventy-five, after years of being tended to by Shirley, she told her, "You've been a good daughter." That was it. Gussie's marriage was largely a sham. Her husband, Abe, drank and was unfaithful. He had a lifelong cough that was said to have been contracted in the Old World when his mother hid him in a well so the Russians would not take him. When their son Meyer was stricken with polio, Gussie seemed to give up on life. The family lived on welfare. Gussie too had her secrets. Shirley remembers a broad scar across her mother's stomach. She once asked her about it, believing it to be from a Cesarean section. Her mother dismissed it as a birthmark.

Gussie's early life and Sam's were marked by such losses. Their mother, Hilda, had suffered at least two miscarriages, and a daughter named Rozlah died as a child in Romania. The children were led to believe her death was the result of an evil eye put on the child by Gypsies. So when Shirley was pregnant with her daughter, Eva, Gussie insisted that red ribbons be placed all around the house to ward off evil. But the real curse on the family came from within—it was their iciness of heart. Upon the death of her son Meyer, Gussie declared, "Well, God punished him because he got married and left me alone."

Shirley was the only relative of Sam's he felt he could trust. She was a lifelong confidante of his and knew some of his secrets. When Shirley was a young girl living in the projects of Pittsburgh, Sam gave her a powder-blue Dan Millstein designer suit, which she wore to the few special occasions she attended in her early life.

Shirley is warm and caring, but she too inherited the familial insecurities rooted in the long-ago pogroms of Romania and reinforced by the Nazis. "Jewish people now think we're good here in America," she tells me. "Don't believe it. All it takes is one rough leader and we are all gone."

For many of the descendants of Jacob and Hilda Finkelstein, 107 years of relative safety and acceptance in this country counted for little. As eager as they were to put the past behind them, they do not let go of history. Gussie's mother was part of the Finkelstein conspiracy that took an oath not to reveal the family's past. Her daughter, Shirley, to this day remembers her words, spoken in Yiddish: "Don't say anything. I was born in America. The whole family was born in America." She also remembers her telling her never to utter the name Finkelstein or they might send her back to the world from which they had escaped. My own mother said that not once in her entire life did she hear her father say the word *Romania*.

Finally, there was Sam's youngest brother, Al. On his August 31, 1934, marriage license, he lists his place of birth as "Pittsburgh, Pa." But unlike Sam, in 1941 he applied for U.S. citizenship and disclosed that he had been born in Dorohoi, Romania. He had a son, Jack, and a daughter, Ferne. Al bore some of the same emotional scarring as his siblings. He never spoke of his father and rarely of his childhood. "They certainly were not emotionally healthy adults," says Ferne. "I felt that my whole life, I fought to not be like my father who was—I was the apple of his eye—I loved him absolutely—he was an amazing father—but he was a workaholic. He could not easily be with other people. He really never had friends. His entire life was working."

In time, the enmity that simmered between Sam and his siblings in the thirties passed. Over the years, Sam and his brother Al reached some reconciliation. His name appears on Minna's gift list, as do Esther's and Gussie's and Sarah's. But there was no armistice with Mack. It was as if he never existed. I never met any of Sam's siblings and did not learn of their existence until well after they were all dead and gone. That decision had been made for me.

Somehow, Sam Stone navigated through all the same treacherous shoals—economic and emotional—that claimed his siblings. He did not emerge wholly unscathed. His attitude toward money, his determination to erase his childhood and place of birth, his fixation on anti-Semitism and the Nazis, were all vestiges of early trauma. And there were doubtless wounds of which even today I am unaware. But his capacity to feel and express love, his compassion and humor, these were largely intact.

To salvage these traits, he had had to reinvent himself, and not only by claiming to be native-born. "Mr. B. Virdot" was the gift he gave others, but it was also the gift he gave himself. It was the right to a second chance, to be reborn as someone else. He had spent his youth under the thumbs of two tyrants—the state and his own father. As a child and an adolescent, he had been largely impotent in the face of the terrible want and injustice that surrounded him. To finally be in a position to help others represented a sea change in his life. It was not external recognition that he hungered for, but the internal affirmation that such giving conferred upon him. It was a statement not of net worth but of his own personal worth, and the value of others with whom, despite a world of differences, he shared so much.

VII.

An Opportunity to Help

A Dog Named Jack

Mr. B. Virdot didn't just spring into being that week of December 1933. He had been taking shape for decades, in the person of Sam Stone and, before that, the refugee Sam Finkelstein. Sam always believed in repaying his debts, and by 1933 he knew he owed much to his adopted country. He also was a man of some compassion, though its source is not so easily identified. As a child no one in his family showed affection or took care of him—even a broken leg did not command sympathy. He knew what it was to go it alone, to have the world rebuff him. For years it was all he knew. But instead of hardening his heart to the world, his own hardships seemed to have made him all the more open to treating the wounds of others.

Having endured so much himself, he developed a soft spot for anything that was unable to care for itself. In Canton, he once came upon a pigeon with a broken wing. He took it home, filled the tub with water, and over the course of many days nursed the bird back to health. As long as he tended to the bird, the bathroom was off-limits to family members. It was one of many such tender acts his children remember. He also brought home an array of stray dogs, mangy and unwanted creatures to which he devoted himself. Indeed, the more neglected they appeared, the more determined he was to make room for them. His favorite was a mutt named Trixie. He first found her in the middle of the road, bloodied from having been struck by a car.

He felt that same compulsion to reach out to people in distress. He knew how even the smallest of gestures of kindness could make an otherwise brutal landscape habitable. In this he was not alone. The more overwhelming the Depression grew, the more important became these myriad small acts of caring and giving. Every child of that era has a memory of someone doing something that lifted the pall, if only for a moment. Sometimes, it was something that was not done—an act of restraint—that counted for much. The children of Roy Teis would come to learn this.

In Roy Teis's letter to Mr. B. Virdot, he wrote:

> I have been out of employment for 15 months and I have a family of eight children ranging in age from 2 yrs. To 16 yrs. We have always had a nice Christmas for the children but this year seemed to be a bad one. . . .

In the end the Teis family could not sustain itself. The eight children were scattered among nearly as many foster homes, and would not see one another for a decade. But each of the surviving children says their lives were the better for it.

One of the daughters was assigned to a "foster farm" on the edge of town, where she and a dozen other girls "orphaned" by the Depression formed their own family. To this day, they, "the sisters," gather to celebrate the good fortune that brought them together. Another sister enjoyed sixty years of a solid marriage and two children, one of whom is mentally disabled. But she has cherished caring for that son, and their relationship has come to define the meaning of *family.*

That was part of the legacy of the Depression, an appreciation of family that was more expansive than it had previously been. Families dissolved and reconstituted themselves sometimes years later. Neighbors, aunts and uncles, even complete strangers, stepped in to provide food, shelter, and stability to those whose own homes had not withstood the ravages of the Depression. And when the children of that era became parents themselves, they knew, having seen their own families scattered by want, not to take togetherness for granted.

But as the Teis children would be the first to admit, it was often the small acts of kindness that made all the difference in their lives. The children had a dog named Jack, a police dog that wasn't much to look at but was all they had in those terrible years as the family was dissolving from poverty and marital disputes. Back then, there sometimes wasn't enough food to go around for the children, much less for a dog, so pets were left to wander the back alleys and streets to fend for themselves, foraging among the trash.

A neighbor didn't like Jack showing up on her property and notified the dog catcher, who promptly responded with a visit to the Teis home.

He searched for the vagrant mutt, but at first could not find him. The Teis children were hiding him in the dark under the front porch. One daughter secured his hind legs, another his front paws. A brother muzzled him with his hand lest he bark and give the hiding place away. The dog catcher thought he heard something stirring under the porch and bent down for a closer look. In the shadows of the porch he saw the children desperately trying to silence their beloved Jack. The children knew they had been discovered and braced themselves to lose the last thing they had left. But what the dog catcher could see in the children's eyes, even in those shadows, convinced him not to do his duty and he pretended he hadn't seen them. When he drove off down the street the children celebrated.

Sometime later, when the family collapsed and was parceled off among many different families across the city, Jack somehow disappeared, not to be seen again. It would have been a crushing blow for the young ones, but in their new homes awaited other dogs, and to them they gave the love they'd lost.

The Milk of Human Kindness

Sam Stone was a silent and minor hero against the vast backdrop of the Great Depression, but he was hardly alone. Among those who wrote to Mr. B. Virdot was Lloyd B. McLain, an out-of-work executive with Ervin Manufacturing, an upholstery company. For five months in 1930 he and his wife, Florence, had taken in a family of five, providing them food and shelter. "Our happiness was greater for it," McLain wrote on stationery that listed him as the company's secretary-treasurer. Every street in Canton—and across the land—had families who put themselves at financial risk for others and who asked for little or nothing in return.

In the absence of cash, a barter system evolved. Goods and services of all kinds were freely exchanged without a dollar changing hands. Shopkeepers, physicians, butchers, bakers, plumbers, shoe repairmen, all traded their talents and goods. And it wasn't only the merchants who came to accept the bartering of goods and services. One of those who wrote to B. Virdot was fifty-three-year-old Clifford P. Boylan, a landscaper and grading contractor who was falling behind in his mortgage payments. In lieu of interest payments, the bank allowed him to spend the summer working on improving its property. Otherwise, wrote Boylan, "I would have lost everything."

Across Canton—across the country—this ad hoc system was built upon mutual trust and mutual need. (Leading economists of that era even proposed a federal barter scheme, so paralyzed were businesses and banks.) But it was the informal system that evolved, bonding neighbor to neighbor, and creating personal loyalties that long outlasted the Depression. Such a system helped form the dense core of community that became a hallmark of the Hard Times.

By extending credit, indebtedness of another kind was created. Earl J. Billings, a forty-seven-year-old unemployed plasterer, wrote: "If it was not for my grocery man J. E. Grove to carry me, would be on charity now as I can't make ends meet. There is six in my family and that means something." The grocer, James Groves, was sixty and lived above the store along with his wife, Mary, three children, and a grandchild. His grocery on Eleventh Street Southwest was but a few doors away from the home of Earl Billings. Many of the letters to B. Virdot are oblique tributes to such individuals:

DEC. 18, 1933
MR. B. VIRDOT:

Dear Sir:

After reading your article in the paper tonight, it seems too good to be true.

Many a day in the last year we thought we must ask for charity but we managed to get by.

Mr. Beggs is a salesman and has been for seven years and we always made a good living until a year ago. We were buying our home in the N.W. end on Frazier Ave., but lost that. Then a year ago in September we lost a baby boy and I was sick nearly the whole winter which meant doctor bills. In April of this year our little girl 2 years old had to have a mastoid operation. Dr. Underwood was just grand and said he would operate and would wait on his money and we have been unable to pay him a cent yet. We do have a large Dr. bill at Dr. Maxwell, a hospital bill, grocery at Mr. Brown's on Navarre rd. The last two I have been paying a dollar on whenever possible. Also owe $16 at Jacobs funeral home yet. The Superior Dairy was just wonderful and let us have milk for seven months without paying anything. We have been able to pay our monthly milk bill for the last six months but are unable to pay any of the back bill. We live in a Timken house and they have left us in a year without paying rent which we were surely thankful for but the first of

September we either had to pay or move so we have managed to pay the last three months and sure do hope we are able to some day pay back the $260 we owe them. We have four children, three boys and a girl and it sure takes some managing to provide for them.

My husband is selling sweepers and he surely works hard and what he does make it is mostly on repair jobs.

It surely looked like we would have to disappoint our children on Christmas for we didn't know where the money was coming from to buy them something. They wrote their letters to Santa Claus and it looks like he may be real and I am so sorry to burden someone else with our troubles.

We want to thank you for helping all these people and if we are not included in the 75 we will only be glad you are helping someone else. Sincerely Yours,

MR. & MRS. R. M. BEGGS
1390 ROSLYN AVE. S.W.

The letter was written by Ora Beggs. She and her husband, Raymond, like everyone they knew, were struggling. The letter refers to a home on Frazer Avenue that they had hoped to buy, but after years of making payments on the property they simply had no more money and were forced to let it go—with a mere nine hundred dollars remaining before it would have been theirs. Raymond Beggs continued to struggle as a Hoover sweeper salesman, going door-to-door at a time when no one was buying and even repairs were out of reach for many.

Not long after the Beggses wrote to Mr. B. Virdot they decided to call it quits in Canton and moved out to the country, to Middle Branch. There they had no indoor plumbing. In winter the water pump froze and would function only after they poured a teakettle of boiling water into it to free it up; son Don, now eighty-one, remembers that he had to grow up fast. At seven, he and his older brother Dale took a job with the farmer across the street and put in a full day picking corn, gathering potatoes, milking cows. For twelve hours' work he was paid one dollar. It went to helping the family make do. When the farm chores were done, he delivered newspapers—the *Canton Repository*—for a penny a copy. He sometimes supplemented the route by selling skinned and cleaned rabbits and big Red Rock chickens he'd raised and killed and cleaned and wrapped in wax paper. He carried them in the basket of his bike, along with the day's newspapers, delivering them to the few who could afford a whole chicken or a rabbit.

Like many of those who appealed to B. Virdot,

the Beggses' letter is replete with mention of merchants who carried them or accepted meager monthly payments of a dollar or less. Around the city, doctors delivered thousands of babies with little or no prospect of payment. Just as many caskets and funerals were provided with the thinnest hopes of being repaid. The Beggses' letter refers to the Jacobs Funeral Home. "It was a little brother of mine," says son Don Beggs. "He had a name but I haven't thought of it for so many years, I can't remember his name." The death certificate shows it was "Jerry G. Beggs." He was born on September 11, 1932, and died the next day. The death certificate lists the cause of death as "premature—8 mo."

In countless cases, those in business risked all to help those who could not help themselves. Desperation spawned creativity. Once the Beggses had moved out of the city to Middle Branch, their milk was delivered by Firestone Dairy. But once again the Beggses fell behind in their payments. Don Beggs remembers: "The bill got up to twelve dollars and my mother's father had an old Model T sitting in a barn in Marlborough Township and it would barely run but we went up and got it running—you had to crank it—and drove it down and put it in front of the house, and the next morning 'Cap' Firestone, who owned Firestone Dairy—he was delivering milk—he saw the old Model T and said, 'What do you want for that?'

Mother and Dad heard him say it. They said, 'We want twelve dollars so we can pay you.' He said, 'Well, I'll just take the car and the bill's paid,' and that's what they did."

But earlier, while they were still in Canton, the milk had been delivered by Superior Dairy. The letter mentions both their indebtedness and their gratitude to the company. It deserved special mention because nothing was more indispensable to a growing family than milk. Superior Dairy extended credit to many such families, and in so doing reserved for itself an esteemed place in the hearts of many of Canton's neediest.

The founder and owner of Superior Dairy was Joseph Soehnlen. An immigrant from Alsace-Lorraine, he had come to America at age eighteen and with his brother founded a wine and brandy import business that flourished until Prohibition, when revenue agents uncorked his casks of brandy. Decades later he told a grandson that watching his brandy being poured out was like watching his life go down the drain. In 1922, he lost his wife, Anna, to tuberculosis and was left with five children. Unable to support them, he farmed them out to relatives across the region. That same year, he bought a dairy route from a farmer, some empty bottles and brushes to clean them out with, a horse, and a milk wagon. Over the years his children returned to him and his business prospered. But even in the depths of the Depression, when longtime customers could not pay their debts, he did not lose faith in them.

His grandson Joseph remembers his grandfather telling him that during the Depression many families couldn't pay for their milk, but he would not allow the deliveries to be interrupted. A family needed its milk. But families like the Beggses eventually made good on their debts. In the 1950s, Joseph Soehnlen received a payment for several weeks' milk delivery that had been in arrears since the Depression—a debt long since forgotten and forgiven.

Call it solicitude or faith or simply shrewd business, Superior Dairy later reaped the benefits of its largesse in unexpected ways. In March 2005, it was struck with a devastating fire that destroyed its original building. Some twenty-nine firefighting units responded, retirees came forward offering help, the company received a tax break to rebuild, and a competitor, Smith Dairy, even stepped forward and provided milk under the Superior name to protect the company's customer base while it rebuilt itself. True to its character, though the company struggled in the aftermath of the blaze, it let none of its employees go.

Today the company is run by the grandsons of Joseph Soehnlen, serves eleven states, and employs more than 250 people. Its innovative ways have been written up in the *New York Times*.

And in these difficult times it continues to help soup kitchens and other organizations providing for the needy. "What we do we do very, very quietly and we seek out people who need it most," says Soehnlen's grandson Dan, Superior's president.

"Too Big-Hearted"

Many of those who wrote to B. Virdot, though barely able to pay their own bills, had routinely extended credit to desperate neighbors. My grandfather had been both a lender and a creditor during the hard years. Were it not for several large clothing suppliers extending him credit in the depths of the Depression, his business wouldn't have survived. They carried him well beyond what prudent business practices might have dictated, but it was predicated upon a belief in his character. That was often all a person had left. If there was an aversion to charity, there was also a predisposition to leniency in collecting what was owed. Such compassion helped the neediest survive, and in better times sometimes laid the foundation for financial recovery for the business. *Sometimes,* but not always. There were also times when such shows of compassion pushed the benefactors over the precipice themselves. Charles Winters knew about this.

Dear Sir:-

I am writing you in regards to your piece you had in the Evening Paper that you were willing to help any Canton Families that were in need, and I feel as I am one of them and when you read this letter I think you will agree with me. I am a disabled American World War veteran; and I have a family of 5 to support but find it is very hard to do with the small income I have; let alone giving my children a Christmas which they are looking forward for. But they will be very much disappointed this Christmas unless the good lord gives me a way to give them a little something for Christmas if it is only a Dinner. Two years ago I was in business of my own. I had a grocery store at the corner of 7th st. and Correll Ave. N.E. But during this Depression I had to close the doors because I was too big hearted and could not tell my Trade No, and keep on carring [carrying] them on the books with the expectations that it would soon end and I would get my money back. But instead I went farther in debt and finely had to close my doors and then move. And I have not worked for one year until the C.W.A. put me to work three weeks ago at $15.00 a week of which I take $10.00 and pay on my bills I made while I was in the Grocery. For I don't want to see anyone go through what I have in the last 2 years. And with the good lord's help and my good health, I will struggle to get them paid weather my children have Christmas or not. Last July I spent in Aultman Hospital and several times I thought I would have to break up my family but with God's help and my struggling I have held them together.

   After reading this letter if you think I need your help it will be very much appreciated; And I thank you very much for helping me give my children a Happie Christmas.

I AM AS EVER YOURS,
MR. CHARLES. A, WINTERS
1016 6TH ST. N.E.
CANTON
OHIO.

That Charles Winters could not say no to his neighbors in need is no surprise to his surviving grandchildren, who remember him as a man of meager means but a bountiful heart. Sandra Jordan considered herself one of his favorite grandchildren. "I walked to his house every Sunday after church and he always gave me a silver dollar," she recalls. "I still have them to this day. I would never spend those."

Charles Winters couldn't help but identify with those in need. His father, Amos, was a cobbler who, according to the 1900 U.S. Census, at thirty-five could neither read nor write. But a decade later, he could proudly check "yes" to both reading and writing. Perhaps he had been tutored by his literate wife, Alice. Son Charles was born in July 1892 and married Florence Bair when he was twenty-two and she was twenty-one.

Florence wore braces on both legs, having been stricken with polio as a child. She limped, but there was nowhere she couldn't reach. She was stern, not the softy that her husband was, and the children and grandchildren gravitated to Charles for affection. They muddled through each setback and difficulty, determined to keep the family together. In the midst of the Depression, Charles's widowed father lived with the family, still working as a cobbler and taking in repairs until his death.

It could be said that Charles's willingness to help others eventually cost him his life. He had a severe heart condition but insisted on pitching in to paint his son's new home on Tyler Avenue. It was then, in 1959, that he was felled with a heart attack, from which he died soon after. "Grandpa had a big heart," says his granddaughter Sandra.

Charles Winters and his descendants have never had it easy, but they didn't expect it to be otherwise. Tragedy, illness, layoffs—and big hearts—run in the family. (One of Winters's sons, Arthur, was killed in World War II.) Charles Winters's son Charles Jr. had five children—four biological, one adopted. But he could never afford a car—he walked or took the bus everywhere. He was often furloughed from his job, even when it seemed the rest of the country prospered. He worked at Canton Drop Forge, grinding steel for a living. He never fully recovered from an industrial accident there that shattered his leg.

His daughter Sandra, now sixty-seven, manages a convenience store and filling station, and is saving money to visit her son in Dallas. "My husband worked at a steel mill and got laid off quite often," she says. "I just learned to live frugal. Most of my kids are the same way. They have learned when there are hard times you got to be careful."

Like many children whose parents grew up during the Depression, sisters Sandra and Carol inherited a scaled-down map of life. Christmas in the Winters home was special, never because of the volume of presents but because it was time shared. "What we got was enough for us," says Carol.

Enough was a byword of the Depression. It was less a measure of what one had than what one was made of. It was about conservation, not consumption. *Enough* was a word around which an entire family could rally, a gesture of faith but also of defiance. It was to count one's blessings aloud, to shore up the soul, and to hold despair at bay.

"We had a good life, whether my dad was out of work or not," remembers Carol. "We are happy. We have each other. We love each other. We survive, we survive."

It was and is enough.

Shipmates

Sam learned many lessons in the first years of the Depression when he saw his business wither, his debts deepen, and his way of life imperiled. None was more important than the realization that the town's survival and return to prosperity was tied to the well-being of the entire community. The old clannish alignments by class, ethnic group, and national origin would no longer suffice. No one, not the Timkens, the Hoovers, or the Beldens, was immune to the poverty and despair engulfing the city. Like rising waters, it threatened to wash away one and all. The storefronts would remain vacant, the mills and plants nearly deserted, the town an economic wasteland, as long as so many were down-and-out. There was a new imperative emerging and it was based on community. B. Virdot's gift, while voluntary, recognized that something was both expected of every citizen and due every citizen. Before the Depression drew to a close, the generation that came of age in the Hard Times would soon be called upon to make extraordinary sacrifices, but they had already come to appreciate both the importance of individual courage and the indispensability of common purpose.

Such values were a part of everyday life in the home of Nora Romesberg. Her letter to B. Virdot:

Dear Sir, a kind neighbor showed me this article in the paper and I believe in prayers being answered.

My husband has been out of work, he even applied on the CWA thinking he could get a pay check before Christmas but it is of no avail. My children are like any other children but instead of toys they need clothing.

If you doubt this statement come down and investigate because if you see our living conditions you will certainly understand. . . . Sorry to say but I do not know where my next month's rent is coming from. If you don't help us in this way maybe you could aid in getting my husband some kind of employment.

SIGNED
MRS. NORA ROMESBERG

Nora Romesberg lived to be ninety-four. Her son Clyde, now eighty-eight, was thirteen that Christmas of 1933. Always when he returned home from school he took off his shoes to conserve the soles. The boys slept on the floor—there were no beds or mattresses, just blankets. At night before the kerosene lamp was doused, their mother and father would take turns reading to them from the Bible. Clyde remembers being embarrassed by the bright patterns in the shirts he wore to school, cut from his mother's worn-out dresses. He remembers that his birthday was an occasion for joking, not presents. But as part of his job for Western Union, he would bicycle to the city's outskirts, a telegram in his hat, and sing "Happy Birthday" to wealthier citizens. Dressed in a snappy uniform, he also worked as an usher, taking patrons down the aisles of the fabulous Palace Theater.

He remembers too how neighbors pulled together to get through those times. The homes were heated by coal, but there was seldom enough money to buy it. So the neighborhood boys would go down to where the B&O Railroad ran and search along the tracks for coal that had fallen off passing trains. They carried burlap sacks and divided among themselves what they could scavenge. "We all worked together," recalled Romesberg. "You had certain obligations." A policeman was stationed at the rail yard to ensure that no one took coal off the open cars, though he often pitied the boys and, with his arm, appeared to "accidentally" bump a few extra lumps of coal onto the tracks. They quickly disappeared into the closest burlap sack.

For Clyde Romesberg and his family, the desperate search for coal to keep warm carried with it a personal irony. Clyde Romesberg's father was an out-of-work coal miner.

The hardship Clyde Romesberg experienced and

the fellowship that was borne of sharing those hardships with so many others defined him as a man and prepared him to endure with quiet dignity even the worst travails of World War II. During his two and a half years in the navy, Romesberg served on an aircraft carrier, the USS *Santee*. At 7:40 A.M. on October 25, 1944, a Japanese suicide bomber carrying a 63-kilogram bomb hit the *Santee*'s flight deck. Romesberg took shrapnel to the head and hand. Blood poured from his wounds. Sixteen minutes later, a torpedo fired from a Japanese sub struck the ship, flooded compartments, and caused it to list 6 degrees. Flames erupted and crew members were burned clear down to the bone. Romesberg, the shrapnel still in his forehead, found himself applying ointment to other men's burns and dressing their wounds. They were worse off and needed tending, and only by acting together could the ship be righted and the crew saved.

Today Romesberg is said to be a part of the Greatest Generation, but it is a generation whose cohesiveness and grit took shape during the Great Depression. Romesberg saw his actions aboard the *Santee* not as heroism but as an extension of the lessons he learned along the railroad tracks. "There was a different feeling then," he says. "You felt united. You endured the same thing." He is a humble man, but unable to resist an observation about the present. "We were made of better stuff," he says.

Doctors

Whatever could befall a soul in good times—illness, loss of loved ones, disabling injuries—did so in bad times as well. No one understood that better than Florence Cunningham, unless perhaps it was the doctor who tended to her family. On December 19, 1933, she took out half of a sheet of lined paper and a pencil and wrote to B. Virdot:

> I am righting in regards to the piece in the Repository about helping some unfortunate people. I am a widow with 5 small children. My husband has been dead a year last Aug. He had no work for two years before that and I was left pennyless no insurance. I am not able to work myself. For the last 8 weeks have had sickness. The children have had chicken pox. The one child had pneumonia. 3 boys yellow jaundice and now 2 are down with the gripp. Dr. Werley has taken care of them. And so far I have not had any income for a year and it surly is heart breaking to have children whom is use to having a nice Xmas and to no that so far There is no signs of any here this Xmas. The Family Services gives us grocers and coal and god

no's I am glad for that but the help you offer would be a god send to us or any one in my condiction. You can investicate as far as you'd like. My husband was a painter contractor and we saw better days but I have had to sell most everything I had for help.

MRS. JOS. CUNNINGHAM
CITY, 1030 CHERRY AVE, N.E.

At the time Florence Cunningham wrote her note she was thirty-eight. Her husband, Joseph, who had helped paint the interior of the Palace Theater, was forty-seven when, on August 29, 1932, he succumbed to kidney failure. Now widowed, Florence was left with daughters Margaret, eleven, and Virginia, five; and sons Joseph, ten, Willard, eight, and Robert, three.

To her aid came Dr. Lloyd H. Werley, a Canton physician and surgeon who, like many of his peers, ministered to the poor knowing payment was unlikely. Amid such emotional and financial desolation, Florence Cunningham and her children looked to Dr. Werley for more than just medical care. He and his kind provided sorely needed evidence that someone cared about them.

OTHER PHYSICIANS TOO donated their time to the needy. In the early years of the Depression, the Stark County Dental Society repeatedly hosted clinics to treat the poor in Canton's municipal auditorium. Several times a year, dentists walked away from their private practices and devoted afternoons to seeing those unable to pay for such visits. In 1932, physicians saw some twenty-three thousand patients at a Canton city clinic—seven thousand more than the year before.

During those toughest of days in 1933, thousands of surgeries were performed across Canton without any prospect of payment—and there was no Medicaid reimbursement. There were many such unheralded heroes, and their names crop up in letter after letter. Among these was Dr. Guy B. Maxwell. He died three years later. Other physicians too were appreciatively mentioned in the B. Virdot letters for tending to those who had no means of paying for their services. Among these were Dr. John H. Underwood and Dr. Zadock Atwell.

Deep into the Depression, Dr. Atwell was overcome by debt, and he and his wife sought to collect from those whom he had treated without payment. Atwell's wife, May, called upon the homes of those whose babies he had delivered for free. But the families had nothing to pay her with, and Atwell ultimately lost his own home. It was a crushing blow. In 1933, at the time the letters cited his kindness, he was sixty-seven.

• • •

BUT FOR THE small acts of kindness by ordinary citizens, whether the dogcatcher, the dairyman, or the doctor, the Depression might well have been insufferable. Every family that endured the Hard Times had a memory of someone who took a chance on them, carried them on credit, or looked past their tattered coats and overalls and treated them as they would have wished to be treated. That was the message B. Virdot sought to send that Christmas, that even those most down on their luck were part of the community and that the well-being of one was of concern to all. It was the message Clyde Romesberg carried with him from the Depression—the fate of his embattled ship rested in the hands of the entire crew.

For Sam Stone, unlikely Santa that he was, the B. Virdot gift was, I believe, a reflection not merely of a Yuletide spirit but of what he had come to believe was part of the character of the nation that had taken him in. In the Old World, no one had been less wanted than the wandering Romanian Jews, but even they had found a home here. Reaching out to the dispossessed was a quintessentially American act, and though Sam never acknowledged that he was himself an immigrant, he often cited the country's willingness to take in those of other lands. By extending a hand to the needy that Christmas, I believe he was both making a payment on an old debt and participating in a distinctly American rite—that of sharing the bounty of the new land with others.

His faith in America could only have been reaffirmed by the selflessness of the letters addressed to B. Virdot. Many came from those who had little themselves but sought help only for others—neighbors, friends, family. Frances Lindsay, whose husband, James, was a clerk for the Pennsylvania Railroad, hoped B. Virdot would help out their neighbors, the family of Willis and Minnie Evans, who for years had put away every spare penny in the bank only to lose it all when the bank failed. Evans was a carpenter who'd been out of work for three years. Her letter concluded, "folks like us have no reason to ask for help . . . but you can inquire anywhere here and you'll find these folks 'All Americans.'" So genuine was their concern for others that the Lindsays did not even include their own return address.

Mr. B. Virdot's Story: A Second Gift, 1940

There was little Sam Stone wanted more than to be a part of his adopted country, but perhaps he did not always understand or appreciate what that required of him. America was a country of laws and processes. It offered a clear path to naturalization. But he had come from a place where the rights of citizenship could be conferred or withdrawn at the state's whim. Generations could live on the same plot of land, and, in the time it took to sign an edict, be reduced to trespassers and aliens. His early years had taught him to distrust the state. I can't say with certainty what was in his mind when he chose to create that fictional autobiography. It was clearly unlawful, but it may have had some rationale rooted in the insecurities of his youth. If the state could take away so much with the stroke of a pen, why should he not be able to restore it with the stroke of his own pen?

In 1921, Sam Stone had persuaded suspicious government bureaucrats to issue him a passport. At the time, it seemed a triumph. The matter of his citizenship had been disposed of once and for all, he thought. After all, a passport is proof of citizenship—unless it's obtained by fraud. For two decades the matter of his citizenship went unquestioned. Sam was living an exemplary American life, a good and loving father and husband, a veteran, a solid provider to his family—immediate and extended—a highly respected member of the community, a man of deep patriotic feeling.

But not even snug little Canton provided safe haven from the events unfolding a world away. In 1940 the specter of another cataclysmic war crept across the Old World. Sam had hoped he had left such horrors behind. Now those same forces threatened to unravel all that he had won—his position, his identity, his honor, and even his freedom.

In June of that year the United States enacted the Alien Registration Act, or Smith Act, as it was known. Coming on the heels of the annexation of Czechoslovakia and the nonaggression pact between Germany and the Soviet Union, it criminalized calls for the violent overthrow of the U.S. government. But it also required all those of foreign birth over fourteen years of age and residing in America for thirty days or more to register and be fingerprinted. Failure to comply meant prosecution, fines, and up to six months in prison. Those who were found to make false statements on the forms and had been in the country for five years or less faced deportation. The provisions sent a chill through the immigrant community. Within four months of its passage, 4.7 million aliens had registered.

But Sam Stone was not among them. He had let the four-month window come and go, undoubtedly tormented by the dilemma he now faced. It was a situation entirely of his own making. If he continued to ignore the registration requirements and cling to the fallacy of his Pittsburgh birth, he risked being found out, prosecuted, and jailed. But if he came forward and admitted that all the affidavits, birth records, and passports were the products of his own deception, he would have to face possible legal consequences as well as public humiliation.

Either way, the stakes were enormous. How would he explain himself to his three young daughters, to his wife, to the community? And just as weighty, after so many years, would he find himself reduced once again to Sam Finkelstein, the penurious Romanian refugee, the undesirable? There was that word again—*alien*—the word that Romania used to strip the Jews of all rights and legitimacy. Now it was the U.S. government that used the word and threatened to take away all that he had.

It is not clear how much even his wife, Minna, knew. Given her legal acumen and ability to slice through deception, it is likely that she knew at least some elements of the truth. The protective way in which she responded to my questions decades later—her demand that I drop my inquiry—was further evidence that even if she did not know the particulars of Sam's deception, she knew something was amiss about his past. Whatever she knew would have made her profoundly uncomfortable. She vigorously defended and supported Sam, but she was also a stickler for the truth. When I was five or six, I once told her a lie and was found out. She marched me into the bathroom and washed my mouth out with Ivory soap while lecturing me on the corrupting nature of lies.

And yet, from the correspondence that was discovered among her personal papers in 2009, it is clear that she played a role in counseling Sam and acted as a liaison between him and the lawyers he retained to help him decide a course of action. In 1940, after the four-month registration deadline had passed, Sam retained a Dayton, Ohio, attorney named Samuel Finn. He was a perfect choice—the son of Russian Jewish immigrants, and just far enough removed from Canton so as to not attract his neighbors' attention or suspicion. In the succeeding months Finn would meet privately with the Immigration commissioner exploring Sam's options, but without revealing Sam's identity. The commissioner told him a legitimate passport was itself proof of citizenship. The operative word was *legitimate*.

Apparently unaware of Sam's innumerable deceptions, Finn attempted to track down the proof that Minna and Sam had provided him documenting Sam's birth in Pittsburgh. The chief piece of evidence was an official-looking birth certificate, which had been signed April 25, 1921, in Pittsburgh, Pennsylvania. The record gives his name as "Sam Stone," and says that he was born at 29 Gum Street in Pittsburgh on March 9, 1889. His parents are listed as Jacob and Hilda Stone, both born in Russia. It even lists the midwife who delivered him—"H. Sandusky." Three weeks after his birth, on April 1, 1889, the record indicates that he left America with his parents and returned to Europe. At the bottom of the document appears the name of "J. H. Harkins, Clerk, Department of Public Health, who attests that the record is to be found in the Birth Register." The record even included the exact site of the original document—volume 376, page 291.

But Pittsburgh authorities informed Sam's lawyers that there was no such record of his birth on that page or any other page. There was indeed a famous Pittsburgh midwife named Hannah Sandusky, known variously as "Bobba Hannah" (Bobba is Yiddish for "Granny"), "the Angel," and "the Saint." The Lithuanian immigrant delivered more than thirty-five hundred babies in Pittsburgh, the last one in 1909 when she was eighty-two. But she had died in November 1913, eight years before Sam submitted the birth certificate. With her death and the absence of any public record, there was no support for the legitimacy of his certificate. Finn and his associates conducted a thorough search of Pittsburgh records and found nothing to bolster Sam's claim. They apparently were unaware that they had been sent on a fool's errand. Sam knew full well that his documents were fabricated.

Two decades earlier, in creating this fictional autobiography and the records to support it, he had allowed himself to act out of fear or impatience, or both. Whether he had been spooked by the hysteria of the Red Scare or duped himself into thinking that he could confer citizenship on himself with a drawer full of false documents, I will never know. What is clear is that the decisions he made that had once seemed expedient would later cause him untold anxiety. B. Virdot had been a role he could assume one week and discard the next. He defined that part; it did not define him. That was not so with the tangled autobiography he had created as a young man. What he had authored long ago would not release him from its grip. In middle age and later years it continued to threaten him, to put his public reputation, his stature in the family, and even his personal freedom at risk. By the 1940s, he recognized it for what it was: a Faustian bargain that could come due at a moment's notice.

It appears that Minna and Sam had a heart-to-heart about what to do. Among Minna's papers is the alien registration form, filled out in pencil. In it, Sam wrote that he was born in Pittsburgh, but added this revealing sentence: "My family and my personal recollections are these: my parents had emigrated in or about 1888 and during their residence here I was born but having no proof am registering in a desire to comply with the law in any eventuality." But by then Sam had become hopelessly ensnared in his own scheme. He could not fall back on a faulty memory when he had personally fabricated a fraudulent birth certificate, complete with forged signatures, and then parlayed that into a series of passports and other sworn declarations that were patently false and contradictory. The registration form filled out in pencil was never submitted.

There was now no innocent explanation and no way to invoke confusion or faulty memory as a defense. The record was one of deliberate and calculated deception. At that late date, the web of lies would not admit good-faith error or parental miscommunication. In the end, he fell back on his old strategy: holding fast to the lie. And he got away with it, if you can call living decades in uncertainty and anxiety getting away with it.

Reading the correspondence between Minna and the attorneys, I finally understood why she had felt so threatened by my inquiries into Sam's past, and was so insistent that I give her my word that I would not pursue it. It was not only Sam's good name at stake but her own as well. Out of her desire to protect her husband, she had allowed herself to be compromised, to enter into a kind of conspiracy with him. Her entire life, Minna had been a model of probity and forthrightness. Taking up Sam's cause must have pained her greatly. The prospect of having the truth discovered by her own grandson, an investigative reporter, the one in whom she had invested so much ethical energy and teaching, would have pained her greatly. The promise she extracted did not bar me for life from pursuing the truth, but only protected her for the duration of her life from having to answer to me.

AT THE SAME time that Sam fretted over the Alien Registration Act, a world away in Dorohoi, things were quickly unraveling for the remaining five thousand Jews. The Christians in town received warning that the Jews were to be targeted and were advised to put religious icons in their windows so that the mayhem would pass them by. The next day, July 1, 1940, as many as two hundred Jewish residents were murdered, their homes looted, their bodies picked over and left in the streets. The victims' families were forced to sign statements that the assailants had been unknown to them. The pogrom was only the first step in what would become a systematic effort to exterminate Dorohoi's Jews. Such actions were being played out across the continent. Hitler was on the move. For Sam Stone, such news rekindled his worst childhood nightmares.

Sam and his siblings, indeed even many of their descendants, were so scarred by the experience of Romanian persecution and the accounts of Nazi horrors that they forever feared being sent back. Among them there was a sense that no matter how calm the surface, there always stirred, just beneath, the very real threat of a violent anti-Semitic eruption—even here in America. My grandfather said as much to me more than once. Call him paranoid or irrational, but history suggested otherwise. Against this wider canvas, the specter of persecution and the fear of prison or deportation, baseless or not, rose up inside him. The dread of being returned to that world against his will—or of it now reaching into the New World—was part of the Stone family's emotional makeup. There weren't enough miles to place them beyond such fears.

But rather than cower at the news, Sam chose to express his solidarity with those who were trying to stop Hitler and put an end to his maniacal anti-Semitism. In late May and early June hundreds of thousands of French and British soldiers had been evacuated from the shores of Dunkirk, and London had become a target of German bombing. So on October 5, 1940, even as he was mired in his own citizenship issues, Sam Stone wrote a letter to the British ambassador to the United States, Lord Lothian:

Honorable Sir:-

The punishment and torture inflicted on the London civilians seems incredible for human beings to endure, and yet these civilians endure them with a courage that compels admiration for everyone that still values freedom.

Impelled by such admiration plus the realization that your struggle today is a barrier to our struggle tomorrow, it is my desire that in addition to a cash contribution (see enclosed copy of letter) to forward direct to London civilians fifty new overcoats, and I will greatly appreciate your informing me of the proper agencies to whom these garments can be forwarded so that they can be distributed to London civilians,

I pray for your worthy cause. . . .

That week, Sam Stone anonymously paid for an Allied Relief Fund ad to appear in the October 13, 1940, *Canton Repository*, which produced additional contributions. And though the British Embassy in Washington knew his identity—a concession he made to the necessity of arranging the shipment of wool coats—no one else did. Once again, the *Canton Repository* wrote an article about this anonymous donor, under the headline, A

GESTURE OF FREEDOM—DEMOCRACY LOVING CANTONIAN SENDS 50 COATS TO ENGLAND.

Into a pocket of each of the coats bound for London, Sam Stone placed a typed letter. It read:

CANTON, OHIO, U.S.A.
DECEMBER 26, 1940

To a Briton:-

This gift comes to you from one who is fortunate to live in a country where faith in democracy—in decency and dignity of men can still be reaffirmed. Please accept it not in a spirit of appreciation, but as a humble thanksgiving for your heroic efforts, so the enslavement, the political and social regimentation would not be extended throughout the continent of Europe and possibly the world.

Here in the United States we realize that our heritage of Democracy and freedom is at stake, and greatly depends upon the outcome of the battle across the sea, impelled by such realization, Americans who believe in the things which make life worth living for free men, have banded together in a great cause of "AID TO BRITAIN".

. . . I hope that you continue your spirit,

high and strong, and with firm belief in
"THAT WHICH IS RIGHT WILL
SURVIVE, THAT WHICH IS WRONG
WILL PERISH", I will close with unshaken
faith in the British, who have risen as by a
single impulse—to Defend.

YOURS FOR VICTORY, I AM

Sam was an able wordsmith, especially considering his limited formal education, and he often spoke in dramatic tones about the virtues of democracy. But the eloquence of this letter, with its rhetorical flourishes, was likely also the work of my grandmother Minna, who was widely read and had a formidable vocabulary. Most likely, they authored the letter together, Sam providing the passion, and Minna, the oratorical high notes. From Sam's point of view, the British were all that stood between the darkness he had grown up with and the America he had grown to love.

But Sam Stone's concern for the British was not unique. By the end of 1940, the English War Relief Society reported that some twenty-five thousand coats were ready to be shipped from America to England, many of them coming from this nation's clothiers and manufacturers. And among those who pitched in to aid the Brits were Sam's daughters, Virginia and Dorothy, then twelve and ten. They are pictured in the *Canton Repository*

410

among twenty-five girls "bending earnestly over knitting needles, working white, navy blue and olive green colored yarns into sea boots, scarfs, sweaters, wristlets and caps and mufflers," all of which were to go to the British War Relief Society.

It was not only the individuals of Canton who reached out to the vulnerable but businesses as well. The Hoover Company arranged for eighty-four British children of its employees in England and Scotland to live with Hoover Company families and others in Canton for the duration of the war. Around town that Christmas Eve, in keeping with their homeland's customs, the children hung pillowcases from the bedposts (instead of stockings) in expectation of Santa's arrival.

VIII.

A Merry and Joyful Christmas

Not long after the war ended, Sam and Minna bought a home in Florida, wintering in Golden Beach and spending their summers at the lake house in Ohio. Sam sold his clothing stores and, taking advantage of the real estate boom in Florida, helped develop Hollywood and Miami Shores. By the early 1950s they were living in an oceanfront apartment in the Carlton Terrace in Bal Harbour. That a man whose childhood was rooted in such hardship should come to enjoy such a retirement was a testament to his resourcefulness but also to that of the country that had made a place for him and so many other immigrants undesired by other nations. Throughout Florida, there were others from Canton who had written to B. Virdot in the terrible years of the Depression and who now, two decades later, shared in a retirement that had once seemed unattainable.

For Sam, those years were filled with irony. From his balcony he could look out across the Atlantic from where he had come half a century earlier. But in another sense, he did not have far to look to see where he was from. The building next door was the eight-story Kenilworth House, and it was, in the vernacular of the late fifties, "restricted." That meant Jews were not allowed to live there. It was something of an anomaly in that area, which had drawn so many Jews, including many Holocaust survivors, that here in plain view was a testament to the New World's brand of gentrified anti-Semitism.

From his terrace, the building nearly filled Sam's southern view, but he chose to look past it. Its residents were affluent. Some were prominent, including restaurateur Howard Johnson and radio and television celebrity Arthur Godfrey. It is said that years earlier a sign was posted at the Kenilworth that read, NO DOGS OR JEWS ALLOWED. The story may well be apocryphal, but it reflected the fears and experiences of many of the Jews who lived in its vicinity.

Sam was well aware of the building's status, but seemed to accept the idea of living next door to people who would rather be much farther away from his kind. The same could not be said of me. As a child visiting my grandparents, I was always hyperaware that I was unwelcome next door. When I took walks down the beach and crossed the Kenilworth's property or came within its chill shadow, my pace quickened and I felt a tremor as if I were standing in some forbidden area.

But the ironies of Sam Stone's residence did not end there. In 1974, my father, the son of a rabbi, dropped dead of a heart attack. He was fifty. My mother left Canton and moved in with her parents, Sam and Minna. A year after my father's death, my mother, then a slim and attractive forty-seven-year-old, met a man on the beach and fell in love. His name was Donald Sharpe. They were married on Valentine's Day, 1976.

But there was a problem. Don lived in the Kenilworth. Worse yet, he was a member of its co-op board, which had enforced the policy against Jews. If my mother—Sam Stone's daughter—were to live there, concessions would have to be sought from the board. A waiver was granted (to my chagrin), and my mother moved in. Equally troubling was the fact that Don, now my stepfather, belonged to La Gorce Country Club, which was notorious for excluding Jews. For Don, the club was his home away from home.

Given my grandfather's traumatic youth in Romania and his obsession with Hitler and the Nazis, one might imagine that he and Don would have had a frosty relationship. In fact, they quickly became best friends. They were both from humble beginnings in Pennsylvania, had no stomach for pretense, and enjoyed a good joke. When Don told my mother he was going to give Sam a present—a light blue windbreaker with the crest of La Gorce Country Club emblazoned on the pocket along with the letters "LGCC"—my mother predicted he would refuse it on principle.

But when Don jokingly told Sam the letters *LGCC* stood for "Large Gains Could Come," Sam laughed and proudly donned the jacket. By then, Sam was well into his eighties and had made a curious peace with the world and its prejudices. The jacket became a favorite of his, a symbol of an unlikely friendship between my grandfather, the refugee Jew, and Don, the Gentile who lived where Jews were not welcome.

Years later, the Kenilworth fell to the wrecker's ball. I made no attempt to conceal my pleasure to know that the building had been reduced to rubble. Much has changed. In 1990, La Gorce Country Club admitted its first Jews. Today the club is 40 percent Jewish, and in 2008 it hosted its first Seder dinner.

For Sam and Minna, memories of the Depression and their years in Canton gradually faded, though their friendships there did not. Even after so many years, neither of them shared with me the story of B. Virdot. There were occasional vague references to Sam's generosity, and in later years I was told of his gift of wool coats to the British in World War II, but nothing of B. Virdot. The passage of time also wiped away Cantonians' memory of that gift. It seemed obvious that all those who wrote the letters had since gone to their graves. But the years have yet to fully erase the last vestiges of the good that B. Virdot did.

The Doll

It is hard to measure the impact of even the smallest unexpected gift on a child who has nothing. Against the dire landscape of the Depression, holidays often went unmarked, and were occasionally marked by violence. At Easter of 1930, a ten-year-old Canton boy was shot to death by an eleven-year-old playmate in a dispute over a chocolate bunny. Such treasures were all but unheard of in many homes. For hundreds of parents and children that Christmas of 1933, B. Virdot was their only hope of having something on the Christmas dinner table, in the stockings, or under a tree. Twenty-eight-year-old Olive Hillman asked for little and had even less. She wrote:

Dear Mr. B. Virdot,

Read your announcement in this evening's paper about wanting to spread Xmas cheer among 75 families. We are Americans.

My husband is a cripple and hasn't worked for seven years. But had a good job when he did work. I have two children and my husband dependent on me. I am employed at Timken's factory.

Manage to live on my salary but winter is always so tough.

The children need so many things and the extra coal and light bills to pay. Don't have any money to buy the children any thing for Xmas this yer. We have our own home. Was left to us by Mr. Hillman's mother. Also had a few hundred dollars but that has been gone a couple years ago.

I get very much blue and discouraged when you work and then never have only your eats and nothing extra for clothing. We all need clothes bad. I don't mind myself but am writing this in hopes that my children may have a nice Xmas.

Certainly would appreciate your good will and Xmas cheer in our home this year. My little girl is 8 years old, the little boy is 10.

Glad to know that the depression is over for you and prosperity is back. Wishing you a Merry Christmas and a brighter New Year.

MRS. PAUL HILLMAN
1431 3RD ST S.E. CITY

B. Virdot's check arrived just days later and Olive Hillman sat down on Christmas Day and wrote this note in response:

Dear Mr. B. Virdot,

Your check you sent us was received and want to thank you kindly for it.

We have had a Merry Xmas through your kindness. We also received a basket from the church.

The children were made happy by the things they received from the check. I bought the girl a pair of shoes and stockings also a doll.

The boy a pair of stockings a new cap and a train.

Thanking you again for your Xmas cheer and wishing you a happy New Year.

MRS. PAUL HILLMAN.

Today, that little girl is eighty-four. Her name is Geraldine Laura Hillman Fry and she lives just eighteen miles east of where she lived as a child, in the hamlet of Minerva, Ohio. "Gerry," as she is called, knew nothing of her mother's letter to B. Virdot, but she does remember the doll—it was to be the only doll she would have as a child. She remembers its arms and legs of leather and its porcelain face. That surprise gift could hardly have been forgotten in such a childhood as hers. The only other gift she could hope for came from the mission—some candy and a few oranges.

"What became of that doll?" she mused aloud. "I wondered that so many times. The only thing I can think of is when my mother divorced my father it got left behind. When we left we took just the clothes on our back."

Her mother had married Paul Hillman, the son of German immigrants, when she was seventeen. Not long after she wrote the letter to B. Virdot she left him and moved into an apartment with the two children, Gerry and Paul Jr. They had but one bed to be shared by the three of them. In some ways it was fortunate that they had one another to stay warm. It was often cold enough in the bedroom to see their own breath. Each morning at four-thirty Olive would quietly get up, get dressed, and walk several miles in the dark from their home to the Timken plant on Dueber Avenue, where she worked as an assembler in the roller bearings department and where she would continue to work for twenty-nine years.

Before leaving she would make sure the alarm clock was set for the children to get up in time to walk to school. Gerry had two blouses and two skirts, which she wore over and over. It was her responsibility not to soil them. Their breakfast, their lunch, and their dinner took on a grinding monotony. There were beans, there was milk— canned, never fresh—and some hamburger.

"I remember one time when things were really,

really bad and she didn't know where she was going to get enough money till the next pay day and as she was walking she found a dollar bill on the ground. She went to the store and bought some bread and lunch meat and came home. She was very happy that she had enough to feed us."

Throughout Gerry's childhood, there was never a car, a telephone, or a refrigerator—just a wooden "window box" that was placed on the outside sill in the cold months and kept things chilled (or frozen).

There were a few bright spots in her early life. One of these was Meyers Lake Amusement Park, a place where many Depression-era children had their best moments. Each year, as a Timken employee, Olive Hillman and her two children were invited to a picnic there. They packed a lunch, swam in the lake, and all the rides were free. Gerry never tired of watching the antics played out on Monkey Island.

Gerry knew little about her father. Her mother rarely spoke of him. He drank, and he could be abusive. At one time he had a good job, but he lost it. As for the cause of his crippling injuries, Gerry knew nothing until many years later, when her older brother, Paul Jr., dying from cancer, told her that their father, at age twenty-two, had closed himself inside a closet and shot himself in the head with a rifle. But the suicide attempt went awry and he was left paralyzed. He lived another forty-eight years in that condition, dying on May 28, 1970.

In 1946, Olive remarried. Her husband, Lawrence Gipe, worked in a foundry and wielded tongs handling steel and working around the blazing furnaces. It was a good marriage, and Olive put the Hard Times behind her.

Her son Paul Jr. would find work with the Civilian Conservation Corps in Washington State, join the navy, and later find work in one of Canton's steel mills.

Gerry's life too took a very different turn. She graduated from Timken Vocational High School in 1943 and went to work in Canton's Hercules Motor Plant. There she met a coworker named Romain "Bud" Fry, whom she would marry in June 1945. She was twenty; he was thirty and had two children. But Fry was an ambitious man and soon left Hercules Motor to try his hand in business. He began in the furniture business, became a developer, built a golf course, and founded a community bank. He became president and chairman of the board of Consumers National Bank, based in Minerva, Ohio, and presided over its expansion to seven branches. Gerry Fry, who had grown up with so little, was now a millionaire, a banker's wife. The Frys enjoyed fifty-four years of marriage and four children.

"I never really thought of myself as being rich, because of my background," Gerry says. "I always appreciated everything I got. I am not a big spender. I hate to spend money."

The dark Christmas of 1933 and the doll that was part of it seem taken from another life. In 2009 she watched over a family whose relative abundance she can scarcely believe. It is one of her great pleasures to do the Christmas shopping early. By mid-November she had already purchased a gift for her one-year-old great-granddaughter, Ivey Julia Rettig, and hid it in the basement. All that remained to be done was to wrap it. It is a lifelike baby doll, something, Gerry says, "she can cuddle."

A Special Time

It would be hard to say just when Elizabeth Bunt's childhood ended, if ever it began. One of three children, she experienced an early life that was pocked with hardship. Even the joys were snatched away. On July 20, 1930, when she was eleven, her mother gave birth to a baby boy, named after her father—Martin William Bunt. But two months and three days later, on September 23, 1930, the child died. The death certificate notes, "hare lip & cleft palate, unable to eat." The infant was buried in Canton's West Lawn Cemetery.

Barely a year later, on October 13, 1931, Elizabeth's father succumbed to liver cancer. A Dr. G. B. Maxwell—the same doctor who signed his son's death certificate—noted cause of death as "general exhaustion." Bunt was buried alongside his namesake and infant son in West Lawn.

Widowed at thirty-eight, Delia Bunt and her children, Elizabeth, George, and Thelma, moved in with her parents on a rented farm on the edge of Canton. They lived in the summer kitchen, a tiny two-room structure they used to can vegetables and cook in summer. There was no indoor plumbing, just a pump and an outhouse. No electricity, just oil lamps. To bathe, they relied on rainwater they collected and heated over a coal-burning stove that often went out in the middle of the night, leaving them shivering. Elizabeth shared a bed with her mother and sister.

Later they moved into the city of Canton and the children attended a one-room schoolhouse, with eight classes divided into two groups by a black curtain. In winter, when the snow was deep, Elizabeth's older brother, George, led the way and the two girls followed in the footsteps he'd left for them.

There were no presents at Christmas, at least not at home. At school, Elizabeth was given a small bag of Hard Tack candy (a mix of sugar, corn syrup, and food coloring) and an orange. But as Christmas 1933 approached, Elizabeth hoped for something more. And when she saw Mr. B. Virdot's offer of help in the newspaper, she could not resist. She took out a pencil and manila paper and secretly wrote this letter:

Dear Mr. B. Virdot

My father has been dead 2 yrs ago last October. We get $3 a wk from the County. There is 4 of us. My brother tried to get a job from the CWA but is to young. He is only 16. and my mother can't get no work. We live in my Grandmother's summer kitchen. We would appreciate whatever you give us.

YOURS TRULY
ELIZABETH BUNT
AGE 14
WARNER RD. S.E.
R. 5.
CANTON, OHIO

A few days later, Mr. B. Virdot's check for five dollars arrived in the mail. It is not known what Elizabeth Bunt did with the money. Her sister, Thelma, has no recollection of that Christmas and had no knowledge of her sister's letter to Mr. B. Virdot. What is known by everyone who knew Elizabeth Bunt was that she would come to regard Christmas as her special day and the high point of her year. Perhaps it was just that her fortunes improved modestly over the years. No one can say. But after years of holidays more hollow than happy, she came to embrace that day, to prepare for it long in advance. She believed that God would provide.

And he did. Throughout the year she would play bingo at area churches and stash away her winnings as her Christmas fund. Christmas was a pleasure she shared with everyone. When she married Bernard Haren in June 1941, it continued to be the pivot around which her entire year

428

revolved. And there was no need to explain to Bernard what the Great Depression had meant to her. As one of fourteen children, he understood only too well. Because Elizabeth did not drive, Bernard, and later the children, would be asked to make endless trips with her to the store to gather presents for an ever-expanding brood.

Even when her own shopping was done, she liked nothing better than to go out among the crowds on Christmas Eve and bid strangers a merry Christmas.

From out of the Great Depression, Elizabeth carried with her a faith that things would work out but also a determination to help them along, to conserve and make use of whatever was at hand. Her children recall being deployed each spring to gather up the dandelions in the yard. She would mix them with vinegar and bits of bacon and it would be dinner. "She could make dinner out of nothing," recalls her son William. And during the Depression, nothing was often all there was. Like so many of her generation, she was frugal and insecure about the future. Two years after she died, son Bill removed a huge painting of sunflowers from her living room wall. Behind the painting, he discovered a twenty-dollar bill taped to the back.

And yet, when it came to Christmas, the purse strings came undone. Son James can still reel off the Christmas gifts that spanned the years: a Schwinn bike, a Lionel train, an Erector Set. And it was not only her own family that concerned her. She wept to read in the newspaper of children who endured hardships. For years, her son James and she arranged for a Christmas turkey or ham to be taken to a needy family and she prided herself on learning the names of their children and having small gifts for them.

Elizabeth Bunt Haren's last Christmas was in 2005. Stricken with pancreatic cancer, she insisted on celebrating the holiday as she had every year. She died on October 20, 2006, at the age of eighty-eight. To her son James Haren she left her Christmas china decorated with holly berries. At her funeral a niece named Laura read a letter in which she spoke of Elizabeth's singular passion for Christmas. As they sat there in St. Louis Catholic Church listening, Elizabeth's son and others say they imagined Elizabeth sitting on a sofa, surrounded by her family and handing out presents one by one, making sure no one was left out. That was quite a feat. When she died, she left behind her husband, two daughters, five sons, a sister, twenty-two grandchildren, thirty great-grandchildren, and two great-great-grandchildren. None of them ever wanted for a gift.

The Pony

Just outside of Canton, on a tumbledown farm, lived Edith May, her husband, James, and their three young children.

"Mr. B. Virdot," thirty-nine-year-old Edith May began her letter, dated December 18, 1933:

Maybe I shouldn't write to you, not living right in Canton, but for some time I have been wanting to know somebody who could give me some help.

We have known better days. Four years ago we were getting 135 dollars a month for milk. Now Saturday we got 12. This 12 has to go as follows: Pay for the gas to hall the milk, get chopping, pay for coal we had to trust—during the cold spell, buy an axe to make wood, buy a tire for a dollar & I had two dollars to buy grocery. Imagine 5 of us for a month. If I only had five dollars, I would think I am in heaven. I would buy a pair of shoes for my oldest boy in school. His toes are all out & no way to give him a pair.

He was just 6 in October. Then I have a little girl will be 4 two days before Xmas + a boy of 18 months.

I could give them all something for

Xmas + I would be very happy. Up to now I haven't a thing for them. I made a dolly for each to look like Santa + that's as much as I could go. Won't you please help me to be happy?

Have you got any ladies in your family could give me some old clothes.

We all took a cold by not having anything warm to wear — it is the children's first cold & my first in ten years. So you can imagine our circumstances.

My husband is a good farmer but we have always rented & that keeps us poor. When we were making good money he bought his machinery & paid for them, so we never wasted anything. He is only 32 & never had anyone to give him a help in starting.

We now live on the "Hills and Dale road" and close to Massillon. The buildings are unpainted. We are supposed to pay 20 dollars a month & since we can't we are ordered off the place — we could just get a place to farm on the shares we could make a go of it — the trouble with us is that lots of people think we don't need anything & if Mr. was to apply on the CWA to get a few hours work a week they would say we don't need it.

And oh my I know what it is to be hungry & cold. We suffered so last winter & this one is worst.

Please do help me! My husband don't know I am writing & I haven't even a stamp, but I am going to beg the mailman to post this for me.

OBLIGE
YRS TRULY
MRS. EDITH MAY

Edith May was one of a half dozen African Americans to write to Mr. B. Virdot. But her story begins far from the cold of the Midwest and far from the hardscrabble farm where she and her family scratched out a living in the winter of 1933. Her story begins in 1925. Edith May—then Edith Thompson—was a thirty-two-year-old Jamaican teacher and governess, the daughter of a teacher and one of seven sisters, all of whom worked in the classroom. For many months, she had been pen pals with an American named James May, eight years her junior and the grandson of Virginian slaves. Over time, they shared their lives in letters, exchanged photographs, and imagined a future together. In October 1925, twenty-four-year-old James May went to Kingston, Jamaica, to meet this intriguing older woman with whom he had already shared much. They married there, and

433

though James returned to America, it was understood that his bride, Edith, would soon follow.

Two months later, on December 11, 1925, Edith May boarded the SS *Santa Marta*, waved good-bye to Kingston, its sunny climes, and a life of relative comfort, and headed first for New York and then the Midwest, where her husband, a farmer, awaited her. She arrived in America on December 17, 1925, and made her way to Ohio.

Even in the best of times, their lives were difficult, but by the time the Depression descended upon Edith and James May and their little family, there was no margin of error, no buffer to keep out the cold and the hunger. Felice May, their daughter, remembers the wind whipping the snowdrifts and burying the narrow lane that led to their rented farm. She remembers her father hoisting her upon his shoulders and carrying her for a mile to where the school bus stopped. She remembers him chopping firewood and loading it into the back of a Model T and driving off to sell what he could to the few who could afford to buy it. The vehicle's canvas roof was torn and leaked, and icy water spilled down upon him.

And she remembers how the smell of skunk was the smell of money. He would trap skunk and sell the pelts for food, clothing, and feed for the animals. "We could smell him coming because he had a skunk in the back," recalls Felice. "Back then a skunk hide was worth a lot of money. The smell would sting your eyes in the house if they got him good. One time his eyes were all shut and he wanted my mom to get a pan of water to wash his eyes out. He came in the house half-blind and the house was permeated by the smell."

What lessons Felice May learned from the Depression and the farm did not prepare her fully for what existed beyond its confines. She knew she was "colored," but she did not understand what barriers that would create for her. An A student in high school and a voracious reader, she applied for many jobs for which she was qualified, but never did she get a call back.

Instead she resigned herself to working as a live-in housekeeper, and after graduating from high school in 1948 she did just that, working for eight dollars a week. But as rough as her time was on the farm, she gravitated back to a country lifestyle, and the pattern she chose for herself—or perhaps that was chosen for her—was the same, often harsh struggle on the land. She worked for years heading a nutrition program for the elderly, but even today she has supplemented her living with the same resourcefulness that her mother and father exhibited. For years she trapped animals—raccoons, fox, mink, possums.

Today she has a bakery called Mom's Kitchen, and each Saturday she takes her banana and honey wheat breads, cookies, and cupcakes to shops and fairs. And at eighty, she still traps an occasional raccoon at her rural home outside Bowerston, Ohio, and sells the pelt. Nor does anything get thrown away. Old clothes become rags to keep the draft out of the barn. The daughter of a teacher, she remains an avid reader. In winter she reads scores of books.

The life of James May, Edith's husband, never did get any easier. A swarm of yellow jackets stung him in the leg, which turned gangrenous and had to be amputated. He died in 1975 and is buried in Canton. As for Edith, she developed diabetes and went to live in California with one of her sons. That is where she died in January 1975 and where she is buried.

There was some irony that Edith May could not afford even a postage stamp to mail her letter to Mr. B. Virdot: her aunt Grace was the postmaster of Kingston, Jamaica. How different her life might have been had she remained there. A taste of that other life arrived in the mail from time to time—a box of cashews from a sister.

The descendants of Edith and James May have many memories of hardship and struggle, but they also have memories of mutual support and pride and of triumphs large and small. From her Depression-era childhood, difficult as it was, Felice has one memory in particular that is almost magical. It was the week before Christmas 1933. She was to turn four years old on that December

23. Ordinarily, neither Christmas nor a birthday would have been occasion for much celebration. But something unexpected happened that day. It was dark and the farm chores had been done, but instead of turning in early, Edith and James May piled the family into their rickety old car and drove into the town of Massillon. The streets were brilliant with Christmas lights, and Edith and James May ushered their daughter into a five-and-dime.

"My eyes bugged out," remembers Felice. "I had never been in anything like that before and she took me back in that toy store and she said I could have my choice between the horse on a board that you pulled with a string or a doll. I chose the horse." It would become her most prized possession. "I pulled that horse up and down the lane."

"I've loved ponies all my life," she says. Even today, at eighty, she has fifteen Welsh ponies that she raises and intends to sell, and she likes nothing better than to ride in her horse-drawn cart.

A check from a stranger named B. Virdot bought that little pony and made such a memory possible. It changed a life.

The Unexpected

By March 8, 2010, my research into the B. Virdot letters was complete. My book was finished; the manuscript was edited and in my publisher's hands. I had cleared my desk of the mountain of papers—a ritual of mine upon completing a project—and had, at last, begun to tidy up my office. I had conducted more than five hundred interviews. I had sifted through thousands of pages of deeds, marriage licenses, census reports, obituaries, and death certificates. Together, they filled six drawers of a file cabinet.

Still, I felt that there was something yet to be done. I had focused on scores of letters and successfully tracked down the descendants of all but one of the writers, a fourteen-year-old girl named Helen Palm. She was the one writer whose life narrative had managed to elude me. With a few minutes of free time, I decided to try once more to locate her descendants. What exactly I hoped to find, I can't say. I just felt a need to close the circle. With the help of the genealogy staff at the Stark County Public Library, I located her parents' obituaries. Her father, Ralston Palm, had died in 1973; her mother, Carrie, in 1984. One of Helen Palm's daughters, Janet, seventy years old, was said to be living in nearby Magnolia, Ohio. I called her to learn what had become of her mother in the years after her letter to B. Virdot, and to fill out the particulars of her life—marriage, children, work, date of death, place of burial. I was not prepared for her response.

Helen Palm was alive.

The fourteen-year-old author—the last and only living link to the B. Virdot letters—was now ninety, a great-great-grandmother who lived at the Laurels of Masillon, a nursing home just outside Canton. Three hours later I received a call from Helen Palm, now Helen Palm Kintz Grant. Her voice was strong and clear.

Helen had been the second-youngest of all those to have written to B. Virdot. I wondered if she had any recollection of his gift. "I remember the ad," she said without hesitation. "I wrote to him and told him I didn't have any money. I think he sent me five bucks." I read her the letter she wrote in pencil on a five-by-eight-inch slip of paper with a return address of "RFD#4":

Dear Sir,

When we went over at the neighbors to borrow the paper I read your article. I am a girl of fourteen. I am writing this because I need clothing. And sometimes we run out of food.

My father does not want to ask for charity. But us children would like to have some clothing for Christmas. When he had a job us children used to have nice things.

I also have brothers and sisters.

If you should send me Ted Dollars I would buy clothing and buy the Christmas dinner and supper.

I thank you.

HELEN PALM

"Oh, my God," she said when I finished reading her seventy-seven-year-old letter. After a pause, she added, "I wanted to do something for my family." And what did she do with the money? "Oh, gee whiz," she said, sounding more like the fourteen-year-old who wrote the letter than the ninety-year-old on the other end of the phone line. Well, I asked, do you remember? "You better believe it," she replied, "because I went right down and bought a pair of shoes." That would have been December 21, 1933, when the check was cashed. Until then, having a decent pair of shoes—ones that fit and didn't have holes—had been a constant problem, as it was for hundreds of thousands of others during the Hard Times. She would cut out the shape of her sole from an empty shredded-wheat box and insert it into her badly worn-out shoes. But true to her word, Helen Palm used the rest of the money to take her family out to eat.

It gave her and the entire family a welcome lift in a holiday season that was marked as much by anxiety as by joy. December, even without the Depression, was a somber time for the Palms. On December 16 more than a decade earlier, a brother, Harold, had been born and died just fifteen days later. His mother would later say that in an effort to keep him warm, she had shared her bed with the infant and inadvertently suffocated him. Helen's own birthday was December 3, 1919, but the holidays were clouded by uncertainty. Her father had worked at Republic Steel but got laid off repeatedly. Her mother, Carrie, went door-to-door trying to sell Christmas cards. "She walked, God love her—she had such bad legs, I felt so sorry for her."

Helen also walked for miles delivering the *Canton Repository*. Many of their meals came from the garden, particularly the fried potatoes that appeared often on their plates. The upstairs of their small white frame house on Genoa Street was unfinished, and a curtain divided her parents' bedroom from the children's. She and her sister, Bernice, shared the room and brother Richard had a cot in the corner. By 1935, the Palms had lost their home and been forced to move. Three years after writing the letter, at age seventeen, Helen got married.

Her memories of Canton echo those of many others who wrote to B. Virdot. She too went to

Myers Lake to see the marathon dancers, drunk with exhaustion, staggering to the music. She recalls the vice and the crime that beset Canton, and how her father would point out the spot where the Mob gunned down Don Mellett, the crusading editor of the *Repository*. In later years her family would convert their front porch to a tiny grocery they called Palm's Variety Store.

But seven decades later, the B. Virdot gift stands out against the pall of the Depression. "I thought that was so wonderful of that man," she gushes. "Oh, you're his grandson! Well, God love him. You should be so proud of him. I was so happy. That anyone could be so kind to help people at that time. I know I made those dollars stretch because I tried to make a lot of people happy with it."

For years, Helen Palm assumed that B. Virdot worked in a bank, perhaps because he had money enough to share with others. She wouldn't have guessed that B. Virdot was the short man at Stone's Clothes where her father bought his clothes and where she would pick out a tie for him in less grim Christmas seasons. "Oh, I'll be darned!" she exclaimed when I told her that B. Virdot was Sam Stone. From among so many who reached out to him in need, she is the only one to learn the secret of Mr. B. Virdot.

Mr. B. Virdot's Story:
The Bridge

Sam Stone never did know the impact of his gift on the lives of Geraldine Hillman, Elizabeth Bunt, Felice May, Helen Palm, or any of the other recipients of his largesse. He had his own three daughters to dote upon, a business to run, and a crush of other matters to occupy his attention. Besides, he understood from the beginning that he could not inquire into the circumstances of those he had helped without compromising his own anonymity and their privacy. What little he did learn came in the trickle of thank-you notes in the days after his gift arrived.

Nearly fifty years later he was still in robust health, still working, and still thoroughly enjoying life in his oceanfront apartment in Bal Harbour, Florida, where he lived with Minna. At ninety-three, he woke up early each morning, went for a dip in the Atlantic, diving headlong into the oncoming waves, then showered in his cabana, donned a pressed white shirt, tie, and jacket, and drove himself to work. He owned a small shop in North Miami that sold marble pen sets, clocks, trophies, and executive knickknacks. He didn't really need the income. He had owned a chain of clothing stores, and later, a plastics plant and a real estate company that helped develop Sunset Isles in Hollywood and Miami Shores. But the tiny shop provided a focus to his days, and procuring the marble stands gave him an excuse to travel the world.

On Thursday morning, January 29, 1981, he set off as always, cruising down Collins Avenue, and eventually turning onto the Broad Causeway, which connects the mainland's North Miami with the Bay Harbor Islands. He paid the quarter toll and proceeded. But on this morning, the drawbridge was already rising and the pike descended toward his windshield. Instead of braking, he panicked, put his foot to the accelerator, and shot forward, slamming into the rising concrete span. He died instantly. The time was 10:15 A.M.

The *Miami Herald* obituary appeared under the headline, ENTREPRENEUR SAMUEL STONE, 93. The city sent my grandmother a bill for the repairs to the bridge, but she would have none of it, and told them as much. Faced with the choice of badgering an aged widow or absorbing the costs, the city relented.

Sam's body was made presentable and flown to Canton. His casket was the color of pewter, and his head was pillowed on a silver crepe interior. I viewed it in the front parlor of the funeral home. The actual service was at three P.M. in the sanctuary of Temple Israel. Just before the casket was closed, his son-in-law and best friend, Don, folded the light blue windbreaker jacket from La Gorce Country Club and gently tucked it into the corner of Sam's casket, a contradictory symbol of both the New World's anti-Semitism and the struggle to rise above it. It was the gift that had sealed their friendship.

Sam was buried in Canton's West Lawn Cemetery in grave number 5, lot 31, section 6, in the ivied company of deceased friends and family. Not far off in all directions were the graves of those whom, nearly fifty years before, he had helped as B. Virdot. Minna had her own name chiseled on the stone, with her birth date and a dash that would hold its breath another quarter century before exhaling. I pinched a green leaf from the arrangement on the casket and put it in my wallet. I still have the leaf. During the funeral I remembered Sam's favorite toast.

> He was a simple honest man. He never strayed,
> He never drank, he never smoked, and he
> never kissed a maid.
> And when he passed away his insurance was
> denied.
> Because he never lived, they claimed he never
> died.

I'd heard him offer that toast scores of times, and always with the same piratical glint in his eye. For us grandchildren, that toast was a welcome manifesto, a license from the patriarch to raise a little hell.

Two decades later, I came upon Sam's death certificate. It cited the cause of death as "multiple blunt impact injuries." His occupation was "Executive." It said he was born on March 2, 1887, in Pittsburgh. Only my grandmother knew otherwise. And so it would remain for nearly thirty years.

Knowing what I now know of Sam's life, I see in his death, if not the perfect exit, at least the perfect metaphor for how he lived. He died crossing a bridge, which was only right given that for my family he *was* the bridge between the old and new worlds, between the pogroms of the past and the promise of the present. His haste in escaping that former life and embracing the new misled him into thinking he might secure that future sooner by creating a web of lies, but ultimately, those lies put him at permanent risk and proved to be the final obstacle to his own security. How appropriate, then, that the barrier that descended upon him that day triggered panic and, instead of waiting, he sped forward hoping to clear the rising span. Three decades later his descendants cannot cross that causeway without thinking of him and paying homage to the man whose crossing brought us all to this place.

IX.
True Circumstances

Final Reflections

The gifts that Sam Stone gave that Christmas 1933 came from a man who understood what it was to be down-and-out. But there was more to it than that. It was no accident that he chose Christmas, a holiday marked for Christians, not Jews, and that he specifically wished his Gentile neighbors a "merry and joyful Christmas." For Sam, the gift marked a kind of final arrival for him. No longer the object of persecution, he was a respected citizen and a welcomed member of the community.

That nearly all the recipients of his largesse were Gentiles represented a measure of acceptance long denied him. Canton had embraced him in ways he had never thought possible. To the suffering of his fellow townspeople, the act had brought relief and hope. But to Sam, it signaled a personal triumph in which he could finally believe that he had escaped the persecution, rejection, and poverty that had defined his past. In Canton, a small midwestern industrial town against the ropes during the Great Depression, he found what had eluded him all his life—a sense of belonging, a home.

He had strayed as far as he could from the stifling orthodoxy of his youth, but he never severed his ties with Judaism. He was proud of his faith. He repudiated only the rituals that had weighed upon him and with which he associated so much suffering. At Christmas, in his Market Street home, he always had an enormous tree that he delighted in helping to decorate. On Christmas morning he insisted that he be allowed to open his gifts first. And yet, even as he celebrated his freedom from the past that Christmas of 1933, the manner of B. Virdot's giving was an homage to that past.

Raised an Orthodox Jew, he knew well both the concept of *tikkun olam* and that of *tzedakah*. *Tikkun olam* is Hebrew for "repairing the world." *Tzedakah* is a Hebrew word embedded in notions of basic justice, but also one that has come to mean caring for the poor. It is not charity but the debt we owe one another and ourselves as human beings. In the world into which Sam was born, it was customary for a new father to make a gift of money to the poor. It was a way of consecrating the newborn to a life of compassion, justice, and observance. "Tzedaka," observed Professor Reuven Kimelman, "may not save us but it makes us worth saving." And that was the power of B. Virdot's gift. It telegraphed to an entire community that it—and he—were indeed worth saving.

The Bible speaks often of such matters:

"When you cut down your harvest in your field, and have forgotten a sheaf in the field, you shall not go again to fetch it; it shall be for the stranger, for the orphan, and for the widow; that the Lord your God may bless you in all the work of your hands. . . . And you shall remember that you were a slave in the land of Egypt; therefore I command you to do this thing" (Deuteronomy 24:19–22). Sam too had come out of a land of bondage. The exodus from Romania was, in its day, often compared to the exodus out of Egypt. And with him he had brought an ancient appreciation of the commandment of *tzedakah*.

He named his pseudonymous donor "B. Virdot" after his own young daughters, speaking to the hope that they would inherit a world free from the bigotry and Old World hatreds that had marked his childhood. Yet, ominously, the year he made his gift, 1933, was the same year Adolf Hitler came to power and Dachau opened its gates. Indeed, the day Sam Stone's ad appeared in the *Canton Repository*, the *New York Times* reported how anti-Semitism was once more inflamed in Europe. A headline in the December 18, 1933, edition read: VIENNA NAZIS IN ATTACK: EXPLODE TEAR GAS BOMBS IN JEWISH-OWNED DEPARTMENT STORE. That same day, another *Times* headline read: NAZI COURT ANNULS MIXED MARRIAGE: SUSTAINS "ARYAN" HUSBAND ON THE GROUND THAT IT VIOLATES THE DOGMA OF BLOOD KINSHIP. It was a landmark case. In granting a husband a divorce from his Jewish wife on the ground that it tainted his Aryan blood, the court wrote in part: "He could not have understood the essential implication involved in such a union at a time when the significance of race, blood kinship and folkdom was recognized by a small minority only."

These were the sorts of accounts that made Sam Stone shiver with boyhood fears. He knew firsthand where such stories inexorably lead. But his faith in America was not misplaced. The sons and daughters of those he'd helped, and millions like them, raised during the Great Depression, would soon march off to defeat Hitler and risk their lives to bring an end to the prejudices and tyranny that had defined his youth. Roy Teis's sons enlisted the day after the bombing of Pearl Harbor. Nora Romesberg's son joined not long after. So too did the sons of Rachel DeHoff. And scores more enlisted from among the families B. Virdot aided. They had learned during the Great Depression that they were all in this together—rich and poor, black and white, Jew and Gentile—and that only by acting in concert could they prevail. B. Virdot had sent them five dollars. They repaid his faith in them ten-thousand-fold.

Epilogue:
Canton Revisited

Over the thirty-five years since I last lived in Canton, I have returned many times. Almost always, it is for a funeral or to pay my respects at the graves of my family. Each time, I stand before Minna's and Sam's graves and gather up four pebbles. I place them on their gravestone—one for myself, one for my mother, Virginia, one for my sister, Audrey, and one for my wife, Peggy. It is how we Jews express remembrance. It is a way to continually build a monument to memory and it is a signal to those who come after us that we were there and that these souls have not been forgotten. Even the smallest pebble says it all.

Four generations of us are buried on a green hillside in West Lawn Cemetery, almost within the shadow of President William McKinley's monument. Returning home—I still consider Canton my home, even after four decades away— I rarely miss a chance to eat at Bender's or drive past Sam and Minna's old home on Market Street. But with the discovery of the suitcase, I began to see things anew. And on each successive visit, researching this family or that, I sought out the landmarks that routinely cropped up in their letters—the places where they had lived and worked and, when they could, played, wondering what had become of them in the intervening seventy-five-plus years. It felt less like a self-guided tour than one directed by the ghosts of December 1933.

The Canton they knew is there still, but smaller. The industrial city of 105,000 has shrunk to 78,000, and the uncertainty of its financial future has done little to stem the exodus of its young. Those in whose hands the city now rests have done what they could to put a positive face on things, but the present increasingly looks like the troubled past. Today Canton must cope with the burdens that weigh on all Rust Belt cities: outsourcing, layoffs, plant closures, and a recession that for many bears an uncanny resemblance to the Hard Times.

In August 2008, *Forbes* magazine listed Canton among the ten fastest dying cities in the nation. In the Canton News Depot on Market Avenue, where decades earlier I had purchased the Harvard Classics, there were few books, but shelves of Dream Books—pamphlets used by those who play the illegal numbers racket and seek to convert their dreams into a winning combination of numerals. These Dream Books are one more sign of Canton's hard-luck history, in which gambling and superstition seem as likely a course of salvation as any. Allen Bennafield, the dry-cleaner-turned-bookie, would have felt right at home.

Empty storefronts abound. At night, Bender's still prospers, but much of the downtown is what one local banker calls "a dead zone." Canton's prostitutes never left, but they no longer claim entire streets. And if education is one of the paths out of difficulty, Canton has a ways to go. Only one in ten adults living there holds a bachelor's degree.

Dollar stores, evangelical halls, bail bondsmen, vacant houses, and boarded-up storefronts proliferate. More than seventy-five years ago the *Canton Repository* ran B. Virdot's offer and made its own appeal to help the needy. Now it is doing so again. In December 2008, the newspaper began a feature called "Community Help" that lists clothing giveaways, soup kitchens, and homeless shelters. As Christmas 2008 approached, more than three thousand people contacted the Salvation Army in search of shelter, food, and help with paying for heat and lights. Like those in 1933, the anguish and humiliation was written on their faces. In the lobby of the Salvation Army a part-time chef and father of six-year-old twin boys sat and wept, in part out of embarrassment, in part out of gratitude, as he waited to receive toys for his sons and food for his family.

Plants closed, factories cut back on hours, benefits were reduced or eliminated, and the growing uncertainty of continued employment took its toll. In March 2009, the posting of a single janitorial position at a junior high school drew 835 applicants. The one-year contract paid fifteen to sixteen dollars an hour. The *Repository* hailed the winner as possibly "the luckiest man in Stark County." By early 2010, Canton's unemployment rate was approaching 15 percent. The only thing that seemed to be expanding was the anger aimed at politicians of both parties at all levels of government.

One of the large downtown storefronts on McKinley Avenue is boldly called "The Recovery," but it has nothing to do with the city regaining its economic standing, and everything to do with serving the growing number of addicts and alcoholics. The old McKinley High School still stands, but is now a nursing home. The first floor once hosted wedding receptions and parties and featured a restaurant. No longer.

Still, it is remarkable how, even today, so much of Canton's landscape and life are defined by the Depression. Fawcett Stadium, where the National Football League kicks off its season each fall and where for generations high school teams have battled under the lights and families cheered, was itself a creation of the Depression and the Works Progress Administration. And much of Canton's parks system owes its existence to the WPA.

Canton's arts also took root during the Depression. The Canton Players' Guild, a theatrical company, came into being in 1932, the

Canton Art Institute in 1934, and the Canton Symphony Orchestra in 1936. Thirteen prized murals that glorify the steel industry and its workers inside Canton's Frank T. Bow Federal Building were done by artist Glenn Moore Shaw under the Works Progress Administration.

But the Depression also scarred this city. At one time, no building was more precious to Canton than the home of President William McKinley. From the front porch of his house at 723 North Market Avenue, he launched his 1896 campaign for the White House. But eventually the house was moved to make room for the expansion of a hospital. During the Depression the home was neglected and became an eyesore. One attempt after another to solicit public and private funds for its restoration during the Hard Times failed. A grainy photo shows a sign in the window of the home that reads, SAVE THIS HOUSE. But there was no savior. Ultimately, the Health Department condemned it. In January 1935 the McKinley home rendered its last pitiful act of service to the city, providing jobs to a Federal Transient Service Bureau crew who tore the dilapidated house apart and hauled it away. The wood that was usable went to building shelters, picnic tables, and benches in the city parks.

Where the McKinley house originally stood, the Stark County Library now stands. It is where, day after day, I pored over old documents and directories, searching for what became of the descendants of those who wrote to B. Virdot.

Canton still has its Jewish community, but it too is smaller and older than the one Sam Stone knew. It was not anti-Semitism but assimilation, not poverty but opportunities elsewhere, that siphoned off the young. In June 2008, Canton's Temple Israel agreed to be acquired by a Christian college, though Jewish services will continue to be hosted there. The Jewish country club, opened because Jews had been shunned by others, became a public golf course.

Canton remains a place of considerable diversity. The descendants of Germans, Italians, Irish, English, French, Greek, sub-Saharan Africans, Polish, and a dozen other nations have made it their home, just as Sam Stone did nearly a century ago. He would have drawn comfort to learn that, according to one survey, the most common place of birth for the foreign-born—11 percent—is Romania.

The house where Sam and Minna lived, 2129 Market Avenue Northwest, is now the home of Larry and Carol Williams. I knock on their door and introduce myself as the grandson of Sam Stone. His name means nothing to them. Carol Williams was born in 1942. But even now, she says, the Depression is a presence in the house and in her life. She knows that in the Hard Times her family had lived off the land and that her grandfather Clem Huth had gone off to work with little more than potato peels in his lunch box.

"My character has been formed and molded partly through the Great Depression, my lifestyle, how I choose to purchase things," she says. "It does shape our character and the way we think. I can't say it's been a bad thing. My parents were able to teach me how to get by, how to manage money. It was one of the gifts they gave me. It was a gift in disguise, how to make the best of what you have. It was a terrible time and yet it was a good time, and I feel like we are maybe coming into that time again because we lost some of the understanding."

I tell her she and Sam would have gotten along just fine. Later I return with my mother. We walk through the house as she narrates from memory. Little has changed. We have lemonade and fruit on the patio and say good-bye.

Beyond the door of that home, in what had once been the industrial strength of Canton, little is the same. The fortunes of the Hoover Company, whose products Raymond Beggs sold, had always been inextricably linked with those of Canton itself. By 1933, Canton produced more vacuum sweepers than any other city in the world and "Hoover" had become synonymous with "sweeper."

For generations, the company's sprawling plant in North Canton defined the landscape, economically and culturally. Some twenty-five hundred residents worked there. Today, Hoover is part of a Hong Kong–based firm, Techtronic Industries. In September 2007, the massive one-million-square-foot plant was closed. Today, the sweepers are assembled in Juarez, Mexico. The towering smokestack still carries the name Hoover in white bricks, and massive letters along the front of the building still proudly proclaim it to be THE HOME OF HOOVER APPLIANCES.

Timken, where Donald Jury and countless others had worked, has gone through its own wrenching changes. Seventy-seven years after B. Virdot's gift, the company boasted sales of $5.7 billion and 25,000 employees, with 61 plants and 103 sales offices and warehouses across six continents. But in May 2004 it announced it was closing three plants in Canton. Together, they employed 1,300 people. In April 2009, the company announced that worldwide it was slashing its work force by 25 percent, eliminating 7,000 jobs. "Here we go again" was a phrase that came to the minds of many who had grown up in the Hard Times.

In 1933, no tour of Canton would have been complete without a visit to the Palace Theater and Meyers Lake Amusement Park, the two great escapes from the Great Depression. Today the theater enjoys a place in the National Register of Historic Places, but it is ailing. Once it was the most ornate edifice in the city. Even at ninety-six,

Marjorie Markey, daughter of "Gray the Painter," remembers the fabulous organ rising out of the pit, Banks Kennedy playing the keys. But today, at eighty-two, the theater's plaster is falling, the tapestries are tattered, the furniture is broken, and the marquee has been allowed to go dark—deemed too expensive to feed its forty-eight hundred lights. An appeal to passersby for contributions to help with the utilities is posted on the door.

Meyers Lake Amusement Park, which hosted the dance marathon and was where Betty Gissiner and her beau would find relief and laughter, was itself not immune to the Depression. When business fell off, its owner, George Sinclair, secretly extended a plank across the moat to Monkey Island and let the monkeys escape, then breathlessly phoned in the story to the *Canton Repository*. "I don't know how they got out," he told the paper. The next day, attendance at the park soared as people came to watch monkey mayhem. Today, nothing remains of Meyers Lake Park except the lake for which it was named and the cottages and condos that sprang up around it.

But even today, B. Virdot's gift enjoys a half-life in Canton. At Christmas 2008, following my discovery of the suitcase, the *Repository* ran an editorial citing Sam Stone (a.k.a. Mr. B. Virdot) and his generosity:

"Stone himself was not a wealthy man, but he had done well enough for his time. He also had experienced the loss of a business and had benefited from the help of others in getting back on his feet. And so, just before Christmas in 1933, Stone reached out to help others, with no wish for acclaim. Our own time is tough enough. There is no better role model than Samuel J. Stone."

And as Sam Stone himself would have been the first to note, numbers themselves do not tell the whole story. Five dollars was so little and yet so much. Today's unemployment numbers are real enough, but so too are the character and resilience of Canton's people. Hard Times come and go, but even in these difficult days they are showing the same grit, compassion, and resourcefulness that have always defined the city and held out the prospect of better days ahead.

Acknowledgments

The place to begin dispensing thanks is with the descendants of those who wrote to B. Virdot that Christmas of 1933. Children and grandchildren, siblings, nieces and nephews—all who allowed me to enter their lives and the memories of those who were loved (and, more difficult still, those who were not). To you, I owe much. You gave me not only a book but a lesson in both history and the character of the country. For most Americans, 1933 was not a good year, and, though hardly comparable, neither were the years in which this book took shape. Still, your courage and humor were themselves a powerfully needed stimulus package for trying times. I defy anyone to spend time with you and not emerge an optimist.

To my many relatives—all those (especially Shirley Cohen) who helped me piece together the riddle of Sam's life but also shared with me the stories of his siblings—I want to say thank you. Their story is not always pretty, and I have made no attempt to gussy it up. It is what it is. That we as a family, the descendants of two displaced Romanian immigrants named Jacob and Hinde, have come into such a life is a testament to their dream of what could be and also what we ourselves have made of it. It is my hope that whatever bad blood stood between our forebears, founded or not, is finally consigned to the past. Consider this a belated olive branch.

To the many good and gracious people in Canton—shopkeepers, steelworkers, city officials, police, social workers, retirees, and the unemployed—who spent innumerable hours with me, your contributions to this story were invaluable. Though I have not lived in Canton for decades, you made me feel as though I were home again.

Deepest appreciation must go to the staff of the genealogical division of the Stark County Public Library, without whose tireless support and resourcefulness this book would have been vastly more difficult and less complete. Lauren Landis was the consummate professional.

I am also indebted to Char Lautzenheiser of the Classic Auto Museum both for her insights into Canton and for her research aids that made it possible for me to track the descendants of those who wrote to Mr. B. Virdot.

At the McKinley Presidential Library & Museum, curator Kimberly Kenney and librarian Karl Ash were of immeasurable help. For her valuable assistance and indefatigable research—and for introducing me to Nicholas Lane, my fabulous guide to the city—I thank Susan M. Melnick, archivist of the Rauh Jewish Archives at

Pittsburgh's Heinz History Center.

Thanks too to any number of friends and family whose suggestions and enthusiasm were invaluable, and whose tolerance in hearing me prattle on about these stories was heroic. A few deserve special mention: Mike Riley, Katie Jordan, Alex Jones, Howard Landau, Thrity Umrigar, Cyrus Taylor, Bill Siebenschuh, Doug Struck, Regina Brett, my thanks to each of you. Thanks too to Jared Bendis, whose tech savvy was exceeded only by his patience with me. And to the late "Bidey" Bryant, who lovingly introduced me to a Canton I might otherwise never have known.

To my many mentors—Ben Bradlee, Bob Woodward, Len Downie—special thanks. To Terry Oblander, for helping me find a place in journalism, for taking my pencil and forcing me to learn to type, and for showing me what a lede should look like, I will be forever grateful. To the legions of others—the late and beloved Frank Longstreth, Eleanor Roundy, Allen Grossman—abiding appreciation. I am particularly indebted to my dear friend Peter de Roetth, whose insights and texual questions proved invaluable.

To the late Susan Tifft, dearest of friends, a note to say your confidence in me made all the difference. Your friendship was itself "A Special Gift."

To my agent, David Black, thank you hardly seems adequate. That he is a superlative agent is well known. That he is a friend, a demanding editor, and a thinly disguised psychologist on constant call makes him so much more than an agent. And to Susan Raihoffer, who works with David, my gratitude for your belief that such an account was not meant for American eyes alone.

To my editor at Penguin, Eamon Dolan, who made sense of my words, there are no words adequate to express my debt. From our first conversation, I knew the book was in the best of hands, that I could trust his judgment, and that his insights and instincts would enrich the book immeasurably. For stretching me to the limits of my capabilities, I say thank you. A nod too to Penguin's Nicole Hughes, whose close reading of this manuscript was deeply appreciated.

The list of those who contributed to this project is longer than time or space allows, but no one was of greater help than my wife, Peggy Watts Gup, whose counsel and guidance left an indelible impression on the book. With candor and passion she influenced the project from initial proposal to final draft, helping me select which letters to include, and creating spreadsheets and organizational systems to manage the information. She asked the questions that ultimately helped shape the narrative. Thanks too to my two teenage sons, David and Matthew, for sleeping late and letting me work.

This book owes everything to my mother,

Virginia, and not just for giving me birth and then handing me the suitcase with the B. Virdot letters, but also for teaching me (contrary to prevailing parental wisdom) that I should always talk to strangers, that there is no such thing as too many questions, and that sticking my nose in other people's business could be turned into a gratifying and even lucrative profession. My father's hand was in this too, though he has been gone for decades.

For Dorothy, my mother's sister, thank you for fielding endless questions, sharing your memories, and combing through mountains of old photographs, legal documents, correspondence, and yellowing newspapers in aid of this story. Thank you for not throwing out the suitcase and its letters while they were in your possession. Without your enormous help, this book would have been much diminished.

Deep appreciation for my sister, Audrey, whose support and enthusiasm mean so much to me.

The final thanks go to my grandparents, Sam and Minna Stone. Though they both passed before they could have possibly imagined their grandson undertaking such a project, it is their hands, their hearts, their words, and their genes that gave life to this book.

Twenty-eight years after Sam Stone left us, I still cannot quite bring myself to believe he is gone. A part of me imagines that, as he did so often, he is merely holding his breath under the water, ready to explode on the surface, expelling a spume of water and a hearty laugh. Sam Finkelstein, Sam Stone, Mr. B. Virdot, Sambo—whatever name you went by, we, your descendants, thank you for your gift.

Author's Note

Digital copies of the letters to B. Virdot are to be given to the William McKinley Presidential Library and Stark County Historical Society in Canton, Ohio, as well as to the Franklin D. Roosevelt Presidential Library in Hyde Park, New York. A Web site features more of the letters as well as additional photos, research materials, and links to related sites and upcoming public appearances by the author. It is hoped that the Web site will be of use not only to the citizens of Canton but to students and scholars who study the Great Depression. Please visit www.asecret giftbook.com.

—T.S.G.

Mr. B. Virdot: A Timeline

CIRCA 1859
Sam's father, Janne, or Jacob, Finkelstein, is born in Romania.

CIRCA 1863
Sam's mother, Hilda, or Hinde, Bacall, is born in Romania.

1888
Sam is born in Romania. He would variously give his birth year as 1888, 1889, or 1890, but nearly always listed the date as March 2.

1888 OR 1889
The years Sam Stone claims in midlife that his parents came to America and then returned to Romania, and that he was born during their visit to the United States. There is no documentary evidence to support that claim.

1902
Romania passes the Law of Guilds, barring Jews from practicing many professions. It comes on top of numerous earlier anti-Semitic pieces of

471

legislation. In September, the United States protests Romania's treatment of Jews. That is the same month Sam and his father set sail for America from Le Havre, France.

OCTOBER 6, 1902
Father Janne (Jacob) Finkelstein, age forty-three; eldest son, Sam, fifteen; eldest daughter, Hana Sure (Sarah), seventeen; and Moses (Morris, Mack), eleven, arrive in the port of New York and make their way to Pittsburgh to join a growing community of displaced Romanian Jews.

SEPTEMBER 1903
Sam's mother, Hinde, age forty, and four younger children—Gusta (Gussie), eleven; Tina (Esther), nine; David, seven; and Isadore (Al), an infant—emigrate to the United States aboard the SS *Ivernia*, leaving from Liverpool, England, and arriving in the port of Boston. The family reunites in Pittsburgh.

DECEMBER 23, 1907
Minna Adolph, Sam's future wife, is born.

1910
U.S. Census for Pittsburgh makes no mention of a Sam Finkelstein or a Sam Stone, but lists his father, Jacob Finkelstein, age forty-eight, born in Romania; spouse Heldia [*sic*], age forty-five;

daughter Goldie, seventeen; daughter Ester, fifteen; son Dave, thirteen; and son Isidor, seven.

1914

The Kenosha, Wisconsin, City Directory records that Samuel Stone, a salesman, is living at 328 Fremont Avenue and working at the Block Brothers department store.

1916

The Kenosha, Wisconsin, City Directory records that Samuel Stone is living at 375 Durkee Avenue and managing S & J Gottlieb Company Dry Goods.

1917

The Chicago City Directory lists Samuel Stone as an advertising agent living at 3000 Ellis Avenue. He works for David Seiden, who runs a millinery shop at 81 East Madison Street.

JUNE 5, 1917

Twenty-nine-year-old Samuel J. Stone signs a military registration card in Chicago, Illinois, giving his birth date as March 2, 1888, and his birthplace as Bucharest, Romania. He lists his legal status as "Alien." Sam serves in the U.S. infantry for two years.

1920

The U.S. Census records that Samuel J. Stone,

age thirty, is a "roomer" living at 930 Tenth Street Northwest in Canton, Ohio. He is listed as emigrating to the United States in 1900, and gives his birthplace, as well as that of his father and mother, as Germany. His occupation: advertising.

1920
The Canton City Directory lists Samuel Stone as a boarder at 1121 Walnut Avenue Northeast working for the Quality Shoppe at 226 Market Avenue South.

APRIL 25, 1921
A birth certificate allegedly signed by J. H. Harkins in Pittsburgh shows that Sam Stone was born in Pittsburgh, Pennsylvania.

JUNE 15, 1921
A U.S. passport is issued to Sam Stone. It gives his place of birth as Pittsburgh and birth date as March 1, 1889. Shortly afterward, he embarks for France, Italy, Romania, Switzerland, and the Kingdom of Serbs, Croats, and Slovenes.

1923
Minna Adolph graduates from McKinley High School at age fifteen. Her graduation is a front-page story.

1924

Sam's eldest sister, Sarah, and her husband, Jacob S. Berman, join Sam in Canton. Jacob goes to work for Sam.

MARCH 14, 1926

Sam's father, Jacob Finkelstein, dies in Pittsburgh at age sixty-seven. Shortly thereafter Sam meets Minna Adolph and they begin their courtship. Sam's brother Mack joins him in Canton and goes to work for him.

APRIL 24, 1927

Sam Stone marries Minna Adolph, a woman who, at nineteen, is half his age. On the marriage certificate, Sam claims to be thirty-five, not thirty-nine, and born in Pittsburgh. He gives his father's name as "Jacob Stone," though his father steadfastly refused to change his name to Stone.

JUNE 20, 1929

Sam purchases a clothing store in Buffalo, New York.

1929

The stock market crashes. The Great Depression begins and Sam Stone suffers his own severe financial reversals.

1930

Sam and Minna Stone and daughters Virginia, two, and Dorothy, four months, live at 1009 Seventeenth Street Northwest in Canton. Sam lists his birthplace as Pennsylvania, and his parents' birthplace as "Bohemia."

1931

Sam's brother Mack, his wife, and perhaps others steal from his inventory and open their own store—Stone Brothers—in direct competition on the same city block in downtown Canton.

1932

In an envelope are notes from Minna in shorthand and an alleged copy of Sam's birth certificate giving the birthplace of his parents as Russia and claiming that Sam was born on March 29, 1889, at 29 Gum Street in Pittsburgh. The midwife is listed as H. Sandusky and the certificate is said to be recorded in volume 376, on pages 291–98. No such record appears in Pittsburgh's birth registry.

NOVEMBER 1932

Mack Stone, Sam's brother, attempts to blackmail him with trumped-up allegations of arson.

1933

Sam Stone acquires the Kibler Clothing chain,

which consists of nine retail stores in Ohio, West Virginia, and Illinois.

CHRISTMAS WEEK, 1933
The B. Virdot letters and gifts are sent.

SEPTEMBER 1938
Sam Stone goes to bankruptcy court.

SEPTEMBER 15, 1939
Sam's mother, Hilda Finkelstein, dies at age seventy-six.

OCTOBER 1940
Sam donates fifty wool coats to British civilians and takes out a full-page ad in the *Repository* soliciting help for the Allied Relief Fund: "The Homeless Poor of Europe Cannot Wait." That same month, because of the Smith Act and its provisions requiring aliens to either register or face prosecution, Sam retains an attorney and agonizes over whether to continue the ruse of citizenship or come clean.

JULY 1, 1941
The Jews of Dorohoi, Romania, where Sam is from, are systematically rounded up and exterminated.

EARLY 1950S
Sam retires from the clothing business and moves

to Golden Beach, Florida. He enters real estate, helps develop Sunset Isles in Hollywood, and acquires the Florida Vacuum Metalizing plant.

DECEMBER 1953
Issues of Sam's citizenship arise again as he seeks to renew his passport. A Washington attorney advises him to avoid raising questions that might provoke suspicions about his legal status.

JANUARY 1958
A passport is again issued to Sam Stone and again he lists his birthplace as Pittsburgh.

JULY 1967
Sam returns to his native town of Dorohoi, Romania, but makes no mention of what he finds, who he sees, or what feelings he has for the town.

JANUARY 29, 1981
Sam Stone dies after crashing into a rising drawbridge in North Miami. He is buried in Canton's West Lawn Cemetery.

JUNE 24, 2008
The B. Virdot letters are passed to Sam Stone's grandson.

About the Author

Ted Gup is the author of the best seller *The Book of Honor*, winner of the Investigative Reporters and Editors Book-of-the-Year Award, and *Nation of Secrets*, winner of the Shorenstein Book Prize. A Pulitzer finalist and recipient of a Guggenheim Fellowship, he is professor and chair of the Journalism Department at Emerson College. A former investigative reporter for *The Washington Post* and *Time* magazine, he has taught at Case Western Reserve University, Georgetown, Johns Hopkins, and the Chinese Academy of Social Sciences in Beijing as a Fulbright scholar. He has written for publications such as *Smithsonian*, *National Geographic*, *The New York Times*, *The Boston Globe*, *Village Voice*, *Sports Illustrated*, *Slate*, *GQ*, *Mother Jones*, *Audubon*, *Columbia Journalism Review*, and *Newsweek*, and for NPR.

Center Point Publishing
600 Brooks Road ● PO Box 1
Thorndike ME 04986-0001 USA

(207) 568-3717

US & Canada:
1 800 929-9108
www.centerpointlargeprint.com